Inclusive Localities

Contributions to Socio-Spatial Research /
Beiträge zur Sozialraumforschung

edited by / herausgegeben von
Monika Alisch
Michael May

Volume/Band 27

Sabine Meier
Lena Bertelmann
Lars Wissenbach (eds.)

Inclusive Localities

Perspectives on Local Social Policies
and Practices

Verlag Barbara Budrich
Opladen • Berlin • Toronto 2024

© 2024 This work is licensed under the Creative Commons Attribution 4.0 (CC-BY 4.0). It permits use, duplication, adaptation, distribution and reproduction in any medium or format, as long as you give appropriate credit to the original author(s) and the source, provide a link to the Creative Commons license and indicate if changes were made.
To view a copy of this license, visit https://creativecommons.org/licenses/by/4.0/

The use of third party material in this book does not indicate that it is also subject to the Creative Commons licence mentioned. If the material used is not subject to the aforementioned Creative Commons licence and the action in question is not permitted by law, the consent of the respective rights holder must be obtained for further use. Trademarks, company names, generally descriptive terms etc. used in this work may not be used freely. The rights of the respective rights holder must be observed and use is subject to the rules of trademark law, even without separate reference.

This book is available as a free download from www.budrich.eu (https://doi.org/10.3224/84743017).

© 2024 by Verlag Barbara Budrich GmbH, Opladen, Berlin & Toronto
www.budrich.eu

     ISBN   978-3-8474-3017-9 (Paperback)
     eISBN 978-3-8474-1954-9 (PDF)
     DOI   10.3224/84743017

Verlag Barbara Budrich GmbH
Stauffenbergstr. 7. D-51379 Leverkusen Opladen, Germany
86 Delma Drive. Toronto, ON M8W 4P6 Canada
www.budrich.eu

A CIP catalogue record for this book is available from Die Deutsche Nationalbibliothek (The German National Library) (https://portal.dnb.de)

Cover design by Walburga Fichtner, Köln, Germany
Typesetting by Anja Borkam, Langenhagen, Germany – kontakt@lektorat-borkam.de

Table of Contents

Sabine Meier, Lars Wissenbach, Lena Bertelmann
Inclusive communities, local policies and their spatial dimensions 7

Inclusion – Space – Communities

Michael May, Monika Alisch
The relationship between inclusion, social space development
and social space organisation. A theory-based concept for research
and social work 25

Marcel Schmidt
Opportunities for inclusive community development 37

Ivan Nio
Dilemmas of the inclusive city: Amsterdam as a case study 51

Elles Bulder
Small-scale community-based care initiatives in the Netherlands 65

Arnold Reijndorp
Strengthening the vitality of neighbourhoods: Countercultures
and self-evident meeting places 81

Martin F. Reichstein
Lessons (not) learned from pandemic times. Individual, socio-spatial
and organisational aspects of digital transformation in the disability
field 95

Inclusion – Governance – Participation

Rebecca Daniel
Participation of persons with disabilities in local political decision-
making: Insights from the Second International Disability Alliance
Global Survey on Organisations of Persons with Disabilities'
participation in policies and programmes 109

Matthias Kempf, Albrecht Rohrmann

Inclusion and political representation of marginalised groups.
The example of self-advocacy of people with disabilities 127

Lena Bertelmann

Moderation, coordination, mediation – Participatory implementation
of the UN Convention on the Rights of Persons with Disability
under the leadership of the municipal administration 141

Matthias Laub

"Giving space to the inner existence" – what to learn from
inclusion-oriented action planning for local empowerment
strategies 159

Johannes Schädler, Lars Wissenbach

Innovation in local social service infrastructure – eco-rational logics
and collective learning 177

Giulia Brogini, Thomas Schuler

Towards a participatory disability policy in Switzerland:
Confederation, cantons and municipalities in exchange with civil
society 197

Alexander Hobinka

Putting citizens into the centre – concepts and lessons learnt
for inclusive local governance from German Development
Cooperation 211

Paul Kwaku Larbi Anderson

Enhancing participation at the local level toward inclusive
communities. Presumption of the subsidiarity principle for local
decision-making from the perspective of Ghanaian decentralisation
and local government policy 227

Authors' Details 239

Index 243

Inclusive communities, local policies and their spatial dimensions

Sabine Meier, Lars Wissenbach, Lena Bertelmann

The political debate on inclusion spans a wide range of demands to improve the lives of those, in particular, who evidently have few options for responding to higher requirements in terms of mobility and education or to the negative effects of rising housing and energy costs. Depending on the national context, these demands are being addressed in different ways, with the 2030 Agenda for Sustainable Development (UN 2015) and the New Urban Agenda (UN 2016) regularly cited as important, but not the only, global milestones for achieving inclusion and equal opportunities. They were preceded by other landmark discussions and legal resolutions, such as the adoption of the UN Convention on the Rights of Persons with Disabilities (CRPD), which laid down in law the right to self-determination and equal opportunities for people with disabilities (UN 2006).

From a systems theory perspective, *inclusion* is usually discussed in conjunction with its opposite, *exclusion* from social subsystems (Kronauer/Häußermann 2016), whereby inclusion and exclusion are not so much mutually exclusive as dialectically interrelated (Stichweh 2009). This pair of terms can be traced back to research conducted in English and French, which has been dealing with socio-spatial exclusion and poverty since the beginning of sociology and social work (cf. Schütte 2012). Attempts have been made to theoretically distinguish the concept of inclusion from that of *integration* and *participation* (Kastl 2018). Following the idea of a functionally differentiated modern society, inclusion encompasses the aspect of the "structural involvement of persons [...] in social contexts (systems), in particular in functional subareas of society, which are covered and protected by fundamental rights" (ibid.: 675)[1]; whereas the concept of integration refers to the type and extent of "the inclusion of persons [...] in social relationships or in the cohesion of social contexts". Albert Scherr (2019:1) states that the concept of integration is linked to an assumption of "a society-wide standardised regulation of the participation of individuals", which is replaced with the concept of inclusion as an "understanding of independent and heterogeneous structures of inclusion/exclusion of the subsystems". "Inclusion does not take place as a comprehensive integration of individuals, but as a selective utilisation and regard for individual abil-

---

1 Within this chapter, all German quotes were translated into English by the authors.

ities and achievements" (ibid.: 1). According to Kastl (2018), participation is primarily focused on the aspect of participation in "social resources (e.g., education, economic resources, political participation, 'connections', prestige, social recognition in various forms)" (ibid.: 675). He goes on to argue that it is not individuals but structures that put in place certain arrangements (dispositions) to ensure access to social systems. These dispositions include human rights, fundamental rights, civil rights, and the distribution of social roles. Based on these definitions, inclusion can be understood as the totality of social processes in which dispositions must be utilised and necessary resources must be accessed by those involved to actually be able to experience an equal distribution of social roles and the right to political, social and socio-spatial participation (in the respective subsystems of society).

1. Inclusion, intersectionality, disability

Notwithstanding the critical importance of this theoretical framework and the political demands, the practical implementation is challenging. According to Degener and Mogge-Grotjahn (2012: 67f), this is not least since inclusion has so far "neither been perceived as a political cross-sectional task nor as a joint professional challenge and task of various professional groups but has been addressed in different functional systems." This manifests itself in the allocation of inclusion projects for different target groups to different ministries or municipal departments. Moreover, expert knowledge is still limited to individual fields of action, such as anti-racism, intercultural communication or accessibility, instead of several fields at the same time. As a result, questions of multidimensional discrimination, which often affect one and the same person in everyday life, are overlooked (ibid.: 71). In addition, in the context of a profit-oriented economic model and the associated reorganisation of social services, cultural and physical characteristics run the risk of being "industrially and politically exploited as a growth-promoting consumptive and productive factor" (Raab 2011: no page). New forms of appropriation of 'the other' are developing that exoticise people rather than actually including them.

Based on these findings, the addition of the issue of intersectionality to the concept of inclusion was long overdue (cf. Penkwitt 2023). Initial research on intersectionality was already undertaken in the US Black Feminism movement from the late 1980s onwards, with Kimberlé Crenshaw as its central representative. In the German-speaking world, several researchers have initiated and carried out studies on intersectionality since the early 2000s (Dederich 2014; Schildmann/Schramme 2017). Degele and Winker (2007), for example, propose researching accessibility to social systems through an intersectional multilevel analysis of structures such as local government institutions, while at the same time relating them to identity narratives. Identity narratives are socially constructed in the context of unequal power relations as valuated categories of difference such as gender, disability, age or migration background. Thus, the concept of intersectionality "explicitly focuses on the social position and the social inequality that accompanies it [...]. At the same time, through a performative perception in the sense of 'doing', difference is understood as socially constructed and not in an essentialist sense as a supposed 'given'" (Penkwitt 2023: no page). Socio-cultural constructions of difference are thus also social practices that (re)produce categories of difference in relation to the body and the space surrounding it, and in interaction with social structures, resources, and places. This interaction is also reflected in the WHO's International Classification of Functioning (ICF) and the CRPD in relation to the category of difference 'disability': Disability arises from the interplay between a person's impairment and barriers in the environment. The accessible design of the environment thus has a direct impact.

The socio-cultural construction of disability as a category of difference is also widely discussed in the field of Disability Studies. At its core is the question: Why and for what purpose is 'disability' produced, objectivised and practised from a historical, social and cultural perspective? Impairment and disability are seen as the product of social and cultural mechanisms of exclusion and oppression and not as the result of medical pathology. In this context, the production and reproduction of disability in everyday interactions is discussed as 'Doing Disability'; the structural embeddedness and social objectification of ability and disability as dispositions as 'Making Disability' (Waldschmidt 2011). These perspectives are supplemented by the additional dimension of 'Being Disabled' or 'Being Able', which refers to the habitual encoding of the category of difference in the context of symbolic power. This allows us to observe how disability and non-disability as habitually encoded forces enable the acceptance of attribution and thus become a category of the self and of the way of being. Such an internalisation of symbolic power generates, in a sense, an acceptance of difference. In this way, socio-culturally constructed difference and the exclusion and inclusion associated with it are turned into something supposedly 'natural' and, to a certain extent, removed from the realm of critical discourse (ibid.).

Considering these aspects, socio-culturally constructed difference has a structurally exclusive effect when people with certain attributed characteristics are systematically and permanently denied access to structures, spaces and resources. Conversely, this means that there can be no inclusion without inclusive spaces and cities, communities and local policies that provide the necessary resources and access for people to be able to assume social roles and for fundamental rights to become effective.

2. Inclusive cities and localities

What inclusive cities, communities and structures should look like has been discussed on an international level at the latest since the Global Report (UN 2001) was published by the United Nations Centre for Human Settlements. Here, the concept of *inclusive cities* was introduced and, as the second main topic of this Habitat Agenda, was applied to sustainable urban development strategies: "Sustainable urban development will depend largely on the capacity of cities to manage efforts to redress" problems such as "rising poverty, violence, unsustainable environmental practices and social exclusion of the poor and minority groups". These are problems which are "closely linked to the functioning of urban governance and the active participation of citizens in it" (ibid.: 211) and therefore there is a need for legal frameworks and policy reforms that are above all decentralised and democratically organised. Fifteen years later, the OECD (2016) published the report 'Making cities work for all: actions for inclusive growth' in which, in addition to possible tools for evaluation, a 'framework for action' is proposed to ensure improved access to work, education, housing, health and public transport. The 2030 Agenda for Sustainable Development, in particular Sustainable Development Goal (SDG) 11 'Make cities and human settlements inclusive, safe, resilient and sustainable' (UN 2015) also refers to the particular importance of local public-sector goods and services for inclusive development. It is estimated that 65% of the 169 goals underlying the 17 SDGs cannot be achieved without the effective involvement of stakeholders at the local level and effective coordination by local governments (cf. Cities Alliance 2015; UN Sustainable Development Solution Network 2016). The UN Habitat III New Urban Agenda (UN 2016) further differentiates this requirement and addresses the particular importance of inclusive local planning and change processes. It calls, firstly, for inclusive forums and local policy measures that enable the effective participation of all people in local decision-making and planning. Secondly, the capacity of local parliaments and administrations needs to be increased in order to be able to cooperate better with self-advocacy organisations and with science in the design of local governance processes. Thirdly, local self-advocacy organisations of vulnerable population groups need to be supported to effectively involve them in local development processes. In addition, the New Urban Agenda calls for more science, research and innovation in the area of local planning, including the collection of disaggregated data on the living conditions of vulnerable population groups. The Asian Development Bank also published a report entitled *Inclusive Cities*, which focuses on addressing the fight against poverty, housing shortages, and pollution in the context of the rapid urbanisation of many Asian metropolitan regions (Steinberg/Lindfield 2011).

Looking at these policy agendas, cities and metropolitan regions appear to play a key role in countering processes of exclusion (OECD 2016; Steinberg/Lindfield 2011). In this context, cities are understood – mostly implicitly – as geopolitically and administratively clearly delineated territories with a certain degree of governance. However, the extent of this governance depends on a variety of factors and, not least, on global developments. This is why some urban researchers argue that cities should rather be understood as *localities* consisting of multiscale levels of power and governance (Brenner 2019: 263ff). A locality is not only determined by its geographical location and legal, political or economic function (Cooke 2009). From a multi-scalar perspective, locality refers, on the one hand, to a physical place where everyday practices take place and through which it is simultaneously formed. On the other, locality is continuously changed by globally organised accumulation (or withdrawal) of economic capital. Besides, supralocal policies and laws can enhance or hinder local developments and scope of actions (Gebhardt 2016). These supralocal aspects influence investment decisions, local governmental budgets and the extent to which public services are provided. Building on this understanding of locality, it is worthwhile to analyse the development of inclusive cities and communities not only from a governmental perspective but also to consider other dynamics of the localities where social inclusion and participation ought to realise (Çağlar/Glick Schiller 2018). This understanding of cities as localities confirms the view stated above that research into processes of inclusion and exclusion should be concerned with the way in which resources are distributed and/or made available, how resources can be accessed by those involved, and the effect this access has on the distribution of social roles and participation.

A review of English language academic literature shows that the concept of inclusive cities consists of numerous dimensions that are increasingly being researched. In a recent paper, Liang et al. (2022) have compiled conceptualisations of the most significant publications between 2000 and 2020. Based on cluster analysis of high-frequency keywords, they first extracted different thematic clusters, each of which discusses two thematic areas and how they interact, such as spaces and rights, participation and citizenship, community (infrastructure) and financial arrangements, segregation and economic regeneration, or migration and access to basic services. Liang et al. (2022) also review relevant studies that analyse forms of exclusion. The first aspect that stands out is that segregation is a driver of exclusion, which is reproduced in cities through habitual strivings toward distinction and the formation of social groups (such as scenes or milieus), as well as through the continuous gentrification of real estate (see Dangschat 2007; Bürkner 2011). Secondly, urban violence, especially in rapidly urbanising cities, counteracts inclusion. Socio-spatial exclusion can only be curbed by "properly designed policies, laws and social institutions, regulated labour markets and honest state officials" (Liang et al. 2022:

71). Thirdly, urban poverty is the result of rapid growth and neoliberal land policies, which steadily reduce investments in affordable housing, basic public infrastructure and inclusive public spaces. In this sense, Waquant (2006) and Bourdieu et al. (2008) also show in their studies that people affected by urban poverty are also criminalised and their places of residence are stigmatised as 'ghettos', thus additionally exposing them to symbolic violence (Meier/Steets/ Frers 2018: 211ff.).

In addition to these studies, an increase in specialised literature can be observed that focuses in particular on social groups with a particularly high risk of exclusion, such as people with disabilities, immigrants, or women (Pineda/ Corburn 2020; Whitzman et al. 2012). Liang et al. (2022: 7) summarise solutions in a multidimensional conceptual framework of the inclusive city, in which the social processes of inclusion are divided into five dimensions: social inclusion as well as spatial, political, environmental and economic inclusion. Each of these dimensions of inclusive cities, which overlap to a great degree, is called upon to provide, for example, more opportunities for political participation (for vulnerable groups), affordable housing, good urban governance focused on sustainability, sustainable urban planning, and economic regeneration and a fairer distribution of labour and resources (OECD 2016; Steinberger/Lindfield 2011).

German-language research on the topic of inclusive cities analyses some of the above-mentioned dimensions, although at the beginning of the 2010s hardly any mention was made of the spatial, environmental or economic dimensions. Initially, inclusion was researched primarily in contexts of (educational) policy, i.e. with regard to social policy, educational infrastructures and policy and their accessibility for people with disabilities (Balz/Benz/Kuhlmann 2012; Bognar 2014; Ottersbach/Platte/Rosen 2016). In addition, we increasingly see studies on local politics and urban governance, which examine the implementation of various requirements of the CRPD at the local level (see below). The connection between the concept of inclusion and cities has only been made sporadically in German-language urban research, whereas processes of inclusion or exclusion of various vulnerable groups are playing an increasingly important role in local planning practice (see Netzwerk Innenstadt NRW 2016). In urban research, these processes have always been discussed using other terms, such as 'Right to the City' (Recht auf Stadt) or a 'City for all/many' (Stadt für Alle/Viele) in the context of gentrification, segregation and urbanity (Holm/Gebhardt 2011; Weiß 2019; Meier/Schlenker 2020). The latter, urbanity, can be seen as a positive precondition for inclusive social processes. Along these lines, Cudak and Bukow (2016) consider the approach and organisation of urban societies with regard to *diversity* and *mobility* as a measure of their capacity for inclusion. In their studies, they prefer the term mobility to migration, as migration is nothing more than a temporary, repeated or irreversible form of mobility (across national borders). In the history of the development of the European city, diversity and mobility are the basis for urbanity, and dealing with diversity (at least in many inner-city, metropolitan neighbourhoods) is an undisputed everyday experience. However, this is overshadowed by discourses in which categories of difference are repeatedly emphasised and, above all, culturalised (Bukow 2020). An urban society is inclusive when a public sphere is created that provides "room for the presentation of different social interests" (Cudak/Bukow 2016: 11). At the same time, a degree of open-mindedness must be developed that, depending on the "context [...], allows "typically different ways of dealing" with lived mobility and diversity (ibid.). Spaces of opportunity for diversity and mobility as experienced in everyday life and recognised in discourse thus form the core of an inclusive urban society, which are (or should be) effectuated by municipal institutions, other organisations and civil society.

3. Inclusive local policies

Taking a closer look at urban societies and urban policy in practice, it is striking that since the publication of the Global Report (UN 2001), many small and large cities around the world have taken up the concept of inclusive cities and have developed action plans. In 2006, the United Nations Convention on the Rights of Persons with Disabilities (UN 2006) provided an important impetus for local policy debate on issues of inclusion. The Convention has been ratified by 186 states worldwide (status: July 2023). It focuses on barriers in the interactions between individuals and their social and physical environment and the resulting barriers to full and effective participation in society on an equal basis with others.

Such barriers usually manifest themselves directly in the person's physical and social environments; in the places where they live, go to school, work, spend their free time, use social and health services, etc. – in other words, the places in which the majority of activities that sustain and support people physically, psychologically and socially take place (De Filippis/Saegert 2012). These are places of reciprocal relationships between people with similar and also very different interests and ways of life. They thus become *shared places* where the co-existence of people has to be managed (Healey 2006). This means that questions of inclusion are inevitably topics of urban and local policy. Local public-sector goods and services and the development and maintenance of a local infrastructure that is equally accessible, affordable and of high quality for everyone are all areas often concerned with questions of co-existence.

Thus, questions of inclusion at the local level arise in the political debate on various areas of local development, such as housing, mobility, education, the labour market, health, politics, culture, etc. These are specific questions of participation in social subdomains, which arise in the concrete political debate and the individual character of local policies with regard to specific localities. Participation is realised through the assumption of certain roles such as tenant, owner, voter/candidate, passenger, pupil or employees, in the social subsystems (Wansing 2015). This often requires interventions in local planning structures, processes and routines to ensure that the rights and needs of all persons concerned are met equally. Necessary changes are thus not so much technical implementation processes as political negotiation processes at the local level, which generate uncertainty and resistance and require debate among a wide range of local political actors (see e.g. Rohrmann et al. 2014; Wissenbach 2019). Local governments are not the only actors in these processes, and often not the most powerful ones. However, they are the democratically legitimised actors responsible for the coordination of local development processes (cf. Romeo 2012), especially with regard to legal and political frameworks at higher levels of government.

Social coexistence in shared places as well as the distribution of resources and life opportunities are largely determined by the values and norms that apply in a society (Wansing 2015). Thus, questions of inclusion also arise concerning local governance as a whole, with regard to the question of a joint concept for coexistence in shared places, a common denominator which provides orientation for debates at the local political level. In many countries, democratic and welfare state principles guarantee civil, economic, social and cultural rights to participation in all social subsystems and areas of life. In this context, inclusion describes the recognition, protection and implementation of corresponding rights and duties – also in the context of local policymaking (ibid.).

From the perspective of social work, in addition to the critical analysis of socio-cultural constructions of categories of difference and their effects on processes of inclusion and exclusion, the focus is on legitimisation processes through institutional structures and local policymaking. In particular, recent studies on community work and the design of *inclusive communities* (inklusives Gemeinwesen) establish a link to the spatial dimension of social inclusion in cities and municipalities (May 2017; Schnur/Drilling/Niermann 2019). The guiding principle of an inclusive community refers to a political approach with which inclusive structures, cultures and practices are developed at the local level (cf. Rohrmann et al. 2014). On the one hand, an inclusive community is a politically defined territory within whose borders the inhabitants have certain rights and duties. On the other hand, more or less informal, dynamic communities are formed based on family, neighbourly or other social relations, which also shape the inclusive community (cf. May 2017: 20ff). According to this perspective, all people, regardless of ethnicity, skin colour, gender, language, religion, political or other views, national or social origin, affluence, disability or other status, or other forms of social attribution are respected

Inclusive communities, local policies and their spatial dimensions 15

as 'members' of a diverse human community. Such an inclusive community does not develop by itself; there is permanent friction with the social contradictions and tendencies towards exclusion that pervade society in all spheres of life. Inclusive community therefore also describes a political mandate for action with which local governments, in participatory processes, actively strive to create the conditions necessary to overcome exclusion. Inclusive community thus also stands for a planning approach that creates conditions in the local community that enable all people to lead self-determined lives within the normal social institutions of the life course (cf. ibid).

The contributions in this edited book look at the development and characteristics of inclusive communities and localities from different perspectives. The authors analyse aspects of community/locality, such as the interrelation between political demands and measures on the one hand and the accessibility of infrastructures, (political) participation and the further development of social relationships and informal networks on the other. The primary analysis of the contributions in the first part of this book deals with the context of *space* and *communities*, while the contributions in the second part focus on aspects of inclusion in the context of *governance* and *participation*. This structure of the contributions does not exclude the possibility that individual contributions combine aspects of both thematic fields.

Monika Alisch and *Michael May* present a comprehensive theory-based concept of social space development and social space organisation that was developed in the context of participative research (and in particular as an element of social work as a profession and its fields of activity). Given the many different understandings of inclusion in the academic debate, their contribution first looks at various interpretations. Following Lefebvre's studies on 'the Utopias' and the 'Right to the City', it is argued that inclusion is only actually lived when the development and organisation of social spaces enables an active subjective appropriation by people (with disabilities). In concrete terms, this means that social space development should always be about enabling people to articulate their own needs and to make (political) interests visible and to assert them; not only on a spatially and temporally limited situational basis but continuously, throughout all administrative and subject-oriented participatory processes. *Marcel Schmidt* defines social space development of inclusive communities in concrete terms by understanding inclusion not only as a structural principle but also as a mandate and planning task of social work. Following a critical discussion of the structural conditions of cooperative organisation and planning processes, he illustrates the development of inclusive communities using real-world laboratory projects. However, Schmidt notes that social work as an 'actor' is still not successful enough in presenting itself in practice as a scientific profession of social transformation, at least in Germany.

Ivan Nio does not come to a definitive conclusion as to whether this is more successful in the Netherlands, although the city of Amsterdam does a great deal to make the participation processes of residents more inclusive in the context of urban renewal. To this end, the local government of Amsterdam makes use of a social-spatial infrastructure consisting of social workers, civil servants and actors of housing corporations, who jointly organise participation processes on the one hand, and meeting places in socially mixed neighbourhoods on the other. Despite these long-established forms of organising participation, Nio argues that these are often on a superficial level with no real influence on, for example, the (re)development of affordable housing. At the same time, there has been a consistent drive towards decentralisation of state tasks in the Netherlands for more than ten years, which is also being carried out in the area of health care and social welfare under the banner of the 'participation society'. *Elles Bulder* analyses how community-based care initiatives in rural areas respond to the so-called Dutch participation society. Using the example of the small communities of Elsendorp and Wedde in the northeast of the Netherlands, she shows how community-based care initiatives have developed through the collaboration of full-time and voluntary actors and healthcare institutions, and how they can contribute in their respective forms to maintaining or improving social living conditions. Among other things, she argues that by stimulating various forms of social capital, these initiatives not only maintain the general well-being of the residents but have also become crucial for a functioning medical care structure. However, this brings with it the risk that they will not be able to fulfil this important role, neither structurally nor in the long term.

Arnold Reijndorp also directs his attention to residents and their social capital. He focuses on the ability of residents to create self-help organisations and inclusive, publicly accessible places. He has however not researched this in rural areas, but in the urban region of the Brugse Poort neighbourhood in Ghent, Belgium. Here, urban policy refers less to inclusive neighbourhoods and more to 'vital' neighbourhoods in which housing, living and working conditions enable a good life for a diverse range of population groups. A vital neighbourhood constitutes resilience, which can be used to react to constantly changing developments. During his one-year stay in Ghent, Reijndorp used ethnographic methods to explore this vitality ascribed to the area, a quality to be cultivated and nurtured. He shows that Brugse Poort consists of a highly dynamic socio-spatial fabric in which political interventions and the self-organisation of spaces, support and interest groups conflict with one another. This contradictory nature becomes particularly clear when regarding the dynamics of diversity and mobility of population groups in a historical context, i.e., from the 1970s until today.

Martin Reichstein takes a look back to the more recent past, i.e., to the time of the COVID-19 pandemic. In his contribution, he addresses the question of the effect that the increase in digital communication has had (up to the present day) on the social lives of people with physical and so-called intellectual disabilities on the one hand and on the working routines of the institutions whose services address them on the other. He argues that the phenomenon of a 'digital divide' – despite an overall increase in the use of digital forms of communication – has widened for these persons in particular. Two main reasons for this are the unchanged working routines of the institutions concerned and the unaltered social and economic living conditions of the people affected. Reichstein concludes that further efforts in research and the organisational development of the institutions concerned are necessary to find solutions that actually meet the requirements of both the (work) routines of the institutions and of the users. Furthermore, Reichstein concludes, that closing the 'digital divide' is a key task for social work in the future.

The contributions in the subject area of *governance* and *participation* take a critical look at the possibilities of participation and, in doing so, examine, among other things, local planning processes. Regarding the possibilities of participation, *Rebecca Daniel* presents the results of a global survey by the *International Disability Alliance (IDA)*, which focused on the participation of organisations of persons with disabilities (OPDs). It can be seen that, at the local level, OPDs are increasingly being consulted on a broader range of issues than in the past (and no longer only on disability-specific issues). They are increasingly involved in (almost) all issues that affect their lives, such as housing, health, employment, environment and climate change. However, even if the conditions for participation have (slightly) improved, in many cases they are still not at all in line with the requirements of the CRPD and hamper the meaningful participation of people with disabilities, especially at the local level. Daniel therefore emphasises the need to combine sector-specific participation opportunities with general efforts of local actors to ensure a more effective participation of people with disabilities in local governance processes and thus promote an inclusive community. *Matthias Kempf* and *Albrecht Rohrmann* also argue in favour of this combination. After a detailed discussion of (extended) forms of participation at the local level, they lay out – based on empirical data from numerous cities and municipalities in North Rhine-Westphalia – three most important aspects of political participation of people with disabilities: participative structures, inclusive culture and political activity. The more extensively these aspects are developed and interconnected within municipalities, the greater the chance of participation in political discourse and successful representation of interests. The importance of an inclusive culture and working on good conditions for participation (for people with disabilities) at the local level is also the central theme of *Lena Bertelmann*'s contribution. The results of a large-scale study on the nature of activities and planning for the implementation of the UN Convention on the Rights of Persons with Disabilities (CRPD) in municipalities in North Rhine-Westphalia show that although certain activities already exist or are being planned in the majority of the municipalities surveyed, there is considerable variation in the nature and extent of these activities. It becomes clear that the municipality as an actor and a place is of far-reaching significance, as it is in a position to mediate between the interests of different population groups and to organise participation itself. In addition, services and infrastructures can be provided that can help facilitate the self-determined appropriation of places and processes. In this context, the expertise, authority and mediation skills of persons or offices within the administration play an important role.

But even local inclusion-oriented planning processes can themselves become places of exclusion. *Matthias Laub* reveals this in his research on people with mental disabilities. Firstly, he illustrates the concept of participation as a core element of the CRPD and establishes the connection between opportunities for participation in social spaces and disability. He notes that people with mental health issues – despite a decades-long tradition of psychiatric care in the community – are virtually invisible in local participation planning. Laub concludes that this invisibility is related to the difficulty of communicating to others one's own 'inner existence', one's subjective experience of reality, which does not necessarily manifest itself physically. Successful participation in planning processes and stigma-free and non-hierarchical communication require empowerment strategies, for example in the form of experienced gatekeepers who are trusted in their mediator role by the persons involved. Laub sees participation in local participation planning as identity-related alignment work for all actors involved. This means that gatekeepers or mediation work on the part of the municipality is an important transfer medium. *Johannes Schädler* and *Lars Wissenbach* examine the implications of the transfer of innovative local social policies into existing structures and routines in the field of social services at the local level. Using the empirical example of a German administrative district and with reference to planning and implementation theories, they retrace its argumentation for implementation both as a process of organisational change and as a reflexive framework for collective learning.

Guila Brogini and *Thomas Schuler* provide insights into the transfer of social policy measures outside German districts and present practical examples of the advancement of participatory policies for people with disabilities in Switzerland. First focussing on independent living as the CRPD's core concern, they then critically examine the relationship between Switzerland's three levels of government – confederation, cantons and municipalities – with regard to the implementation of the CRPD. In addition, current empirical results of a survey among cantonal authorities and civil society organisations on the involvement of people with disabilities as experts in their own right are presented and the practical implementation of projects financed by the confederation for the promotion of independent living is explained. Finally, Brogini and Schuler provide an outlook on the Federal Disability Policy for the years 2023 to 2026, which Switzerland has committed to with reference to the recommendations of the 2022 UN Committee on the Rights of Persons with Disabilities.

Inclusive communities, local policies and their spatial dimensions 19

Alexander Hobinka examines non-European work on participation at the local level by looking at local inclusion processes in the context of International Cooperation (IC). Using concrete project examples from the Western Balkans, Rwanda, Lebanon and Jordan, he shows which approaches IC actors are using to attempt to implement the inclusion goals ('Leave No One Behind') of global policies such as the 2030 Agenda for Sustainable Development or the UN New Urban Agenda in international development practice at the local level. Hobinka argues that to develop inclusive communities, firstly, the availability of disaggregated data on the living situation of marginalised population groups is of major importance, and secondly, there should be close collaboration with local self-advocacy organisations. Thirdly, he concludes that the accessibility of physical and virtual spaces is a necessary precondition for political participation. *Paul Anderson* looks at the development of inclusive communities from a different perspective, namely that of state decentralisation reforms in Ghana. Based on the importance of the principle of subsidiarity, he discusses the role of state decentralisation in the participation of citizens in local decision-making processes. In a critical reflection on the situation in Ghana, Anderson highlights the challenges associated with the transfer of state responsibility to the local level, especially when this is linked to the demand for an expansion of political participation opportunities for the local population.

We would like to thank Kathrin Bennett for editing, proofreading, and translating texts in this edited reader.

References

Balz, Hans-Jürgen/Benz, Benjamin/Kuhlmann, Carola (2012) (eds.): Soziale Inklusion. Grundlagen, Strategien und Projekte in der Sozialen Arbeit. Wiesbaden: VS Springer Verlag.
Brenner, Neil (2019): New Urban Spaces. Urban Theory and the Scale Question. Oxford: University Press.
Bukow, Wolf-Diedrich (2020): Urbanität – ein globales Narrativ wird zur Herausforderung, In: Meier, Sabine/Schlenker, Kathrin (eds.): Teilhabe und Raum. Interdisziplinäre Perspektiven. Leverkusen, Opladen: Barbara Budrich Verlag, pp. 37-52.
Bognar, Daniel (2014) (Hrsg): Inklusion an Schulen: Praxishandbuch zur Umsetzung mit Anleitungen. Köln: Link.
Bourdieu, Pierre et al. (2008): Das Elend der Welt. Zeugnisse und Diagnosen alltäglichen Leidens an der Gesellschaft, Konstanz: UVK Verlagsgesellschaft.
Bürkner, Hans-Joachim (2011): Sozialräumliche Disparitäten und soziale Mischung. Aktuelle Diskurslinien in Forschung und gesellschaftlicher Praxis. In: Belina,

Bernd/Gestring, Nobert (eds.) Urbane Differenzen. Disparitäten innerhalb und zwischen Städten. Münster: Westfälisches Dampfboot, pp. 16-42.

Çağlar, Ayşe/Glick Schiller, Nina (2018): Migrants & City-Making. Dispossession, Displacement and Urban Regeneration. Durham and London: Duke University Press.

Cities Alliance (2015): Sustainable Development Goals and Habitat III: Opportunities for a Successful New Urban Agenda. Cities Alliance Discussion Paper — N° 3. https://www.citiesalliance.org/sites/default/files/Opportunities%20for%20the%20New%20Urban%20Agenda.pdf [accessed: 18.08.2023]

Cooke, Phil (2009): Locality debates. In: Kitchin, Rob/Thrift, Nigel/Falconer Al-Hindi, Karen (eds.): International Encyclopedia of Human Geography, pp. 256-262.

Cudak, Karin/Bukow, Wolf-Diedrich (2016): Auf dem Weg zur Inclusive City. In: Behrens, Melanie/Bukow, Wolf-Diedrich/Cudak, Karin/Strünck, Christopf (eds.): Inclusive City, Überlegungen zum gegenwärtigen Verhältnis von Mobilität und Diversität in der Stadtgesellschaft. Wiesbaden: VS Springer Verlag, pp. 1-20.

Dangschat, Jens (2007): Soziale Ungleichheit, gesellschaftlicher Raum und Segregation. In: Dangschat, Jens/Hamedinger, Alexander (eds.): Lebensstile, soziale Lagen und Siedlungsstrukturen. Hannover: Verlag der Akademie für Raumforschung und Landesplanung, pp. 2-20.

Dederich, Markus (2014): Intersektionalität und Behinderung. Ein Problemaufriss. Behinderte Menschen. In: Zeitschrift für gemeinsames Leben, Lernen und Arbeiten, 37, pp. 47–53.

De Filippis, James/Saegert, Susan (2012): Communities Develop: The Question is, How? In: De Filippis, James/Saegert, Susan (eds.): The Community Development Reader. Routledge: New York, pp. 1-6.

Degener, Theresia/Mogge-Grotjahn, Hildegard (2012): "All inclusive"? Annäherungen an ein interdisziplinäres Verständnis von Inklusion. In: Balz, Hans-Jürgen/Benz, Benjamin/Kuhlmann, Carola (eds.): Soziale Inklusion. Grundlagen, Strategien und Projekte in der Sozialen Arbeit. Wiesbaden: Springer VS, pp. 59-77.

Degele, Nina/Winker, Gabriele (2007): Intersektionalität als Mehrebenenanalyse. https://tore.tuhh.de/bitstream/11420/384/1/Intersektionalitaet_Mehrebenen.pdf [acccessed: 23.02.2023].

Gebhardt, Dirk (2016): When the state takes over: civic integration programmes and the role of cities in immigrant integration. In: Journal of Ethnic and Migration Studies, 42, 5, pp. 742-758.

Holm, Andrej/Gebhardt, Dirk (Hrsg.) (2011): Initiativen für ein Recht auf Stadt: Theorie und Praxis städtischer Aneignungen. Hamburg: VSA.

Healey, Patsy (2006): Collaborative Planning. Shaping Places in Fragmented Societies. 2nd Edition. Basingstoke. New York: Palgrave Macmillan.

Kastl, Jörg Michael (2018): Inklusion. In: Otto, Hans-Uwe/Thiersch, Hans/Treptow, Rainer/Ziegler, Holger (eds.): Handbuch Soziale Arbeit. München: Ernst Reinhardt Verlag, pp. 665-678.

Kronauer, Martin/Häußermann, Hartmut (2016): Inklusion – Exklusion. In: Kessl, Fabian/Reutlinger, Christian (Hrsg.): Handbuch Sozialraum, Wiesbaden: Springer Fachmedien, pp. 1-16.

Liang, Danni/De Jong, Martin/Schraven, Daan/Wang, Lili (2022): Mapping key features and dimensions of the inclusive city: A systematic bibliometric analysis and

literature study. In: International Journal of Sustainable Development & World Ecology, 29, 1, pp. 60-79.
May, Michael (2017): Soziale Arbeit am Gemeinwesen. Ein theoretischer Begründungsrahmen. Leverkusen, Opladen: Barbara Budrich Verlag.
Meier, Lars/Steets, Silke/Frers, Lars (2018): Theoretische Positionen der Stadtsoziologie. Weinheim, Basel: Beltz Juventa.
Meier, Sabine/Schlenker, Kathrin (2020): Teilhabe und Raum. Interdisziplinäre Perspektiven. Leverkusen, Opladen: Barbara Budrich Verlag.
Netzwerk Innenstadt NRW (2016): Inklusion und Stadtentwicklung, Positionen der Arbeitsgruppe Inklusion und Stadtentwicklung, Münster.
OECD (2016): Making Cities work for All: Data and Actions for Inclusive Growth., Paris: OECD Publishing.
Ottersbach, Markus/Platte, Andrea/Rosen, Lisa (2016): Soziale Ungleichheiten als Herausforderung für inklusive Bildung. Wiesbaden: Springer VS Verlag.
Penkwitt, Meike (2023): Einleitung – Intersektionalität und inklusive Pädagogik. *Zeitschrift für Inklusion*, (1). https://www.inklusion-online.net/index.php/inklusion-online/article/view/695 [accessed: 18.05.2023]
Pineda, Victor Santiago/Corburn, Jason (2020): Disability, Urban Health Equity, and the Coronavirus Pandemic: Promoting Cities for All. In: Journal of Urban Health, 97, pp. 336-341.
Raab, Heike (2011): Inklusive Gender?: Gender, Inklusion und Disability Studies. *Zeitschrift für Inklusion*, 5(1). https://www.inklusion-online.net/index.php/inklusion-online/article/view/104 [accessed: 25.02.2023]
Rohrmann, Albrecht/Schädler, Johannes/Kempf, Matthias/Konieczny, Eva/Windisch, Marcus (2014): Inklusive Gemeinwesen Planen: Abschlussbericht eines Forschungsprojektes im Auftrag des Ministeriums für Arbeit, Integration und Soziales in Nordrhein-Westfalen. ZPE-Schriftenreihe 36. Siegen: Zentrum für Planung und Evaluation Sozialer Dienste.
Romeo, Leonardo (2012): Decentralizing for Development: The developmental potential of local autonomy and the limits of politics-driven decentralization reforms. ICLD Working Paper No11. https://icld.se/wp-content/uploads/media/working-paper/icld-workingpaper-11-tryck-low.pdf [accessed: 10.03.2023]
Scherr, Albert (2019): Der Inklusionsbegriff. Theoretische Grundlagen und gesellschaftspolitische Implikationen. In: Pickel, Gert/Decker, Oliver/Kailitz, Steffen/Röder, Antje/Schulze Wessel, Julia (Hrsg.), Handbuch Integration. Wiesbaden: Springer Fachmedien, pp.1-16.
Schildmann, Ulrike/Schramme, Sabrina (2017): Intersektionalität: Behinderung – Geschlecht – Alter. In: Vierteljahresschrift Heilpädagogik und ihre Nachbargebiete, 86, 3, pp. 191-201.
Schnur, Olaf/Drilling, Markus/Niermann, Oliver (2019): Quartier und Demokratie. Theorie und Praxis lokaler Partizipation zwischen Fremdbestimmung und Grassroots. Wiesbaden: Springer VS Verlag.
Schütte, Johannes D. (2012): Soziale Inklusion und Exklusion: Norm, Zustandsbeschreibung und Handlungsoptionen. In: Huster, Ernst-Ulrich/Boeckh, Jürgen/Mogge-Grotjahn, Hildegard (eds.): Handbuch Armut und Soziale Ausgrenzung, Wiesbaden: VS Verlag für Sozialwissenschaften, pp. 104-121.
Steinberg, Florian/Lindfield, Michael (2011): Inclusive Cities. Mandaluyong City, Philippines: Asian Development Bank.

Stichweh, Rudolf (2009) Leitgesichtspunkte einer Soziologie der Inklusion und Exklusion. In: Stichweh, Rudolf/Windolf, Paul (Hrsg.): Inklusion und Exklusion: Analysen zur Sozialstruktur und sozialen Ungleichheit. Wiesbaden: VS Verlag für Sozialwissenschaften, pp. 29-42.

UN (2001) Cities in a globalizing world. Global report on Human Settlements 2001, Nairobi: Earthscan London and Sterling, p. 211.

UN (2006): United Nations Convention on the Rights of Persons with Disabilities. New York: UN.

UN (2015): Transforming our world: the 2030 Agenda for Sustainable Development. UN General Assembly A/RES/70/1. http://www.un.org/ga/search/view_doc.asp?symbol=A/RES/70/1&Lang=E [accessed: 18.08.2023]

UN (2016): New Urban Agenda. UN General Assembly A/RES/71/256. http://habitat3.org/wp-content/uploads/New-Urban-Agenda-GA-Adopted-68th-Plenary-N1646655-E.pdf [accessed: 18.08.2023]

UN Sustainable Development Solution Network (2016): Getting Started with the SDGs in Cities. A Guide for Stakeholders. http://unsdsn.org/wp-content/uploads/2016/07/9.1.8.-Cities-SDG-Guide.pdf [accessed: 18.08.2023]

Waldschmidt, Anne (2011): Symbolische Gewalt, Normalisierungsdispositiv und/oder Stigma? Soziologie der Behinderung im Anschluss an Goffman, Foucault und Bourdieu. Österreichische Zeitschrift für Soziologie, 36, 4, pp. 89-106.

Wacquant, Loïc (2006): Das Janusgesicht des Ghettos und andere Essays. Gütersloh, Berlin: Bauverlag und Basel: Birkhäuser Verlag.

Wansing, Gudrun (2015): Was bedeutet Inklusion? Annäherungen an einen vielschichtigen Begriff. In: Degener, Theresia/Diehl, Elke (eds.): Handbuch Behindertenrechtskonvention. Teilhabe als Menschenrecht – Inklusion als gesellschaftliche Aufgabe. Bonn: Bundeszentrale für politische Bildung, pp. 43-54.

Weiß, Stephanie (2019): Quartiere für Alle. Städtebauliche Strategien sozialer Inklusion in der Planung von Wohnquartieren. Wiesbaden: Springer VS Verlag.

Whitzman, Carolyn/Legacy, Crystal/Andrew, Caroline/Klodawsky, Fran/Shaw, Margaret/Viswanath, Kalpana (2012): Building Inclusive Cities. Women's Safety and the Right to the City. London: Routledge.

Wissenbach, Lars (2019): Planning inclusive cities and human settlements. Entry points for International Development Cooperation. Siegen: Universi.

Inclusion – Space – Communities

The relationship between inclusion, social space development and social space organisation. A theory-based concept for research and social work

Michael May, Monika Alisch

1. On the different definitions of the concept of inclusion

Since the ratification of the UN Convention on the Rights of Persons with Disabilities (UN-CRPD) in Germany in 2009, the term "inclusion" has been on everyone's lips. Curiously, only the English text of the Convention, which has become German law, uses the term 'inclusive', while the German and French translations use the term 'Integration' or 'intégration'.

In the scientific debate, there are highly different definitions of the term inclusion. Stichweh (2009: 29f.) distinguishes between the three paradigms of membership, solidarity and social discipline. According to his research, Talcott Parsons was probably the first to use the concept of inclusion as a key term in connection with the differentiation of social functional systems that characterises modernity, thus founding the paradigm of membership. In terms of content, however, this paradigm follows the British welfare state theory of T.H. Marshall (1992), which already distinguished between civil, political and social forms of social institutionalisation of citizenship. In contrast, the paradigm of solidarity goes back to Durkheim's social theory and emphasises more strongly the interdependence of social relations.

Interestingly, Marshall (ibid.: 53) assumed in his theory that citizenship rights are reserved for those who are full members of a community. Using the example of the right for the poor, he (ibid.: 49f.) emphasises that this right was not understood as an integral part of citizenship rights, but as an alternative to them. Even before Marshall, Georg Simmel (1992: 352f.), also using the example of the poor, had elaborated that on the one hand, they would be degraded to rightless objects through the use of welfare state assistance. At the same time, they could hardly escape the bureaucratised procedures and legal regulations of the welfare state. At least before the ratification of the UN-CRPD, this applied to a much greater extent to people who were subsumed under the category of 'disability' and accordingly provided for by the welfare state.

That those people could hardly escape the bureaucratised procedures and legal regulations of the welfare state is already the third conceptual definition of inclusion in the paradigm of social disciplining. Stichweh (2009: 37) refers to thinkers as diverse as Michel Foucault and Niklas Luhmann. They agreed that under modern conditions, exclusion is only 'permitted' insofar as it is brought into the form of inclusion. For every new form of exclusion, an institution of inclusion has to be created and established, which absorbs the previous exclusion and makes it invisible, because it dresses it in the garment of a resocialising and reincluding intention. Against this background, Stichweh (ibid.: 38) speaks of institutions – mostly these are organisations – of inclusive exclusion. In addition to prisons, this also includes institutions for the disabled. In this context, he refers to analyses that show how these institutions, despite the good intentions they pursue, permanently mark the people they care for with a stigma, even through the attempt to re-include them, and thus erect impassable thresholds between the realms of inclusion and exclusion.

This danger is by no means eliminated by the dissolution of the large 'institutions for the disabled'. For example, the now common categorisation in Germany as an 'I(= inclusion)-child' in day care or school is unlikely to be less stigmatising for those concerned than the term, now declared obsolete, 'Behindertes Kind'. In a critical understanding (cf. Jantzen 2016), this means the child is also disabled by society. The new politically correct term of inclusion tends to obscure this, often accompanied by a lack of self-reflection on the part of professionals with regard to the potentially disabling effects of their surely well-intentioned inclusion pedagogy.

With his concept of inclusive exclusion, Stichweh follows Foucault's (2006) concept of deviance heterotopia as spaces of inclusive exclusion (cf. Diebäcker 2014: 113). As Helga Cremer-Schäfer (2001: 64) also points out, inclusion in the paradigm of social disciplining is often organised and experienced in this way as exclusion, which has been correspondingly problematised by various affected persons' initiatives and the disability rights movement.

The fact that Stichweh also refers to Luhmann in connection with the paradigm of social disciplining is insofar surprising as he assumed in his early writings – similarly to Parsons – that the differentiated social functional systems each aimed at full inclusion. Later – probably not entirely uninfluenced by a visit to Brazilian favelas (cf. May 2012) – Luhmann (1996: 228) came to the conclusion that in a system of functional differentiation, the postulated full inclusion could not be achieved. Functional systems exclude persons in their rational operation or marginalise them to such an extent that this not only has consequences for access to other functional systems. Rather, these would then also often be separated in terms of housing and thus made invisible (Luhmann 1998: 630f.). As an example, Luhmann could have used people categorised as 'handicapped', whose appearance and behaviour do not correspond to the ideas of normality. Despite efforts to dissolve the large so-called 'complex institutions', their living situation is still strongly characterised by spatial segregation of their places of residence, work and education.

This segregation of disability in devalued social locations in the margins of communities is characterised in disability studies by the term ableism. Correspondingly, Bill Hughes' (2014) notion of disablement, which he uses to describe the process by which impairments are transformed into disabilities and bodily differences into social relations of oppression, also targets both confinement through incapacity and deficit of credibility. Hughes, however, does not refer to Luhmann's theory, which theorises the autonomy of social (functional) systems as an evolutionary regularity, but to the human scientist Norbert Elias (2001). Following Elias' theory of the civilisation process, Hughes (2015) shows how ableism becomes predominant in highly civilised societies. But when Luhmann (1998: 632) states that in some regions of the globe, the variable inclusion/exclusion is about to take on the role of a meta-difference and to mediatise the codes of functional systems, this is certainly true for people who are labelled "disabled" and subjected to that invalidating dialectic of ableism.

Beyond Luhmann's thesis that the way in which societal functional systems include or exclude persons is thus overlaid by a much more general form of inclusion/exclusion, Stichweh (2009: 30) shows in what way the distinction of inclusion and exclusion affects the question of how persons are designated or addressed in social systems. He even claims to be able to overturn in this way the different paradigmatic roots of conceptual differentiation of inclusion and exclusion that he has elaborated in an almost dialectical way. Accordingly, he assumes that communicative acts of addressing persons grant or deny membership. Furthermore, they could be accompanied by the activation or denial of solidarity, as well as by an element of control and disciplining.

Sichtweh's attribution of Luhmann to the paradigm of social disciplining can be explained by the fact that his system theory assumes that systems address people in a specific way and that it is precisely in this functionality that they are included in the self-referential, autopoietic systems that reproduce themselves according to a specific rationality. As Albert Scherr (2000: 67) has made clear, this requires the persons addressed to discipline themselves sufficiently to participate in this highly specialised subsystemic communication.

Against this background, Scherr (ibid.: 78) has pointed out that the concept of integration, which aims at the whole individual, as it was used in both the German and the French translation of the UN-CRPD, is systematically deconstructed by Luhmann. Going far beyond the UN-CRPD, the objectives of inclusion propagated by the disability rights movement aim to open up social institutions and organisations to the individuality of each person. Surprisingly, this concept of inclusion does not appear at all in Stichweh's distinction of paradigms. Except for certain intimate systems of interaction, Luhmann (cf.

1993: 158) can only conceive of individuality beyond inclusion in systems as exclusion-individuality.

Despite all the criticism of Luhmann's concept of exclusion-individuality (cf. May 2001), the implementation of the inclusion objectives under the currently prevailing conditions is likely to amount to something completely different than a real community in which individuals in and through their association simultaneously attain their freedom (Marx/Engels 1978: 74). Rather, the vision of full inclusion remains, in the words of Lefebvre (2003: 45), 'imaginarily abstract' – because it abstracts from both – from these ruling conditions in social institutions and organisations and from what the now more or less voluntarily 'included' people 'really really want', as Bergmann (2005) has put it. With this term Bergmann refers to the contingency of interpretations of needs and their contextuality with a view to overcoming adaptive prefectures (cf. May 2020a: 47). Thus, these social systems, which are now supposed to transform into inclusive ones in the sense of the disability rights movement, have emerged largely without the participation of the people who are now supposed to be included in them and are no longer questioned in terms of their social functionality.

Although the political demand of the disability rights movement 'Nothing about us without us' is on everyone's lips as far as the relations of domination in the social systems – which are now challenged to transform into inclusive ones – are concerned, the strict systems-theoretical distinction between audience and performance-roles still prevails. This analytical perspective sees the various professionals in their respective specialisations functioning in the help system in performance-roles, while the addressed users assume an audience-role. Such a perspective remains all too plausible and empirically obvious. The same is true for Stichweh's (2009: 33) thesis that wherever the position of professions is strong, inclusion takes the form of care in the shape of 'people processing' of the audience-roles by the performance-roles of the system. Thus, people diagnosed on the basis of the International Classification of Functioning, Disability and Health (ICF) are still pushed into an audience-role by the professionals in their performance-role. In this role, they are processed back and forth between assisted living, employment-workshop and further leisure offers, which today are apostrophised as inclusive.

The current inclusion discourse is thus very much dominated by experts from the institutions of knowledge production and use (cf. Fraser 1994: 268). In addition to the employment-workshops, for which ableism is out of the question anyway, the largely expertocratically planned barrier-free apartments and residential communities (cf. May 2018) as well as the inclusive leisure activities, where the position of professionals is usually very strong, could also prove to be only slightly differently oriented socio-pedagogical hetero-topias in the sense of Foucault (2006).

Thus, the discourse criticised by Feuser (2013: 3) as inclusionism is not only associated with the formation of professional groups and institutions and with social 'problem-solving techniques'– as Fraser (1994: 269) characterised all expert discourses. Rather, political questions concerning the interpretation of the needs of people who are now to be 'included' are redefined in this discourse as legal, administrative and/or therapeutic matters (cf. ibid.: 237). This is then connected with a management of needs satisfaction that calls itself inclusive (cf. ibid.: 240). Legally, the so-called Federal Participation Act (BTHG) now provides the guideline in Germany.

Accordingly, the welfare associations and other organisations of the welfare state are institutionally implementing these measures, which are actually political with regard to the dialectic of participation and attendance, in a way that appears apolitical. As far as those affected are concerned, they still have a tendency to depoliticise. The question of who interprets their social needs and in what way does not seem to play a role in the current discourse on inclusion. There are indeed independent counselling centres that more or less support people eligible under the BTHG in finding out what they 'really really want' in the sense of Bergmann. However, this has to be translated into the corresponding operationalisations of the BTHG.

Just like the ICF mentioned above, the BTHG demands a breakdown of individuals into variables in which they have a need for support or in which this is no longer required for what is operationalised in the BTHG as participation. This is insofar curious, as it actually stands in contradiction to the inclusion concept of the disability rights movement, which – as outlined – aims to open up the social institutions for the individuality (translated from the Latin, in dividuum means indivisible!) of all. ICF and BTHG thus also tempt inclusion professionals not to focus on the individuality with which (potential) users of their person-related services approach the world and other people. Rather, they are encouraged by these instruments to focus only on the specific needs predefined by their corresponding operationalisations. However, these are not oriented towards what the people to be included really want as individuals, but towards normalisation. In addition, the diagnosis and permanent verification of eligibility is accompanied by the danger of stigmatisation in the sense of Goffman (1967).

Thus, assistance or participation planning imposes a process of permanent evaluation not only on the professionals but also on the users of their personal services as to whether they can (already) cope with certain everyday tasks on their own or to what extent they (still) need professional support. This is accompanied by corresponding reifying self-observations of the users and an impression management, in which they attempt to conform to the objectives more or less imposed on them in the context of participation planning (cf. May 2022).

Here, the maxim of Lefebvre's everyday critique helping everydayness to produce a 'present-absent fullness' (1972: 31) within it opens up a different perspective. This seems paradoxical. However, this impression dissolves against the background of his space-theoretical concept of U-topias (cf. 1999: 163ff.; 2003: 44ff.). For this concept, in the sense of the ancient Greek meaning of u topos – to have no place – aims at objective, i.e. not merely imagined, possibilities as a fullness that is in this sense definitely present, but at the same time absent, because it has not yet had a place to realise itself.

Thus, such a U-Topian has nothing in common with the imaginary abstracts as criticised earlier following Lefebvre (2003: 45) in the vision of a full inclusion. As objective possibilities exposed by domination, to which the adherence of materialistic disability pedagogy to the intransitive disabled refers in contrast to the other wording demanded today in the course of political correctness, this U-topian is real. Yes, it is the core of a concept of reality that does not apologetically reduce these people on the basis of corresponding ICF diagnoses to what could be realised by them so far under conditions of domination – not least ableism and the invalidation associated with it.

It is understandable that the demand for inclusion of the disability rights movement aims at a change of systems. Paradoxically, however, this is accompanied by the fact that (disabled) people are included in these systems, i.e. they implicitly become passive objects. In contrast, Lefebvre's (2016: 189) right to the city explicitly includes the right to the work – i.e. to make organisations and institutions as well as space one's own work – and the right to active subjective appropriation, which he clearly distinguishes from the right to property. Against this background, the right to individualisation in socialisation as another part of this higher legal form of a right to the city would be an objective that describes more precisely than that of inclusion the envisaged dialectic of participation (Teilhabe) and attendance (Teilnahme) of subaltern groups (May 2020b: 23ff.), which also include disabled people.

2. Social space development and social space organisation as community-oriented perspectives beyond the prevailing *Inclusion Discourse*

In order to bring forth Lefebvre's postulate of the *U-Topia* by means of maieutic, which transforms the original meaning of the Greek word as the "art of midwifery" in a way that is critical of everyday life, as a ferment-like reality (cf. May 2017: 129ff.), we have developed (cf. May/Alisch 2015) a concept of *social space development* and *social space organisation*.

The idea of *social space development* is about supporting people who have been hindered by society in their authentic, political expression of their own needs and interests, in creating a social and spatial framework for dialogical, participatory processes. Nancy Fraser (cf. 1994: 240) aptly defined such processes as the *politics of needs-interpretation* by those affected. Because what they 'really really' want can only be found out by these people labelled as 'disabled' themselves on their way out of the excluding institutions or their overprotective family households.

This requires appropriate communicative processes that come as close as possible to the ideals of democracy, equality and fairness (cf. ibid.: 281) and make it possible to recognise, bring up and articulate own needs and interests. It is therefore about much more than the questioning of 'desires' that is embedded in many participatory processes. In contrast to the common concepts of participation planning in the context of the BTHG, we assume that ultimately only those affected themselves can – in a corresponding process of experience – open up for themselves the specific spatial and social framework conditions they would need in order to interpret their needs and then also to be able to articulate these needs publicly as social demands. In this process, social space is developed as an expression of their own life plans.

The concept of social space development is by no means limited to the groups of people that are mostly addressed in the political and social discourse on inclusion. Rather, it aims to ensure that groups of people who are connected through common interests not only have appropriate space in special places created by institutions of social work, social pedagogy or services for the disabled but also appropriate *spaces for the representation* of their life experiences and life plans.

In a first step, this means – if there are not already relevant initiatives for those affected – taking concrete *spatial interest orientations*, as they become clear from so-called disabled people in the practical contexts of their specific groups, networks and initiatives. Michael Winkler (2021) calls this approach to social work *socio-educational local action* (sozialpädagogisches Ortshandeln). With regard to the dialectical relationship between participation and attendance, it is important to realise more social participation with *social space development*, in participatory planning processes with the participation and involvement of those affected, and to do so in an area that is clearly defined in terms of content, space and time. Based on Winkler's distinction, this form of social space development would be assigned to *social work, which abolishes the discourse of social pedagogy*.

However, such processes must necessarily go beyond the spatially and temporally very limited, situational networking of *space-related interest orientations* of the people concerned. This is a self-regulated joint production of social spaces, but nevertheless mostly initiated and also designed by social work professionals. It is part of a comprehensive work on a community that does not exclude and promotes the subjectivity of all its members (Kunstreich/ May 1999). It is therefore necessary to complement this form of *social space development* with an approach *to social space organisation*. In contrast to a legal-administrative-therapeutic management of the satisfaction of needs (Fraser 1994: 240) in the course of the BTHG, as we outlined in the first part of this paper, this approach can certainly be understood as a struggle to integrate institutional arrangements of social administration in order to make the socially bureaucratically managed resources fruitful for the *social space development* of those people.

Such a form of overarching *social space organisation* is not necessarily tied to geographic boundaries of a container space like a neighbourhood or district. Rather, it is based on the socio-culturally very different forms of space use and space appropriation of the by no means homogeneous group of people who are subsumed under the category 'disabled'.

Only on this basis can the process of *social space organisation* be expanded in further steps with regard to democratic negotiation processes with other groups. Social work professionals would have the task of moderation or, in the case of conflicts, mediation. Under the maxim of creating a non-exclusive community that promotes the subjectivity of each member, an attitude of *impartiality* is required. *Impartiality* in this sense means ensuring that all those (groups) involved in these negotiation processes have the same opportunities to assert their needs and interests. In the case of people who have been handicapped in this respect up to now, it is necessary to give them opportunities again and again – also through *local socio-pedagogical action* – to create an appropriate framework for a policy of needs interpretation through *social space development* spatially and socially. This is the only way for this group to be able to appropriate the territory that is involved in an overarching *social space organisation* for the representation of their own life experiences and interests.

The critical discussion of the term and the discourse on inclusion is always in danger of being limited to members of the community labelled as 'disabled'. In our explanations and the attempt to offer an approach for research and practice of social work with the concept of *social space development* and *social space organisation*, the aim is to address all people (groups) inclusively – so to speak – who directly or indirectly experience obstruction of their own interests and needs. Indirect blocking contexts in the form of denied spatial realisation conditions are linked to the fact that these affected people have not yet been able to ascertain their social demands through a *policy of interpreting needs*. In addition, it also applies to groups that are not only brought together because of their interests in the context *of social space development* but who already have their own strategies for acquiring spaces of representation in a social space. These groups must also be able to reassure themselves of their underlying interests over and over again.

It therefore seems necessary to repeatedly open up opportunities for those concerned to use relevant experiences to ascertain whether this or another type of *social space development* enables what they consider to be the most appropriate realisation of their life plans (cf. Alisch/May 2022).

On this basis, a process of *social space organisation* can be expanded in further steps, spirally, so to speak, in its democratic negotiation processes, in order to ensure that all those involved are given the same opportunities for comprehensive participation and participation in society as a whole.

References

Alisch, M.; May, M. (2022): Management. In: Kessl, F./Reutlinger, Ch. (Ed.): Sozialraum – eine elementare Einführung. Wiesbaden: Springer VS. pp. 265-276.
Bergmann, F. (2005): Die Freiheit leben. 1. Aufl. Freiamt im Schwarzwald.
Cremer-Schäfer, H. (2001): Ein politisches Mandat schreibt man sich zu. Zur Politik (mit) der Sozialen Arbeit. In: Merten, R. (Ed.): Hat soziale Arbeit ein politisches Mandat? Positionen zu einem strittigen Thema. Opladen. pp. 55-69.
Diebäcker, M. (2014): Soziale Arbeit als staatliche Praxis im städtischen Raum. Sozialraumforschung und Sozialraumarbeit, Band 13. Wiesbaden.
Elias, N. (2001): Über den Prozeß der Zivilisation: Soziogenetische und psychogenetische Untersuchungen. 1. Aufl., [Neuausg.], 24. [Dr.]. Suhrkamp-Taschenbuch Wissenschaft, Band 158. Frankfurt a.M.
Feuser, G. (2013): Inklusive Bildung – ein pädagogisches Paradox. Vortrag im Rahmen der Jahrestagung 2013 der Leibniz-Sozietät mit der Thematik "Inklusion und Integration" an der Universität Potsdam am 31. Mai 2013.
Foucault, M. (2006): Von anderen Räumen. In: Dünne, J. et al. (Ed.): Raumtheorie. Grundlagentexte aus Philosophie und Kulturwissenschaften. 1. Aufl., Originalausg. Suhrkamp Taschenbuch Wissenschaft, Band 1800. Frankfurt a.M. pp. 317-329.
Fraser, N. (1994): Widerspenstige Praktiken. Macht, Diskurs, Geschlecht. Dt. Erstausg., 1. Aufl. Gender studies, Band 1726. Frankfurt a.M.
Goffman, Erving (1967): Stigma. Über Techniken der Bewältigung beschädigter Identität. Suhrkamp-Taschenbuch Wissenschaft, Band 140. Frankfurt am Main: Suhrkamp.
Hughes, B. (2014): Invalidierung: Eine Theoretisierung der Ausschließung von Behinderung. In: Widersprüche Redaktion (Ed.): Inklusion – Versprechungen vom Ende der Ausgrenzung. Widersprüche. Zeitschrift für sozialistische Politik im Bildungs-, Gesundheits- und Sozialbereich, Band 133. Münster. pp. 51-58.
Hughes, B. (2015): Zivilisierung und ontologische Invalidierung von Menschen mit Behinderung. Teil I. In: Widersprüche Redaktion (Ed.): Sozialraum ist die Antwort. Was war nochmals die Frage? Widersprüche. Zeitschrift für sozialistische Politik im Bildungs-, Gesundheits- und Sozialbereich, Band 135. Münster. pp. 121-131.

Jantzen, W. (2016): Einführung in die Behindertenpädagogik. Eine Vorlesung. Schriftenreihe International Cultural-historical Human Sciences, Band 53. Berlin: Lehmanns Media GmbH.
Kunstreich, T./May, M. (1999): Soziale Arbeit als Bildung des Sozialen und Bildung am Sozialen. In: Widersprüche Redaktion (Ed.): Transversale Bildung – wider die Unbilden der Lerngesellschaft. Widersprüche, 19.1999=73. Bielefeld. pp. 35-52.
Lefebvre, H. (1972): Das Alltagsleben in der modernen Welt. 1. Aufl. Theorie. Frankfurt am Main: Suhrkamp.
Lefebvre, H. (2003): Die Revolution der Städte. 1. Aufl. Berlin.
Lefebvre, H. (2016): Das Recht auf Stadt. Deutsche Erstausgabe. Flugschrift. Hamburg: Edition Nautilus.
Luhmann, N. (1993): Individuum, Individualität, Individualismus. In: Luhmann, N. (Ed.): Gesellschaftsstruktur und Semantik. Studien zur Wissenssoziologie der modernen Gesellschaft. 1. Aufl. Frankfurt am Main: Suhrkamp, pp. 149–258.
Luhmann, N. (1996): Jenseits von Barbarei. In: Miller, M./Soeffner, H.-G. (Ed.): Modernität und Barbarei. Soziologische Zeitdiagnose am Ende des 20. Jahrhunderts. 2. Aufl./Suhrkamp-Taschenbuch/Wissenschaft] Suhrkamp-Taschenbuch Wissenschaft, Band 1243. Frankfurt a.M. pp. 219-230.
Luhmann, N. (1998): Die Gesellschaft der Gesellschaft. Suhrkamp-Taschenbuch Wissenschaft. Frankfurt a.M.
Marshall, T.H. (1992): Bürgerrechte und soziale Klassen. Zur Soziologie des Wohlfahrtsstaates. Theorie und Gesellschaft, Band 22. Frankfurt a.M.
Marx, K./Engels, F. (1978): Die Deutsche Ideologie. Kritik der neuesten deutschen Philosophie in ihren Repräsentanten Feuerbach, B. Bauer und Stirner, und des deutschen Sozialismus in seinen verschiedenen Propheten. MEW, Band 3. Berlin:
May, M. (2001): Wider den Zynismus einer Luhmannisierung der Theorie Sozialer Arbeit. Eine Antwort auf Albert Scherr. In: Widersprüche Redaktion (Ed.): Fragmente städtischen Alltags. Widersprüche, Band 78. Bielefeld. pp. 95-114.
May, M. (2010): Aktuelle Theoriediskurse Sozialer Arbeit. Eine Einführung. 3. Auflage. Wiesbaden: VS Verlag für Sozialwissenschaften/GWV Fachverlage GmbH Wiesbaden.
May, M. (2012): Segregation und Soziale Arbeit:. Ausschluss und Einschluss. In: May, M./Alisch, M. (Ed.): Formen sozialräumlicher Segregation. Beiträge zur Sozialraumforschung, Band 7. Opladen, Berlin, Toronto. pp. 135-156.
May, M. (2014): Zur Mäeutik durch Intersektionalitäten in ihrer Verwirklichung blockierter Vermögen von Heranwachsenden. In: Langsdorff, N. (Ed.): Jugendhilfe und Intersektionalität. Leverkusen. pp. 135-155.
May, Michael (2017): Soziale Arbeit als Arbeit am Gemeinwesen. Ein theoretischer Begründungsrahmen. 1. Auflage. Beiträge zur Sozialraumforschung, Band 14. Leverkusen: Budrich, Barbara.
May, M. (2018): Wohnraum und Wohnzufriedenheit. In: May, M./Ehrhardt, A./ Schmidt, M. (Ed.): MitLeben: Sozialräumliche Dimensionen der Inklusion geistig behinderter Menschen. 1. Auflage. Beiträge zur Sozialraumforschung, Band 16. Leverkusen: Budrich, Barbara, pp. 59–74.
May, M. (2020a): Methodologische Implikationen von Subjektbegriffen unterschiedlicher Theorien Sozialer Arbeit. In: van Rießen, A./Jepkens, K. (Ed.): Nutzen, Nicht-Nutzen und Nutzung Sozialer Arbeit. Wiesbaden: Springer Fachmedien Wiesbaden, pp. 41–58.

May, M. (2020b): Partizipative Sozialraumforschung und gesellschaftliche Teilhabe. In: Meier, S./Schlenker, K. (Ed.): Teilhabe und Raum. Interdisziplinäre Perspektiven und Annäherungen an Dimensionen von Teilhabe. Beiträge zur Sozialraumforschung, Band 20. Opladen [u.a.]: Barbara Budrich.

May, M. (2022): VISION-RA Aufklärung der Interaktionen zwischen Fachkräften der Gemeindepsychiatrie und Nutzenden ihrer Dienstleistungen. Schriftenreihe des Zentrums für Soziale Interventionsforschung, Band 2. Frankfurt am Main: Frankfurt University of Applied Sciences.

May, M./Alisch, M. (2015): Zum Zusammenhang von Normalität, Inklusion, Sozialraumentwicklung und -organisation. In: Alisch, M./May, M. (Ed.): "Das ist doch nicht normal…!" Sozialraumentwicklung, Inklusion und Konstruktionen von Normalität. 1. Aufl. Beiträge zur Sozialraumforschung, Band 13. Leverkusen: Budrich, pp. 7–29.

Scherr, A. (2000): Was nutzt die soziologische Systemtheorie für eine Theorie der Sozialen Arbeit? In: Widersprüche Redaktion (Ed.): Der kontrakulturelle Sozialstaat – Herrschaft des Managements? Ende der Profession? Widersprüche, H. 77. Bielefeld: Kleine, pp. 63–80.

Simmel, G. (1992): Soziologie. Untersuchungen über die Formen der Vergesellschaftung. 1. Aufl. Suhrkamp-Taschenbuch Wissenschaft, Band 811. Frankfurt a.M.

Stichweh, R. (2009): Inklusion und Exklusion. Analysen zur Sozialstruktur und sozialen Ungleichheit. Wiesbaden: VS Verlag für Sozialwissenschaften

Winkler, M. (2021): Eine Theorie der Sozialpädagogik. Neuausgabe mit einem neuen Nachwort. Beltz Juventa: Weinheim Basel.

Opportunities for inclusive community development

Marcel Schmidt

Introduction

Since the UN Convention on the Rights of Persons with Disabilities, which was adopted in 2006 and entered into force in 2008, inclusion has repeatedly been referred to as a human right (Degener et al. 2016). On closer inspection, however, according to Kastl, it "does not create a new human right of 'inclusion' but is based on the 1948 United Nations' 'Universal Declaration of Human Rights' already in existence at the time, as well as the International Covenants on 'Civil and Political Rights' (Civil Covenant) and 'Economic, Social and Cultural Rights' ('Social Covenant') of 1966, which were concluded in its wake" (Kastl 2018: 667). Accordingly, inclusion is not specifically referred to as a human right in the UN CRPD, but as a "structural principle" (ibid.: 675) for the realisation of human rights. In this context, Winkler (2014: 36), too, states with reference to the inclusion debates: "Human rights can only be realised by establishing societal infrastructures and chances as well as open access for all to all imaginable social and cultural opportunities necessary for the fulfilment of human life". The inclusion debate is therefore, according to Winkler, "largely conducted on a level of political debate which is concerned with changing society" (ibid.: 37), in order not to misconstrue inclusion in a reductionist sense as "inclusion in a society which repeatedly and downright systematically produces exclusion" (ibid.: 38).

Based on Winkler's opinions, but also with a view to supplementing them, this article aims to illustrate that inclusion should be understood not only as a structural principle, but above all as a mandate for social work to search for ways to support people in bringing about inclusive communities.

Against this background, the term inclusion will first be examined in more detail (chapter 2), and then placed in the context of community-oriented social work approaches aimed at promoting inclusion (chapter 3). Subsequently, organisational, and structural conditions of inclusive community development in the context of cooperative urban development and planning processes will be discussed (chapter 4) and these in turn examined in the context of transdisciplinary as well as multi-professional real-world laboratory projects, highlighting the special challenges for social work (chapters 5 and 6).

1. Inclusion – from the action plan to the structural principle

Since the 1994 UN statement in Salamanca on "Special Needs Education", which called for "'education for all'" and "'inclusion as the inclusion of all", including disabled children "'within the regular education system'" (UNESCO 1994, VIII, cited in Kastl 2018: 666), the term inclusion has evolved from an "action plan for the school education sector" (ibid.) to a "structural principle of modern, complex societies that consider themselves democratic" (ibid.: 675). Hinz, for example, understands inclusion as a completely new approach to participation and social integration, "which argues on the basis of civil rights, opposes all forms of social marginalisation, and thus wants to see all people guaranteed the same full right to individual development and social participation regardless of their personal support needs" (Hinz 2006: 98). Such inclusion for all, if you will, requires, as Kastl concludes, "reliable and reciprocal arrangements that can be safely expected" (Kastl 2018: 675). In addition to statutory legal rights to access to all areas of community and social life and public service infrastructures, however, citizens must above all also have the opportunity at the lifeworld level to be able to not only have individual access to areas of community and social life and public service infrastructures, but also to develop an individual participatory role (ibid.). In other words, rights alone do not lead to integration in urban development and planning processes, for example, let alone to actually have a voice on the ground that is taken seriously and into consideration during the further development of processes. What is required instead is mutual recognition of the diverse and highly varied needs and abilities of the stakeholders involved, as well as a willingness to engage in social processes of identifying and articulating needs. In other words, inclusion can only be realised through the social development of a common third party, a community that connects people with one another on a level that is no longer merely based on legal technicalities, but on human compassion and subjectivity.

2. Inclusion in the context of community work

The concept of inclusion thus also refers to the necessity of "working on the community" (May 2017b). In the light of current, constantly developing syndromes of "group-based misanthropy" (Grau/Heitmeyer 2011) and "generalised constructions of rejection" (Möller 2016), this must ultimately be seen as one of the fundamental challenges of inclusive community development. The way social work is understood here, namely as support "for the de facto exercise of rights and roles", primarily involves supporting people in their individual and also joint development of "skills, abilities and knowledge necessary for the de facto exercise of roles" as well as "social relationships" (Kastl 2018: 676).

With regard to such work on inclusive communities, Maykus distinguishes between two perspectives, that of "inclusive community" and that of "community inclusion", "which together make up the whole extent of inclusive practice in cities and municipalities" (Maykus 2017a: 33). He describes "inclusive community" as "the practice of social services and planning that aims to ensure that legal requirements and conceptual goals of inclusion are implemented. Inclusive community stands for correspondingly active social services and planning, whereas community inclusion focuses on community as a space of lifeworld communication" (ibid.: 33f). Or to put it differently: "Inclusive community thus stands for the organisation of infrastructure, and community inclusion for the dialogical process of citizens in a municipality as the subjectification and expression of care for the community in a polycontextural society of multiple forms of the present, which demonstrates inclusion in the functional and social dimension." (Maykus 2017b: 110f)

While Maykus' differentiation on the one hand enables a more precise analysis of the processes of subjectification and structure formation inherent in a development of inclusion, it remains, on the other hand, rooted in an ontological separation of system and lifeworld. It is as if systems existed independently of people, instead of them creating, reproducing and also (being able to) change them through their everyday actions. In contrast, the concept of social space development and organisation (Alisch/May 2013, 2015; May 2017b) not only expresses Maykus' distinction between community inclusion and inclusive community, but also places both levels in a dialectical relationship to one another.

Alisch and May understand social space development as designing spaces with pedagogical support and guidance in a way that the people and groups who use these spaces are encouraged to shape them themselves to the greatest possible extent. This includes being able to autonomously appropriate these spaces and redesign them for their own needs. At the same time, this includes the prospect of having to look for ways to share public spaces with other groups and their interests and to resolve conflicts democratically instead of opposing one another (Alisch/May 2013: 19f). Social space development is thus located at the level of subjectification, and thus Maykus' definition of community inclusion (2017b: 110f). With the term social space organisation, Alisch and May link subjectification to the formation of structures. They understand social space organisation as the democratic resolution of conflicts that are located beyond the respective groups and are managed by municipal authorities or local government politics, and which can sometimes severely limit the possibilities to appropriate and shape social space and thus also limit the development of community inclusion. These can be issues concerning ownership, utilisation concepts, structural accessibility, and architectural barriers. Ultimately, Alisch and May's concept of social space organisation aims to establish a co-producing form of urban development and social planning that places all the stakeholders in a social and/or communal space in an organisational relationship that enables them to mutually "interpret needs" (Fraser 1994: 237ff), thereby making it possible to develop and manage the social space of the city while acknowledging the different lifeworlds and needs involved (Alisch/May 2015: 20). The goal is thus "the realisation of a non-exclusionary community that is as social as it is democratic" (May 2017b: 172). In other words, the goal is the development of an inclusive community, in which social space development or community inclusion help to create social space organisation or inclusive community, which is ultimately intended to structurally support the further development of community inclusion, so that inclusive community can also develop further as a result. For Alisch and May too, however, "active social services and planning" that ensure that "legal requirements and conceptual goals of inclusion are implemented" are the prerequisite to enable community inclusion or social space development (Maykus 2017a: 33 f.). At the same time, however, May concedes that such a "non-exclusionary community that is as social as it is democratic" (May 2017b: 172) "can only be realised in a social cooperative form" (ibid.: 176), since only in this way would the relationship between system and lifeworld be placed in an organisational framework that could help to break down the barriers between the two and render more permeable their strict separation.

3. Cooperative community development

Flieger (2003, 2019) specifies five principles of cooperative organisation: the promotion principle (promoting social/cultural concerns of members through collective business operations), the democracy principle (heterarchical opportunities for active participation in the cooperative), the identity principle (identification with the cooperative's product portfolio, production methods, and supply chains as well as with the goals and development of the cooperative itself), the solidarity principle (supporting one another in order to be able to do together what no member could do alone), the community principle (the neighbourhood, the urban quarter, the district, the city as the area in which the cooperatives are active). Social cooperatives are also characterised by the fact that they are starting "to approach economic issues from a social perspective" (Kunstreich 2005: 114). Either as self-organised cooperatives of groups comprising stakeholders with specific statuses to cooperatively deal with shared concerns (e.g. senior citizens' cooperatives) or in order to exercise the rights of third parties (e.g. children or people with disabilities) on the basis of solidarity, be it through the social cooperative alliance of friends and family or by professional specialists (Flieger 2003).

Around 100 years ago, Paul Natorp already went a step further and advocated organising not only certain sub-areas of life and public services on a cooperative basis, but also the entirety of communal life: Starting with (social) cooperative associations and the (social) cooperative merger of these associations into a (social) cooperative of (social) cooperatives, all areas of communal life should gradually unite to form the "cooperative of cooperatives" (Natorp 1922: 113), "up to the most comprehensive whole, the welfare state" (ibid.). In Natorp's proposal of what might be called a community cooperative or community multi-stakeholder cooperative, not only should the various groups of stakeholders and statuses in municipal civil society be able to meet among themselves as equal members, but also the stakeholders providing and using municipal infrastructures (from education, health and housing services to communications and electricity supply, waste disposal, water supply and wastewater disposal, public transport, etc.) as well as local companies and investors. Even representatives of state authorities and local politics would be active cooperative stakeholders in the community cooperative.

The transfer of cooperative and social cooperative principles to the development and organisation of urban space would open up vast potential for inclusive community development. Urban residents, for example, would be entitled to demand spatial, structural, and also financial support from the local government state apparatus, or its representatives, that benefited their subjective development, which would then also need to be negotiated and agreed upon with all the other members of the community cooperative. At the same time, the authorities and local enterprises would be required to implement the decisions taken, in which they as equal-ranking stakeholders will have been involved.

Only in a community cooperative with such a dialogical-reflexive approach would it be possible to speak of an urban quarter, a district, a city, a local government, or generally speaking: a community, as being "shaped in accordance with lifeworlds and not merely an administrative construction" (Richter 1998: 195) – as Richter pre-empted Maykus' (2017a, 2017b) concept of community inclusion.

The goal of cooperatively organised community development is thus a "right to the city" (Lefebvre 2016; Schmidt 2020) that legitimises urban residents to create and use social spaces and infrastructures for themselves through co-producing social and urban planning processes. Spaces and infrastructures that help them to dialogically and reflexively produce a fair (in the sense defined by Rawls 2003, 2012, 1998) form of urban development, i.e. one that is geared to the individual requirements of its members and organised along generally comprehensible rules and procedures, and to deal democratically with the conflicts that arise in the process.

At the same time, however, it cannot be a matter of guaranteeing a right to subjective development in and with urban spaces and infrastructures solely for the proactive stakeholders of such a community cooperative and excluding all less or non-proactively involved urban residents from community development. This would mean failing to achieve the goal of inclusive community development. One could only speak of urban development and planning being organised in a socially cooperative manner when its economic and political policies start to stem from a common good that extends beyond the benefit of its (proactive) members. In other words, when these also base their actions on a principle of solidarity with the lifeworld concerns not only of their less active members, but also of the non-members and beneficiaries of the community cooperative, and look for ways to democratically involve them, advance their interests, and support them in their concerns. Only in this way can they also enable the personal development of people and groups who cannot productively participate in the urban development and social planning process but can only benefit from it: groups of people, for example, who cannot yet be persuaded to participate in a cooperative project due to a variety of experiences of alienation and/or marginalisation. But also, groups of people who, due to physical, mental, or intellectual impairments, are not or no longer able to productively participate in such projects. In a communal cooperative of this kind, all the people and groups of an urban quarter, a district, or a city, whether as members or beneficiaries, would – at least in theory – be granted the cooperative right to receive support and assistance. At the same time, no one could continue to take only their own (group-related) interests into consideration, but everyone would be forced to deal with the other interest groups of the communal cooperative, who have exactly the same rights.

Initially, this may all sound like a distant prospect and theoretically contrived. However, research into cooperatives in Germany reveals three trends that could make these developments possible. First, we can see that for some years now, as a consequence of the long nationwide austerity policy and the systematic collapse of infrastructures as a result of ruinous cost-cutting (Peck 2015; Eckardt 2018), numerous community-oriented social cooperatives have been founded in order to operate local government public service infrastructures in a spirit of solidarity and thus to maintain or rebuild them (Schmale/Ravensburg 2017; Thürling 2017, 2018). Secondly, it is becoming apparent that "in the course of demographic decline, problems in ensuring the provision of services" are becoming foreseeable – and not only in rural regions, but also in urban areas and large conurbations – as a result of which the "supply infrastructure can no longer be guaranteed" (Schulz-Nieswandt 2017: 352). In such regions and cities, municipal multi-stakeholder cooperatives as public-private partnership projects can ensure "services for the public in a very elementary existential sense" (ibid.). And finally – thirdly – it is apparent that, as mentioned above, not only are numerous community-oriented social cooperatives being established, but "more and more local governments are also looking for cooperative models of collaboration. For example, in the form of urban quarter and district cooperatives or municipal multi-stakeholder cooperatives" (Thürling 2018: 27).

However, these developments should not blind us to the fact that while such municipal cooperative projects "take on very important tasks in the provision of public services," they also have a "kind of stopgap function" (Schulz-Nieswandt 2017: 346f). Instead of such municipal cooperative projects being founded in order to proactively organise communal life in a renewed spirit of solidarity, they are still operating on a rather reactive level.

One attempt to proactively develop municipal cooperative projects are real world laboratories. The concept of real world laboratories is a response to climate change and the resulting need for inclusive participatory structures and organisational forms of urban development and planning processes, which at the same time demand educational and development processes that could bring about lasting changes in everyday community life at subjective and structural levels (Schneidewind/Singer-Brodowski 2015; Schneidewind 2014; WBGU 2016).

4. Real world laboratories as places of inclusive community development

Real world laboratories are long-term projects, i.e., socio-culturally, and socio-economically sustainable, civil society-oriented transdisciplinary and transformative research projects, which differ "sometimes considerably" from, for example, (urban or sustainable) living labs or (urban or sustainable) transition labs (Parodi et al. 2016: 15). The real world laboratory projects, developed heterarchically with all the stakeholders and accompanied by professionals from a range of disciplines, have an experimental character and can therefore be described as real world experiments. What is meant, however, are not uncontrolled experiments on the real lives of the stakeholders with a random outcome, but experiments that first are "carried out under at least partially controlled conditions", second are "integrated into a theoretical context" (e.g., inclusive community development), third are geared to the competencies and needs of those involved from civil society, local economy, politics and administration, fourth, in which "conditions, progress, and results are comprehensively documented" and fifth, whose "primary goal and result is new knowledge" (ibid.). Instead of "real world experiments", it would therefore be more fitting to call them "'transdisciplinary experiments'", "'sustainability experiments'" or "'transformation experiments'" (ibid.: 16), which transform urban space and real everyday community life into an experimental laboratory.

In other words, real world laboratories provide the stakeholders involved with a structural framework for scientifically accompanied urban development and planning processes in order to experiment with new forms and hierarchies of participation and to create the necessary conditions for implementation on the level of the stakeholders' lifeworld and biographical experiences as well as on the organisational and socio-structural level and to receive multi-professional support for this purpose. Real world laboratories therefore offer significant potential for the dialectical development of an inclusive community, i.e., for the reciprocal development of community inclusion and inclusive community (Maykus 2017a, 2017b) or social space development/organisation (Alisch/May 2013, 2015; May 2017b). If such real world laboratory projects were then also organised as cooperatives, this would at the same time create a legally binding framework of cooperative urban development and planning which would enable the project to be carried out on an inclusive basis not only during its phase as a publicly funded laboratory situation, but also to continue it after this stage has come to an end.

Social work could support real world laboratory projects, for example, through community-based pedagogical facilitation (Richter 2019: 172f) as well as through practice research initiating social space development and organisation processes, thus making a valuable contribution to the successful development of inclusion. Research could be conducted, for example, on how vulnerable and/or marginalised population groups could be involved in the real world laboratories in a social space-oriented way which is congruent with their lifeworlds. This applies above all to people from subaltern milieus (Spivak 2008) who, due to biographical constellations and/or milieu-specific experiences, are not used to articulating their needs beyond internalised clichés or intersectional barriers and to defending them against others whom they consider to be of a higher status. People, for example, who were socialised in total institutions (Goffman 2020) and/or "greedy institutions" (Coser 1974) and who throughout their lives have had little experience of having a say in the discursive shaping of their structural living conditions. They would first have to (re)train skills such as these with the help of social pedagogical support (Winkler 2006), to enable them to articulate what, from their subjective point of view, should be criticised and changed (in line with Alisch/May, we could speak here of social space development). Only then would the conditions be in place for them, too, to be able to participate in the rhetorically demanding process of real world laboratories and real world experiments. In addition, the reproduction of everyday hegemonies of state institutions and social groups would have to be researched in order to ultimately prevent, at least as far as possible, marginalised population groups and their needs from being ignored

Opportunities for inclusive community development

once again, despite their being structurally integrated, which would have the consequence that the development of community inclusion – despite the best intentions of the stakeholders – would fail to materialise (Maykus 2017a, 2017b).

The goal of community inclusion poses a number of serious problems for social work, which professionals in the field must address through strategic transdisciplinary practice research aimed at social space development/organisation in order to recognise and prevent the (re)production of subjective and structural exclusions – for example, the possibly quite significant differences in terms of competence and experience between the various groups of stakeholders and status groups with regard to cooperative and co-producing work processes. Heterarchical work processes are likely to be particularly difficult for, and possibly alienate, those stakeholders and groups (but not only these) for whom it was/is more natural, due to their social education, background and position, to assert their own interests, needs and privileges instead of putting them up for discussion and thus possibly entering into compromises that may deprive them of privileges. And, with the goal of also including hitherto marginalised population groups, comes the additional difficulty that real world laboratories also include people who have begun to organise themselves – possibly over longer periods of time – in order to deal with their concerns or to pursue their needs and interests, and who will initially reject any cooperation with status groups whose interests and concerns they perceive or have even experienced as being the cause of their marginalisation. Given the experiences in similarly collaborative projects (May 2017a), it is foreseeable that real world experimental cooperation projects that want to include the range of lifeworlds of a district or an entire city, municipality or region will quickly reach the limits of mutual acceptance here, which will then need to be addressed and dealt with through methods of social pedagogical facilitation.

Another problem which should not be underestimated is that broad sections of the population are losing interest in the development of collective strategies in favour of group-focused strategies or "generalised constructions of rejection" (Möller 2016). It can be assumed that this development is also reflected in real world laboratories and needs to be dealt with using facilitation methods, requiring a degree of milieu sensitivity and diversity competence that is difficult to achieve as part of the facilitation process (May 2017a).

In other words, the professionals are confronted with conflicting interests that are difficult to reconcile. On the one hand, hegemonic groups of stakeholders must be curbed in their established dominant positions in order to give others the opportunity to be present in the real world laboratories in a way that is congruent with their lifeworld, which on the other hand always means not assigning due value to the experiential knowledge of some in favour of the experiential knowledge of others. The more attempts are made to avoid this dilemma with a form of facilitation that is very much "geared towards compromise and conciliation" (May 2017a: 154), the more the facilitation also runs the risk of relieving the individual groups of the responsibility of dealing with their conflicts with one another. While such conflicts can certainly lead to the failure of transformative inclusion experiments, they also hold the enormous potential of developing mutual appreciation and productive processes of compromise. Ultimately, however, it is only when these are achieved that community inclusion becomes possible for all the stakeholders from civil society, the local economy, politics and administration, because they are then able to identify with the urban development and planning concepts that have been jointly developed (a process that can sometimes be difficult and fraught with conflict) and are willing to support them. Only then would the strategies and concepts for an inclusive community developed in the real world laboratories be socially sustainable.

5. And social work?

The list of social work's pedagogical and research contributions necessary for the successful development of inclusive, i.e. vulnerability- and subject-centred communities in the context of real world laboratory experiments could be continued ad infinitum. However, outside of its own theoretical and academic discourses, social work is still rarely perceived as a profession engaged in scientific research and practice. Räuchle, for example, observes that "many services offered by social work" are similar to "interventions in real world laboratories, with quite comparable aspirations in terms of transformative goals," however, "they lack scientific conception and supervision" (Räuchle 2021: 299). This is all the more astonishing in light of the fact that Räuchle is analysing a real world laboratory in Hanover (Germany) that has "cultivated relatively close contacts with social work projects since 2018" (ibid.: 297f). Criticism must therefore be directed at the social work professionals themselves, who – at least in Germany – still far too rarely succeed in presenting themselves in practice as a scientific profession of social transformation with the competence to contribute to the experimental development of inclusive communities.

But instead of accusing professionals of being incapable, it would be more important to take a closer look at why they do not succeed in working in a research-based way in practice. To do this, however, the focus would have to be more on the widening gap in terms of the different logics of action and everyday life between the worlds of academic and professional social work, rather than on the lack of competencies and inadequate status policy of the professionals themselves. The question that therefore needs to be asked is which working conditions the professionals need in order to be able to participate in the dialogical process of inclusive community development as community pedagogues on the one hand, and to be able to carry out the necessary research into obstacles and opportunities of community inclusion in situ on the other. This ultimately leads us to the question of the possibilities of a more close-knit cooperation between professional and academic social work, especially in terms of location, as was begun in the founding years of social work in the Hull House Project in Chicago (Staub-Bernasconi 2013) and has since never been achieved again.

References

Alisch, Monika/May, Michael (2013): Von der Sozialraumorientierung zu Sozialraumentwicklung/Sozialraumorganisation. In: Alisch, M./May, M. (Ed.): Sozialraumentwicklung und Raumaneignung von Kindern und Jugendlichen. Leverkusen-Opladen: Barbara Budrich-Esser, pp. 7-28.

Alisch, Monika/May, Michael (2015): Zum Zusammenhang von Normalität, Inklusion, Sozialraumentwicklung und -organisation. In: Alisch, M./May, M. (Ed.): "Das Ist Doch Nicht Normal ...!". Sozialraumentwicklung, Inklusion und Konstruktionen von Normalität. Leverkusen-Opladen: Barbara Budrich-Esser, pp. 7-29.

Biehl, Janet (1998): Der libertäre Kommunalismus. Die politische Praxis der Sozialökologie. Grafenau: Trotzdem Verlag.

Bookchin, Murray (1992): Die Neugestaltung der Gesellschaft. Pfade in eine ökologische Zukunft. Grafenau: Trotzdem-Verlag.

Bookchin, Murray (1996): Die Agonie der Stadt. Städte ohne Bürger oder Aufstieg und Niedergang des freien Bürgers. Grafenau: Trotzdem Verlag.

Coser, Lewis A. (1974): Greedy institutions. Patterns of undivided commitment. New York: Free Press.

Degener, Theresia/Eberl, Klaus/Graumann, Sigrid/Maaß, Olaf/Schäfer, Gerhard K. (Ed.) (2016): Menschenrecht Inklusion. 10 Jahre UN-Behindertenrechtskonvention – Bestandsaufnahme und Perspektiven zur Umsetzung in sozialen Diensten und diakonischen Handlungsfeldern. Göttingen: Vandenhoeck & Ruprecht Neukirchener Theologie.

Eckardt, Frank (2018): Austerity Urbanism. In: Rink, D./Haase, A. (Ed.): Handbuch Stadtkonzepte. Analysen, Diagnosen, Kritiken und Visionen. Wien: UTB GmbH, pp. 23-42.

Flieger, Burghard (2003): Sozialgenossenschaften als Perspektive für den sozialen Sektor in Deutschland. In: Flieger, B./Binding, L./Elsen, S./Göler von Ravensburg, N./Achter, W./Hafner, A./Ohli, M./Pahl, W. (Ed.): Sozialgenossenschaften. Wege zu mehr Beschäftigung, bürgerschaftlichem Engagement und Arbeitsformen der Zukunft. Neu-Ulm: AG-SPAK, pp. 11-35.

Flieger, Burghard (2019): Stadtteilgenossenschaften gründen – Sozialräume gestalten. https://blog.ksoe.at/stadtteilgenossenschaften-gruenden-sozialraeume-gestalten/ [accessed: 17.11.2020].

Fraser, Nancy (1994): Widerspenstige Praktiken. Macht, Diskurs, Geschlecht. Frankfurt (Main): Suhrkamp.

Goffman, Erving (2020): Asyle. Über die soziale Situation psychiatrischer Patienten und anderer Insassen. Frankfurt (Main): Suhrkamp Verlag.

Grau, Andreas/Heitmeyer, Wilhelm (2011): Gruppenbezogene Menschenfeindlichkeit und bürgerschaftliches Engagement. In: Forum Wohnen und Stadtentwicklung – Verbandszeitschrift des Bundesverband Wohnen und Stadtentwicklung, Forum von und für Akteure in den Handlungsfeldern Wohnen und Stadtentwicklung, 6/2011, pp. 301-304.

Helbrecht, Ilse/Weber-Newth, Francesca (2017): Die Abschöpfung des Planungsmehrwerts als Repolitisierung der Planung? Eine neue Perspektive auf die aktuelle Wohnungsfrage. In: sub \ u r b a n zeitschrift für kritischen stadtforschung, Heft 1-2, pp. 61-86.

Hinz, Andreas (2006): Inklusion. In: Antor, G./Bleidick, U. (Ed.): Handlexikon der Behindertenpädagogik. Schlüsselbegriffe aus Theorie und Praxis. Stuttgart: Kohlhammer Verlag, pp. 97-99.

Holm, Andrej (2013): Wir bleiben alle! Gentrifizierung – städtische Konflikte um Aufwertung und Verdrängung. Münster: Unrast-Verlag.

Kastl, Jörg Michael (2018): Inklusion. In: Otto, H.-U./Thiersch, H./Treptow, R./Ziegler, H. (Ed.): Handbuch Soziale Arbeit. München: Ernst Reinhardt Verlag, pp. 665-678.

Kunstreich, Timm (2005): Sozialgenossenschaften. Ein Versuch, eine kooperative Vergesellschaftung im kapitalistischen Sozialstaat zu denken. In: Widersprüche Redaktion (Ed.): Politik des Sozialen – Alternativen zur Sozialpolitik. Umrisse einer Sozialen Infrastruktur. Heft 97. Bielefeld: Kleine Verlag, pp. 105-122.

Lefebvre, Henri (2016): Das Recht auf Stadt. Hamburg: Edition Nautilus.

May, Michael (2017a): Ansätze migrantischer Sozialpolitik der Produzierenden und Dilemmata sie unterstützender Sozialer Arbeit. In: Braches-Chyrek, R./Sünker, H. (Ed.): Soziale Arbeit in gesellschaftlichen Konflikten und Kämpfen. Wiesbaden: VS Verlag für Sozialwissenschaften, pp. 139-158.

May, Michael (2017b): Soziale Arbeit als Arbeit am Gemeinwesen. Ein theoretischer Begründungsrahmen. Opladen: Verlag Barbara Budrich.

Maykus, Stephan (2017a): Inklusion und Kommune. Sozialplanung als (fach-)politischer Prozess. In: Archiv für Wissenschaft und Praxis der sozialen Arbeit, Heft 1/2017, pp. 30-39.

Maykus, Stephan (2017b): Kommunale Sozialpädagogik. Theorie einer Pädagogik des Sozialen in der Stadtgesellschaft. Weinheim: Beltz Juventa.

Möller, Kurt (2016): Entwicklung und Ausmaß gruppenbezogener Menschenfeindlichkeit. In: Scherr, A./El-Mafaalani, A./Gökcen Yüksel, E. (Ed.): Handbuch Diskriminierung. Wiesbaden: Springer Fachmedien Wiesbaden, pp. 425-448.

Natorp, Paul (1922): Sozial-Idealismus. Neue Richtlinien sozialer Erziehung. Berlin: Verlag Julius Springer.

Parodi, Oliver/Beecroft, Richard/Albiez, Marius/Quint, Alexandra/Seebacher, Andreas/Tamm, Kaidi/Waitz, Colette/Institut für Technikfolgenabschätzung und Systemanalyse (ITAS), Karlsruhe (2016): Von "Aktionsforschung" bis "Zielkonflikte". Schlüsselbegriffe der Reallaborforschung. In: Technikfolgenabschätzung – Theorie und Praxis (Ed.): Reallabore als Orte der Nachhaltigkeitsforschung und Transformation. Heft 3/2016. Karlsruhe, pp. 9-18.

Peck, Jamie (2015): Urbane Austerität. Die neoliberale Krise der amerikanischen Städte. In: Rosa Luxemburg Stiftung New York Office.

Räuchle, Charlotte (2021): Zum Verhältnis von Realexperiment und Stadtplanung am Beispiel kooperativer Freiraumgestaltung. In: Räuchle, C./Stelzer, F./Zimmer-Hegmann, R. (Ed.): Urbane Reallabore. Special Issue der Zeitschrift Raumforschung und Raumordnung | Spatial Research and Planning. Ausgabe 04 – 2021. München: oekom verlag, pp. 291-305.

Rawls, John (1998): Politischer Liberalismus. Frankfurt (Main): Suhrkamp.

Rawls, John (2003): Gerechtigkeit als Fairneß. Ein Neuentwurf. Frankfurt (Main): Suhrkamp.

Rawls, John (2012): Eine Theorie der Gerechtigkeit. Frankfurt (Main): Suhrkamp.

Reihlen, Markus (1998): Die Heterarchie als postbürokratisches Organisationsmodell der Zukunft? Arbeitsberichte des Seminars für Allgemeine Betriebswirtschaftslehre, Betriebswirtschaftliche Planung und Logistik der Universität zu Köln. Köln.

Reihlen, Markus (1999): Moderne, Postmoderne und heterarchische Organisation. In: Schreyögg, G. (Ed.): Organisation und Postmoderne. Grundfragen – Analysen – Perspektiven; Verhandlungen der Wissenschaftlichen Kommission "Organisation" im Verband der Hochschullehrer für Betriebswirtschaft e.V. Wiesbaden: Gabler, pp. 268-303.

Richter, Helmut (1998): Sozialpädagogik – Pädagogik des Sozialen. Grundlegungen, Institutionen, Perspektiven der Jugendbildung. Frankfurt (Main): Lang.

Richter, Helmut (2019): Sozialpädagogik – Pädagogik des Sozialen. Grundlegungen, Institutionen und Perspektiven der Jugendbildung. 2. Auflage. Wiesbaden: VS Verlag für Sozialwissenschaften.

Schmale, Ingrid/Ravensburg, Nicole Göler von (2017): Sozialgenossenschaften als Akteure des sozialen Wandels und genossenschaftliche Beiträge zu einer nachhaltigen Sozial- und Daseinsvorsorge. In: Theuvsen, L./Andeßner, R. C./Gmür, M./Greiling, D. (Ed.): Nonprofit-Organisationen und Nachhaltigkeit. Wiesbaden: Springer Gabler, pp. 439-448.

Schmidt, Marcel (2020): Zur Entstehung und Bedeutung des "Recht auf Stadt" im Werk Lefebvres. https://www.sozialraum.de/zur-entstehung-und-bedeutung-des-recht-auf-stadt-im-werk-lefebvres.php [accessed: 01.10.2020].

Schmidt, Marcel (2021): Eine theoretische Orientierung für die Soziale Arbeit in Zeiten des Klimawandels. Von der ökosozialen zur sozial-ökologischen Transformation. Leverkusen: Verlag Barbara Budrich.

Schneidewind, Uwe (2014): Urbane Reallabore – ein Blick in die aktuelle Forschungswerkstatt. In: pnd online. https://epub.wupperinst.org/frontdoor/deliver/index/docId/5706/file/5706_Schneidewind.pdf [accessed: 17.08.2023]

Schneidewind, Uwe/Singer-Brodowski, Mandy (2015): Vom experimentellen Lernen zum transformativen Experimentieren: Reallabore als Katalysator für eine lernende Gesellschaft auf dem Weg zu einer Nachhaltigen Entwicklung. In: Zeitschrift für Wirtschafts- und Unternehmensethik. Heft 16/1, pp. 10-23.

Schulz-Nieswandt, Frank (2017): Genossenschaftliche Selbsthilfe in anthropologischer Perspektive. In: Schmale, I./Blome-Drees, J. (Ed.): Genossenschaft innovativ. Wiesbaden: Springer Fachmedien Wiesbaden, pp. 345-362.

Spivak, Gayatari Chakravorty (2008): Can subaltern speak? In: Spivak, G. C. (Ed.): Can the subaltern speak? Postkolonialität und subalterne Artikulation. Wien: Turia + Kant, pp. 17-118.

Staub-Bernasconi, Silvia (2013): Integrale soziale Demokratie als gemeinwesenbezogener Lernprozess und soziale Vision: Jane Addams. In: Stövesand, S./Stoik, C./

Troxler, U. (Ed.): Handbuch Gemeinwesenarbeit. Traditionen und Positionen, Konzepte und Methoden. Deutschland – Schweiz – Österreich. Opladen: Barbara Budrich, pp. 37-43.

Thürling, Marleen (2017): Sozialgenossenschaftliche Unternehmen in Deutschland. Begriff, aktuelle Entwicklungen und Forschungsbedarf. In: Theuvsen, L./Andeßner, R. C./Gmür, M./Greiling, D. (Ed.): Nonprofit-Organisationen und Nachhaltigkeit. Wiesbaden: Springer Gabler, pp. 459-468.

Thürling, Marleen (2018): Gemeinwohl liegt im Trend. In: enorm – weconomy, Heft Themenschwerpunkt Genossenschaften, pp. 22-27.

Winkler, Michael (2006): Kleine Skizze einer revidierten Theorie der Sozialpädagogik. In: Badawia, T./Luckas, H./Müller, H. (Ed.): Das Soziale gestalten. Über Mögliches und Unmögliches der Sozialpädagogik. Wiesbaden: VS Verlag für Sozialwissenschaften, pp. 55-80.

Winkler, Michael (2014): Kritik der Inklusion – oder: über die Unvermeidlichkeit von Dialektik in der Pädagogik. Ein Essay. In: Widersprüche Redaktion (Ed.): Inklusion – Versprechungen vom Ende der Ausgrenzung. Widersprüche, Band 133. Münster: Westfälisches Dampfboot, pp. 25-39.

Dilemmas of the inclusive city: Amsterdam as a case study

Ivan Nio

Inclusion has been the new magic concept in Dutch policy for about ten years now. The term appears in policy memorandums of many municipalities. At the same time, there is a discussion among scholars about interpretations of inclusion. What is an inclusive city? Is it a city that is accessible to everyone? A city without inequality? A city where everyone feels at home? There are no unequivocal answers. Everyone interprets the inclusive city differently. But it does touch on essential issues. This article elaborates on policies for an inclusive city of the municipality of Amsterdam. I will critically assess the effects of three policy areas aimed at inclusion in deprived neighbourhoods. I will show that the results are not so unequivocal because of obstacles in the system world and the realities of everyday life. Finally, I will indicate what this means for the approach of various practitioners who deal with the principle of inclusion.

1. The rise of the concept of inclusion

Before I show how the municipality of Amsterdam strives towards more inclusion, I will first sketch the rise of the Dutch debate on inclusion. The accessibility of cities is one of the United Nation's sustainable development goals, to which the Netherlands has committed itself. Based on the principles of an accessible city and equality of opportunity, cities should provide opportunities for all its inhabitants to develop, emancipate, progress in terms of income, find a job, receive an education or move to a better place. Since the 1990s, policy for Dutch cities has focused strongly on economic growth and attracting higher incomes. The attractiveness and popularity of Dutch cities has increased significantly over the past thirty years. But due to the retracting government, increased market forces and more emphasis on self-reliance, negative effects like inequality, growing polarisation and segregation have become more apparent (Planbureau voor de Leefomgeving 2016; Raad voor de Leefomgeving en Infrastructuur 2020).

The discussion about inclusion has gained momentum due to exclusion processes in cities. In the past ten years, inequality of access to housing, employment, education, transport and public facilities has increased, especially in the large Dutch cities. The emancipatory lift function of the city is faltering, because of rising housing prices and the diminishing range of public facilities. Victims of exclusion processes are no longer only the most vulnerable groups (such as people with a low income or social assistance benefits, with a physical or mental disability, with debts and/or a small social network), but also people with middle incomes (teachers, healthcare staff), flex workers and self-employed persons (Raad voor de Leefomgeving en Infrastructuur 2020; Boterman/Van Gent 2022). Access to the city as a whole has become more restricted for broad groups. For entire sections of the population, exclusion from the city is a threat, and with it, the prospect of social advancement disappears.

Reflecting a shift in thinking about the condition and future of the city, municipalities apply a broadly defined concept of inclusion (of a city which is accessible to everyone) to emphasise more strongly the social aims of urban policy. This concept of inclusion also concerns housing associations which were partly deregulated in the 1990s. For example, a number of large Amsterdam housing associations are now committed to inclusive cities. This means cities where everyone feels at home, can participate and develop their talents. "Where everyone has access to everything the city has to offer; from a place to live to facilities and from public space to education. Inclusive cities offer a healthy and safe living environment with sufficient greenery and public space in all neighbourhoods. Neighbourhoods invite everyday encounters; a first step towards recognition of the other. Ultimately, it's about creating valuable places, neighbourhoods that people love" (De Vernieuwde Stad 2011: no page).

Private developers now also embrace inclusion. This proves the capacity of this concept to mobilise and enhance the formation of coalitions for new spatial and social assignments, although it will also be part of their marketing strategies. One of the largest developers in the Netherlands, AM, launched a competition in 2018 entitled: 'Towards a more inclusive city'. In their definition, it is also a city with a diversity of population groups, backgrounds and incomes. The city must remain accessible to everyone and be a place where everyone has equal opportunities, with access to education and the labour market. The inclusive city offers amenities and activities that residents feel they are part of. Mixed neighbourhoods are seen as a key to achieving this inclusion (Smit 2018).

Because of its broad scope, normative attractiveness and near-universal application, the inclusive city can be seen as a magic concept (Pollitt/Hupe 2011). The concept of inclusion seeks to support efforts to do something about the increased inaccessibility of cities and the inequality of opportunity. It is striking how quickly the concept of inclusion has become common in the system world of municipalities, housing associations and private developers. However, the above quotes suggest that everyone can find a place in an inclusive city and that this can occur in a harmonious and rational-planned manner. That is why the concept has been criticised. Pollitt and Hupe (2011) warn that magic concepts can dilute, obscure or even deny traditional social science concerns with conflicting interests and logic. Franke and Veldhuis (2019: 69) argue, for example, that the concept of an inclusive city has an overly idealistic and moralistic edge. 'It sometimes suggests the elimination of differences, while the city thrives on difference, contrast, conflict and complexity.' They prefer to speak of the just city. Buitelaar (2020) considers both concepts – just city and inclusive city – to be interchangeable. However, he believes that the concept of justice can draw on a long philosophical tradition, while inclusion is mainly a recent, policy-related invention.

The assumption that inclusion must include conflicts is also reflected in criticism based on the theories of political scientist Chantal Mouffe. According to Mouffe (2005), instead of pinning our hopes for an inclusive city on the rational capacity of humans, we should learn to live together again in a world of division, conflict and complexity. Scholars argue that contradiction and conflict should be part of urban development (Visser 2020). It is not a problem if places are not one hundred per cent inclusive. Then there will also be openness to intergenerational inclusion, for citizens who want to alter a place at a later time (Verloo in: Karnenbeek/Willems 2022).

Some Dutch sociologists argue for a more relaxed view of inclusion, with a focus on initiatives where residents connect because of things they have in common and less on inclusive activities that should be accessible to all residents. The aim should be more focused on inclusive neighbourhoods and less on inclusive activities (Engbersen/Jansen 2022).

2. Amsterdam as an inclusive city?

Inclusion is identified as a value in recent policy documents of the municipality of Amsterdam. In the Environmental Vision 2050, the long-term vision for the spatial development of the city, it is described as follows: 'Amsterdam wants to be an inclusive city. A city where inhabitants of Amsterdam and newcomers can feel at home, and which offers opportunities to develop. An inclusive city is also an undivided city. This means that opportunities to emancipate are the same everywhere in the city. It also means that we combat large differences in perceived quality of life and concentrations of disadvantages and social problems' (Gemeente Amsterdam 2021b: 158).

An important reason the concept is embraced is that Amsterdam as an undivided city is under pressure. The city has experienced strong economic growth since 2000 which has made Amsterdam a more expensive place to live in. The city is struggling with rising land and rent prices, crowds of tourists and the arrival of expats (Milikowski 2018). Housing prices of owner-occupied dwellings and rents in the private sector have risen enormously and there has been a decrease in affordable housing (Christof/Majoor 2021). Not only vulnerable and lower-income households, but also the middle class is finding it increasingly difficult in Amsterdam (Boterman/Van Gent 2022). This is a new situation for this city which has a rich tradition of affordable (social) housing. In the past, Amsterdam was even hailed by Fainstein (2010) as a just city and praised for its social democratic principles of city development. Others claim that Amsterdam no longer deserves this 'just city' status (Uitermark 2009).

Secondly, there is increasing inequality and segregation. The social geography of Amsterdam shows a growing core-periphery divide (Savini et al. 2015). Pockets of poverty and high unemployment have arisen in vulnerable post-war neighbourhoods in the urban periphery outside the A10 ring road. These neighbourhoods have high percentages of non-Western migrants. In these superdiverse neighbourhoods, various kinds of policies are trying to reverse the threat of exclusion and displacement processes.

In Amsterdam, inclusion has been translated into various policy areas. This article focuses on urban renewal in so-called deprived neighbourhoods. These neighbourhoods are characterised by socio-economic problems such as high unemployment, low incomes and feelings of unsafeness. In addition, the maintenance of homes and public space is often delayed or minimal. In the past 20 years, some of these neighbourhoods have been renovated in terms of housing, social facilities and public space. In 2018, 32 neighbourhoods were again designated for large-scale renovation and socio-economic improvement. In the last few years, the aim has been to better align physical investments with the needs of current and future residents. In addition to extra social investments, restructuring and densification are a means of improving quality of life. Inclusion relates to both the process and the outcome of urban renewal. In order to increase the number of affordable homes in the city and therefore inclusion, the municipality of Amsterdam introduced the '40-40-20 scheme' since 2018. For new construction, the requirement is 40 per cent social rent, 40 per cent medium-priced rent and purchase and 20 per cent high-end rent and purchase (Gemeente Amsterdam 2017).

Three aspects of inclusive urban and social renewal in deprived neighbourhoods will be discussed here: resident participation, socio-spatial infrastructure and mixed neighbourhoods. The ambition of the left-wing city council is to involve everyone in participation processes and to make the results in the field of housing, social facilities and public space as inclusive as possible. For inclusive goals at the intersection of spatial and social policy domains – participation, collective facilities and neighbourhoods – I will address two issues on the basis of some examples. First, living together in a city is always accompanied by processes of self-selection, division, conflict and inclusion and exclusion in relation to places. Second, I will contrast the system world of the pro-

Dilemmas of the inclusive city: Amsterdam 55

fessionals with the everyday living environment of residents in neighbourhoods. Based on research of the Amsterdam University of Applied Sciences (AUAS) and research into the socio-spatial practices of residents in the super-diverse post-war neighbourhoods in Amsterdam, I will show what inclusion as a policy goal means and how it actually works in daily life and what dilemmas it poses.

3. Participation as a process

Amsterdam has a tradition of strong government and outspoken civil society. In this constant confrontation, all kinds of – often pragmatic – attempts are made to establish a connection with bottom-up movements (Christof/Majoor 2021). With the change of city government in 2018, a greater focus on democratisation emerged. The municipality of Amsterdam has the ambition to involve citizens as much as possible in decision-making about spatial interventions and urban renewal. New ways of cooperation are being explored for an inclusive city. There is room to experiment with new forms of participation. The policy document on participation states: 'Our participation is inclusive. This means that we match the wishes and possibilities of the target group as closely as possible with the use of language, working methods and means of communication. We also make sure that the buildings where we organise meetings are easily accessible to everyone' (Gemeente Amsterdam 2019).

The city council attaches great importance to the fact that the residents of deprived neighbourhoods are included in the renewal. This implies involving residents in urban renewal, i.e. renovating existing homes and public space, adding new homes and making the neighbourhood low-traffic or natural gas-free. The objective of inclusion implies a high degree of accessibility to participation for the citizens who have an interest in the outcome. In addition, another goal is the broad representation of local residents. However, no specific participation methods are prescribed, thus enabling participation to be customised. Citizens are involved in the planning processes in very different ways.

An important issue for inclusion is how to achieve broad representation. Participation often promotes unintentional selection of participants. Active residents have the time and energy to participate, while it is precisely in deprived neighbourhoods that people do not have (mental) space to participate in this planning because of the many problems with which they themselves are confronted (Van Aanholt et al. 2019). Ethnic minorities, young people, the less educated and women are often underrepresented in participation (Bronsvoort et al. 2020). If it is not a good representation of the local population, a project runs the risk of becoming exclusive rather than inclusive (Jansen 2019). The dilemma is: Will the municipality engage in targeted dialogue with a limited group of residents who are already active and have a network in the neighbourhood, or is it trying to involve as many people as possible?

In the post-war neighbourhood of Banne Noord, an intensive participation process was chosen in the course of urban renewal and densification in order to arrive at a plan (Van Aanholt et al. 2021). 16 meetings were organised – mainly in the neutral context of a primary school – in which about 600 residents participated in one way or another. The municipality's project team approached groups of residents who were largely absent at the first meetings, such as Muslim women, young people and residents of social housing. Because the project team attached great importance to the inclusivity of the process, they went door-to-door at nearby social housing flats to invite residents to the next meeting. In terms of numbers of residents and the inclusion of those residents, the participation process in Banne Noord has been successful. Migrant groups also took an active part here. Shaping inclusive participation gatherings is an art that determines whether it is meaningful to residents (Bronsvoort et al. 2020). Despite the efforts, the older, long-term residents who were involved from the start left a greater mark on the process. The residents had a strong preference for a minimal variant of densification. The municipal ambitions for densification were much greater due to the housing shortage. The municipal team eventually found a balance between city-wide interests and the neighbourhood. The starting point will be the small-scale densification that was preferred by the participating residents. Banne Noord shows that a large-scale inclusive participation process requires a lot of commitment from the municipality and that it also leads to imbalances in the process and new uncertainties and complexities in the outcome.

There are also neighbourhoods in which participation experiments take place where participants form a selection of activist residents. In the K-neighbourhood in Amsterdam Zuidoost, a majority of residents are of an immigrant background. After residents in this neighbourhood went on a 'participation strike' because plans had already developed so far that they no longer had any real influence on them, an organisation from the neighbourhood was made responsible for the implementation and supervision of a participation process. According to some residents and officials, this central role comes at the expense of the inclusivity of the process. Others believe that it is increasing because this organisation has a broad network in the local area (Van Aanholt et al. 2021).

Another issue is the effect of inclusive participation. How interactive is the communication between citizens and government and how influential is the participation? The 'right to the city' (Harvey 2003) – having control and being able to influence your environment – appears to have been realised to a limited extent. Not all residents – e.g., those with limited Dutch language skills or a low education – feel free to think along with the government. Even within an inclusive participatory process, divisions can exist, and certain groups of residents are dominant. And professionals are not always eager to participate, because NIMBY (Not In My Backyard)-like protests can lead to delays. The ideas that are generated through participation often also do not fit with the internal municipal procedures and responsibilities. There is still little willingness among civil servants to work on such participatory projects. Translating civic needs into urban plans requires extensive negotiation, flexibility, and above all, patience among administration as well as civil society (Christof/Majoor 2021). Opinions are therefore divided about the effectiveness of participation in Amsterdam. On the one hand, it has increased involvement in the living environment. On the other hand, the participation mainly concerns adjustments to large-scale plans and has little effect on the affordability of housing and accessibility of the city.

4. Socio-spatial infrastructure

A second policy area of inclusion is the social infrastructure. The municipality of Amsterdam strives for a broad and accessible range of activities and support in each neighbourhood or district (Gemeente Amsterdam 2019). Mayor Femke Halsema of Amsterdam argued that every neighbourhood should have at least three core facilities: a library, a community centre and a basketball court (in Dutch the three B's: bibliotheek, buurthuis, basketbalveld). Here, fairness is the aim of inclusion. The inclusive city is translated into offering personal development opportunities to residents who have had fewer chances than others. The social infrastructure focuses on connectedness and promoting involvement between residents. Everyone is welcome in community centres and they should be accessible to everyone. Initiatives that have their own objectives and target their own group – such as migrant organisations – therefore receive no support from the municipality. The objectives of community centres as places where people can meet are strict. The policy of the municipality is aimed at universal accessibility of these facilities for everyone. Based on this policy, there is a clear hope that community centres will provide universalistic, low-threshold facilities for all residents in highly diverse neighbourhoods. Against the background of increasing diversity and the accumulation of social problems, the community centre should be a place, especially in deprived neighbourhoods, where different groups of residents 'learn to live together'. Bridging contacts should be formed, which should lead to the reduction of prejudice, greater mutual sympathy and possibly mutual support.

That this turns out differently in reality is shown by research (Welschen et al. 2020) which gained insight into what the social basis means in practice for residents and professionals. Vulnerable groups (migrant elderly, refugees with a residence permit, people with a mental health care background or intellectual disability and people from social care) were examined in two community centres in the Amsterdam Nieuw-West district. It has become apparent that there is a great need among vulnerable groups for particularistic facilities and activities: aimed at their 'own groups'. Coming together with one's own group lowers the barriers: for elderly migrants who do not have sufficient command of the Dutch language, for people with a care background who feel unsafe in mixed groups, for refugees who still do not know the way to formal facilities and who seek support from compatriots. Activities in your own circle are important to feel at home somewhere. Vulnerable groups in society have a strong need to continue to come together in their own circle and to reach out to new residents from there. All these different groups of residents first of all want a place for their own group. In Robert Putnam's (2000) terms of social relations: before bridging is possible, the focus is primarily on bonding.

These findings form a nuance of the municipality's policy aimed at universal accessibility of facilities for everyone. Social professionals are often ambivalent about the ideal of inclusion. The ideal image is supported, but on the other hand, practice points to a different reality. Professionals in the community centres are aware of the need for a certain degree of particularism. Otherwise, some groups, such as women with a migrant background, will not be able to leave their houses. Research also shows that elderly people prefer the intimacy and living room-like atmosphere of small-scale neighbourhood rooms instead of a larger community centre (Nio et al. 2020). The location and physical characteristics of a building and the layout and atmosphere also determine its accessibility and for whom it is and is not intended. In ethnically mixed neighbourhoods, native elderly people also have a clear preference for places where they can be among others of their own kind. In community centres of different sizes, it is about the balance between the need for safety of activities in one's own circle, and the possibility of openness for other groups. Social professionals always have to navigate between these conflicting objectives and look for the right balance. As Zacka (2017) states, social work in everyday practice always requires a 'balancing act' between all kinds of conflicting expectations. It turns out that the community centres are mainly used for certain groups of residents, partly as a result of the composition of the neighbourhood. Street-level professionals do, however, play with time and space to create circumstances in which encounters become more likely. An example is the simultaneous planning of activities of two groups who then 'spontaneously' encounter each other during the coffee break.

There is even an important role for a certain degree of particularism in the inclusive city. The inclusive city cannot do without parochial places for specific groups. Parochial places are spaces which (sometimes temporarily) are appropriated by and for a certain group (Lofland 1998). These are spaces that evidently constitute the space of a certain group. Various groups that have something in common have their own places where they feel at home and or-

Dilemmas of the inclusive city: Amsterdam

ganisations where they meet and organise activities. This happens in the working-class neighbourhoods in Amsterdam Noord where older native residents come together during evening events to play cards and bingo. In Amsterdam Zuidoost, Ghanaians and Surinamese help each other. In Amsterdam Nieuw-West, migrants are active in self-organisations and have their mosques and community centres. And new city dwellers meet each other in trendy cafés. Facilities can be (semi)public or have a more parochial character and they work in- and exclusively. Due to high real estate rents, small affordable spaces in renewal neighbourhoods for specific groups and activities are becoming increasingly scarce.

When we talk about inclusive facilities, we think of neighbourhood-oriented meeting places where everyone is welcome. They come in all kinds of forms, from social facilities such as community centres and libraries to commercial facilities such as local shops. These collective facilities – the sociologist Klinenburg (2018) calls them 'Palaces for the People' – are important for mutual contact between local residents. These can be very mixed places. A major concern is the impoverishment of these public facilities. In Amsterdam, the city council now recognises the importance of sufficient public facilities in poor neighbourhoods. Whether these are mixed or closed group facilities or a combination of both is still an open question for researchers. In my research into socio-spatial practices of various groups of city dwellers in post-war districts in Amsterdam Nieuw-West, I have noticed that inclusion as accessibility can also occur in commercial facilities (Nio et al. 2009). For example, various groups with little money visit the department store HEMA which has a popular and affordable built-in restaurant and coffee corner. This chain radiates neutrality and fulfils an important function for residents with a migration background as well as for native elderly people who are familiar with this store. Research even shows that older people prefer commercial spaces like shopping malls to planned and designed activity spaces in care homes or neighbourhood centres (Van Melik/Pijpers 2017). Other examples of inclusive, easily accessible public facilities that attract a mix of visitors are neighbourhood shopping centres, markets, thrift shops, affordable cafés and lunchrooms. Residents can feel at home in their ethnically diverse neighbourhood, thanks to these commercial facilities.

5. Mixed neighbourhoods

In deprived neighbourhoods in Amsterdam, the municipality, housing associations and private parties have been working on inclusive neighbourhoods for more than 20 years. The policy ideal in Amsterdam is mixed neighbourhoods where different groups feel connected and at home, where groups live together and meet each other and where they have equal opportunities. The focus is on social connections and strengthening social cohesion. A great deal has been invested in Amsterdam, in the spatial renewal of deprived neighbourhoods, in order to break through the one-sidedness and improve the quality of life through mixing (more owner-occupied homes). The aim is always a mix of social housing, private sector rental housing and owner-occupied housing. Investments have also been made in new schools, social facilities and public spaces in deprived neighbourhoods. The municipality strives for an integrated approach, spatially and socially. What effect has this had? Urban renewal has led to a heated debate in Amsterdam, because the renewal has also increased gentrification and displacement of residents with low incomes. What does a diversity of population groups, backgrounds and incomes mean in practice for an inclusive neighbourhood?

An example is the Staalmanpleinbuurt, which has been renovated and renewed for 15 years. Many owner-occupied and private sector rental homes have been added, as a result of which the percentage of social rental homes has dropped from 100 per cent to 54 per cent. Social housing has been renewed. Residents of social housing were able to move on to a better home in the same neighbourhood. Residents with a higher income have moved in. The public space has also been renovated. Interviews with residents show that the quality of life has improved and that the mixing at neighbourhood level is appreciated, but that it also leads to new social dividing lines (Nio 2022). The differences in income, education and cultural background are large. A new primary school only attracts children from migrant families, but not children from the newly prosperous households. There is a gym and also a small neighbourhood room which can be used for specific groups. But a lack of connection between the different groups of residents is due to the fact that there are hardly any inclusive social and commercial facilities. There are a few retail spaces with independent entrepreneurs on a recently renovated neighbourhood square. A hopeful new private initiative is a neighbourhood facility with a café that meets the needs of various residents as a meeting place. However, the rent of the commercial space is so high that viability is at risk. Inclusive social and commercial facilities that are also open on weekends can encourage public familiarity in a socially diverse neighbourhood. This concerns lighter forms of living together and feeling at home, observing and recognising each other. An inclusive neighbourhood also demands conviviality. In conviviality, which is a friendly variant of public familiarity, a balance is found between activities within one's own circle on the one hand and cross-group contact on the other, to promote mutual familiarity and friendliness (Wessendorf 2014). What is needed to achieve this are places where that can actually happen: a lively and socially diverse public space and, above all, public facilities.

A lesson from urban renewal in Amsterdam is that an inclusive neighbourhood requires more than just a mixture of housing categories and a mix of population groups. For the inhabitants to be able to live together, it is important that there is also an attractively designed and well-managed public space and public facilities. The task for urban renewal is how to create a neighbourhood where diverse groups of people can live together comfortably. The question is therefore: Which spatial structures, places and programs currently function as neighbourhood carriers and how can these be strengthened and enriched so that different groups of residents feel at home in a neighbourhood and feel connected to it? In a study into the renewal neighbourhood Couperusbuurt, we drew attention to a neighbourhood street that links various public spaces and facilities, such as a primary school, a church, a square with a mosque, a park and a shopping strip (Nio et al. 2020). In Sennett's (2018) terminology, this street is a weak boundary or border where the worlds of different groups of inhabitants come together. It is important to create public domains in socially diverse neighbourhoods. In inclusive neighbourhoods, residents can live peacefully side by side and informal contacts are not excluded, so that more mutual trust can develop. However, high land prices and land exploitation are usually decisive in the renewal of neighbourhoods. The financial-economic significance of space has become dominant at the expense of social use, which cannot be expressed in monetary terms.

6. Conclusions

What does Amsterdam's policy deliver in terms of successful interventions and what makes a process (participation), a place (socio-spatial infrastructure) and a neighbourhood inclusive? Urban renewal is a catalyst to simultaneously work on different physical and social ambitions in terms of inclusion. The Amsterdam examples show that the policy revolves around low threshold accessibility, proportionality and simultaneity of groups, interaction, meeting, bridging and building social capital. From the perspective of the lived city, it is important to take socio-spatial issues into account, such as how groups of residents (want to) live together.

The inclusive city is an aspiration, a state of mind and a way of working. It is a guiding principle. Inclusion is also a magic concept that challenges structures and processes that cause social injustice. The concept makes exclusive effects visible and helps to set agendas of (local) governments and other stakeholders. In this way, policy can take vulnerable groups into account, in particular. In the current opinion of the municipality and housing associations, it is necessary to invest unevenly in order to promote equality. However, the issue of the availability of facilities and the affordability of housing in the city cannot be solved solely with the policy aimed at inclusion. The concept of inclusion has its limitations because it runs into (bureaucratic and financial-economic) obstacles in the system world and in the realities of everyday life.

What can practitioners in the social and spatial domains do to strengthen inclusion in processes, in places and in neighbourhoods? This presents professionals with dilemmas and challenges for their action repertoire, especially because complexity has increased due to a multitude of stakeholders and a greater diversity of residents who are becoming increasingly empowered. The Amsterdam examples show that there are a variety of situations in which professionals in different policy domains can strengthen inclusion and implement knowledge of the residents' way of life.

First of all, policy makers and other practitioners must have an eye for the lived city, for different groups and their ways of life and needs, for socio-spatial issues. In addition, in socially diverse neighbourhoods there are always frictions and processes of inclusion and exclusion. The Amsterdam case shows that there are opportunities and professional scope for action in bringing various groups of residents together at certain times and places. In the social domain in particular, there is room for anticipatory action. Street-level professionals can acquire a position as an intermediary between groups of citizens. They are part of situations and processes in which they have to act as a bridge between professional knowledge and the knowledge of residents and the interests of the various parties involved.

Practitioners also have to navigate between the lived city of residents and the system world. The system world consists of all kinds of requirements, regulations and frameworks. In the case of participation: how can you adopt inclusion into the city's urban planning system? Particularly in the field of urban renewal, professionals have to take into account complex forces and a multitude of parties and interests. The new action perspective for professionals is that of a mediator between the spatial and social domain and between residents, city government and other stakeholders.

References

Boterman, Willem/Van Gent, Wouter (2022): Making the Middle-class City. The Politics of Gentrifying Amsterdam. London: Palgrave MacMillan.
Bronsvoort, Irene/Hoffman, Jesse/Hajer, Maarten (2020): Wat, hoe en wie? Vormgeven aan inclusieve ontmoetingen in de energietransitie. Utrecht: Urban Futures Studio, Universiteit Utrecht.
Buitelaar, Edwin (2020): Maximaal, Gelijk, Voldoende, Vrij. Vier perspectieven op de rechtvaardige stad. Amsterdam: Trancity/Valiz.
Christof, Karin/Majoor, Stan (2021): A City of Strong Government and Active Citizens. Eigenlogik Amsterdam. In: Van der Veen, Menno/Duyvendak. Jan Willem (eds),

Participate! Portraits of Cities and Citizens in Action. Rotterdam: Nai010 publishers.
De Vernieuwde Stad (2021): De Inclusieve Stad als state of mind. Stadspaper, Editie 6.
Engbersen, Radboud/Jansen, Judith (2022): Laten we uit de inclusiekramp komen. In: Sociale Vraagstukken, 2022, 22, 1. https://www.socialevraagstukken.nl/laten-we-uit-de-inclusiekramp-komen/. [accessed on September 22, 2022].
Fainstein, Susan (2010): The Just City. Ithaca: Cornell University Press.
Franke, Simon/Veldhuis, Wouter (2019): Verkenningen van de rechtvaardige stad. Stedenbouw en de economisering van de ruimte. Amsterdam: Trancity/Valiz.
Gemeente Amsterdam (2017): Woonagenda 2025. Amsterdam: Gemeente Amsterdam.
Gemeente Amsterdam (2019): Samen vooruit: Op weg naar een stevige sociale basis in Amsterdam. Stedelijk kader 2020-2023. Amsterdam: Gemeente Amsterdam.
Gemeente Amsterdam (2021a): Beleidskader Participatie. Amsterdam: Gemeente Amsterdam.
Gemeente Amsterdam (2021b): Omgevingsvisie Amsterdam 2050. Amsterdam: Gemeente Amsterdam.
Harvey, David (2003): The Right to the City. In: International Journal of Urban and Regional Research, 2003, 27, 4, pp. 939-941.
Jansen, Céline (2019): Gebiedsontwikkeling voor de inclusieve stad, wat is dat? https://www.gebiedsontwikkeling.nu/artikelen/gebiedsontwikkeling-voor-de-inclusieve-stad-wat-dat/. [accessed on September 22, 2022].
Karnenbeek, Lilian van/Willems, Jannes (2022): De inclusieve stad (No.6) (Podcastepisode). In: Onder planologen. https://podcastluisteren.nl/ep/Onder-Planologen-6-De-Inclusieve-Stad. [accessed on September 21, 2022].
Klinenberg, Eric (2018): Palaces for the people. How social infrastructure can help fight inequality, polarization, and the decline of civic life. New York: Crown.
Lofland, Lyn (1998): The Public Realm. Exploring the City's Quintessential Social Territory. New York: Aldine de Gruyter.
Milikowski, Floor (2018): Van wie is de stad. De strijd om Amsterdam. Amsterdam: Atlas Contact.
Mouffe, Chantal (2005): On the Political. London: Routledge.
Nio, Ivan/Reijndorp, Arnold/Veldhuis, Wouter (2009): Atlas van de Westelijke Tuinsteden. De geplande en de geleefde stad. Amsterdam: SUN-Trancity.
Nio, Ivan/Treffers, Anneke/Suurenbroek, Frank (2020): Buurtdragers in de Couperusbuurt. Een ruimtelijk-programmatische verkenning van een ontwikkelbuurt. Amsterdam: Hogeschool van Amsterdam.
Nio, Ivan (2022): Gemengd maar wel apart. Samenleven in vernieuwde buurten. In: De Hoog, Maurits/De Wit, Anouk (eds). SuperWest. Vernieuwing van de Amsterdamse Tuinsteden 2000-2021. Bussum: Uitgeverij Thoth.
Planbureau voor de Leefomgeving (2016): De verdeelde triomf. Verkenning van stedelijk-economische ongelijkheid en opties voor beleid. Ruimtelijke Verkenningen 2016. Den Haag: PBL.
Pollitt, Christopher/Hupe, Peter (2011): Talking about Government. The role of magic concepts. In: Public Management Review, 2011, 13, 5, pp.641-658.
Putnam, Robert (2000): Bowling Alone. The Collapse and Revival of American Community. New York: Touchstone.
Raad voor de leefomgeving en infrastructuur (2020): Toegang tot de stad. Hoe publieke voorzieningen, wonen en vervoer de sleutel voor burgers vormen. Den Haag: Rli.

Savini, Federico/Boterman, Willem/Van Gent, Wouter/Majoor, Stan (2016): Amsterdam in the 21st Century: Geography, housing, spatial developments and politics. In: Cities, 2016, 52, pp.103-113.
Sennett, Richard (2018): Building and Dwelling. Ethics for the City. New York: Farrar, Straus and Giroux.
Smit, Evamarije (2018): Ontmoeten essentie inclusieve stad. In: Ruimte + Wonen, 2018, 3, pp.18-27.
Uitermark, Justus (2009): An in memoriam for the just city of Amsterdam. In: City, 2009, 13, 2-3, pp.347-361.
Van Aanholt, Jelle/Van den Hende, Harko/Spanjar, Gideon/Majoor, Stan/Suurenbroek, Frank (2019): Ontwikkelbuurten: eerste lessen en aanbevelingen. Amsterdam: Hogeschool van Amsterdam.
Van Aanholt, Jelle/Nio, Ivan/De Nijs, Karin/Van den Hende, Harko (2021): Gedegen keuzes: verder komen bij participatiedilemma's in de Amsterdamse ontwikkelbuurten. Amsterdam: Hogeschool van Amsterdam.
Van Melik, Rianne/Pijpers, Roos (2017): Older People's Self-Selected Spaces of Encounter in Urban Aging Environments in the Netherlands. In: City & Community, 2017, 16, 3, pp. 284-303.
Visser, Jitse (2020): De inclusieve stad. Op zoek naar een werkbaar inclusiviteitsideaal. Masterthesis Filosofie van Cultuur en Bestuur. Amsterdam: Vrije Universiteit Amsterdam.
Welschen, Saskia/Lucas, Pamela/Von Meyenfeldt, Lone/Hoijtink, Marc/Rijnders, Jeremy/Veldboer, Lex (2020): Toegankelijkheid in divers perspectief. Bewoners, verbinders en professionals over de sociale basis in een ontwikkelbuurt. Amsterdam: Hogeschool van Amsterdam, lectoraat Stedelijk Sociaal Werken.
Wessendorf, Susanne (2014): Being open, but sometimes closed. Conviviality in a super-diverse London neighbourhood. In: European Journal of Cultural studies. 2017, 17, 4, pp. 392-405.
Zacka, Bernardo (2017): When the state meets the street. Cambridge, Massachusetts: Harvard University Press.

Small-scale community-based care initiatives in the Netherlands

Elles Bulder

Introduction

Population in the 27 countries in the EU, is rapidly ageing (EuroStat 2020; EuroStat 2017). This demographic process is stimulated by a general increase in life expectancy and an overall decrease in the number of children being born. Ageing will, because of higher age-related public spending (Kiss et. al. 2021: 1), put pressure on the healthcare and welfare system. Furthermore, a gradual decrease in the number of children born results in smaller familial networks. Therefore, more elderly people have to rely on a smaller convoy (De Jong-Gierveld 2011) of family members for informal care. Reversely, chances of someone having to provide informal care to their (grand)parents increase as families become smaller, because of the decreasing number of children, and the joint lifespan increases (Van Gaalen/Van Poppel 2007; Stuifbergen/Van Delden/Dykstra 2008). A convenient occasion for governments to reconsider national care arrangements and some parts of the welfare state. David Cameron's 2010-election campaign for example centred around the Big Society Programme in which the government proclaimed to help society regenerate itself by giving citizens the means to look after their communities. A conservative pamphlet issued for this cause stated: *Government on its own cannot fix every problem. We are all in this together. We need to draw on the skills and expertise of people across the country as we respond to the social, political, and economic challenges Britain faces* (HM Government UK 2010).

Since then, a gradual transition from Big Government to Big Society ideology developed throughout Europe (Meerstra-de Haan 2019: 21). In the Netherlands, this ideology took the shape of what became known as the 'participation society'. The policy accompanying this shift encouraged citizens to take responsibility for their own social and physical environment (Ubels/Bock/Haartsen 2019: 764). Here, this policy was gradually enforced by a legal framework, starting with the 2007 Social Support Act – in Dutch the Wet Maatschappelijke Ondersteuning WMO – developing further during the 2010s. On 17 September of 2013 the king of the Netherlands in his King's speech stated: "Combined with the need to reduce the government deficit, (…) is slowly but surely turning the classical welfare state into a participatory society. Everyone who can do this is asked to take responsibility for his or her own life and environment" (Koninklijk Huis 2013).

In 2015, the decentralisation of the care and welfare domain in the Netherlands, for the time being, was finalised. First by the extension of the Social Support Act, and after that by the introduction of the Participation Act – the latter aiming to help as many people with an occupational disability as possible to find work- and the Youth Act. Following these adjustments to the legal system, a structural shift commenced involving the devolution of responsibilities in the care and welfare and welfare domain from the central government to municipalities. A new – locally orientated – social domain emerged. However, when tasks were transferred to the municipalities, the corresponding budgets were immediately cut. Kim Putters, as director of the Dutch Social and Cultural Planning Agency, in 2018 phrases this shift in the social domain as: "the government's ambition in the social domain is clear: all citizens must be able to participate in society to the best of their ability, while retaining as much independence, self-reliance, and self-direction as possible. Even if they have a disability or a condition" (Putters 2018: 7). He continues in a more critical tone of voice: "In order to realize these objectives – and to be able to provide better support to citizens –, a renewed social contract is needed: a contemporary interplay between the government, social organizations, and citizens in the changing welfare state." (ibid 2018: 8).

This article focusses on small-scale community-based care initiatives developed as a result of the circumstances described above. Initiatives developed by citizens in small villages in rural areas in the Netherlands, with special attention to some interesting case studies in the North and South of the country. These initiatives will be contextualised. First, the demographic processes impacting the Dutch care and welfare domain will be discussed in more detail in chapter one. Subsequently, chapter two will focus on citizens' initiatives, attempting to put them in a broader theoretical framework using theories on voluntary engagement, social cohesion, and a line of reasoning from social capital theory. Finally, in chapter three, these findings will be used to describe and discuss small-scale community-based care initiatives in the Netherlands in general with a specific focus on two relatively new types of small-scale initiatives built around a social support worker.

1. Demographic developments impacting care and welfare in the Netherlands

Since the 1960s, the Netherlands saw a rapid decrease in the number of children born. In 2020 the net birth rate was as low as 9.7 per cent. Combined with

Small-scale community-based care initiatives in the Netherlands   67

an ever-rising life expectancy, 79.7 per cent for men and 83.1 per cent for women in 2020, this meant a gradual ageing of the Dutch population (Statline 1). In 2020 9.5 per cent of the Dutch population was 65 years and over, while 4.7 per cent of the population was 80 years and over (Statline 2). In more peripheral parts of the Netherlands this process is accelerated due to the outmigration of young people, for their studies and better paid jobs, to more economically attractive urban regions such as the Randstad and the Eindhoven region, as can also be seen in other EU-countries (European Commission no year). Therefore, age division in these more peripheral regions shows a more disturbing face. For example, we saw in 2020 that 24 per cent, 22 per cent and 20 per cent of the population in Drenthe, Friesland and Groningen – the three northern provinces in the Netherlands – was 65 years and over. The prognosis for 2040, all three provinces taken together, is that 28 per cent of the population will be 65 years and beyond while 9 per cent of the total population will be 80 years and beyond (Statline 4). When looking at these data we should consider that all three provinces also include medium and larger towns, making the percentages for the more rural areas seem even grimmer.

Furthermore, household structures in the Netherlands also saw, in line with other EU-countries, significant changes, from larger household types with several children and sometimes other relatives living with their parents, to more nuclear household types with sometimes one or two children living with their parents, or single-person households (European Parliament 2010). In 2021 32 per cent of all households in the Netherlands consisted of one or two parents with children, 29 per cent of the households had a couple without children, and no less than 39 per cent of the households were single-person households (Statline 3). Solo dwellers form a very diverse group of youngsters, divorcees, widows and widowers, and people who were never in a relationship. In more urban areas single-person households belong more often to the group of youngsters, whereas in more rural areas they are typically formed by elderly men and women living alone after divorce or the loss of their spouse (Sociaal Planbureau Groningen no year). Combining the process of more rapidly ageing in rural, more peripheral regions with the shift in household structures, especially when focussing on the number of elderly people living in single-person households in those regions, loneliness and neglect are lurking. However, after the decentralisation of the care and welfare domain in the Netherlands, resulting in the devolution of responsibilities from the central government to municipalities, followed by the cut in the corresponding budgets, municipalities had to reconsider their role. This resulted in a cut-down system for people in need of care and assistance. Furthermore, the flow of youngsters and young families to the Randstad and other urban areas weakened intergenerational ties and regional social capital. Consequently, other solutions for the stripped collective care and welfare system had to be found in the delicate balance between collective and indivi-dual responsibilities.

2. Community-based citizens' initiatives, social cohesion and Social Capital theory

In the process of finding a new balance between collective and individual responsibilities, citizens' initiatives became a popular policy tool in the Netherlands (Hurenkamp/Tonkens 2020: 54). In this article we use the definition of Meerstra- de Haan: "These initiatives as formally or informally organized groups of citizens who are active in and contribute to the public domain on a voluntary basis without financial compensation" (Meerstra- de Haan 2019: 8). Most of the time these initiatives are locally based. They know their communities' needs and potential and are therefore well equipped to respond to local needs and challenges (ibid.: 21-24). Whatever legal form these initiatives may take, most of the time they are built around voluntary engagement of residents. Here, we will focus on citizens' initiatives in care and welfare; organizations that are established by a group of citizens with the aim to increase health and welfare within the local community in which the organisation operates while they are not focussing on making a profit (Van der Knaap et al. 2019: 2). But before doing so, the attempt will be made to put them in a broader theoretical framework using theories on voluntary engagement, social cohesion, and a line of reasoning from social capital theory.

2.1 Volunteering: the pros and cons

Voluntary engagement is an important driving force in establishing a wide range of activities in villages and neighbourhoods in the Netherlands (Bulder forthcoming; Bulder/Melis 2021). Fonseca et al. (2019: 246) argue that voluntary engagement is an essential part of the process that binds people together and therefore an essential element in building and upkeeping social cohesion. In addition, some scholars list benefits that can be attributed to voluntary civic activities as compared to activities with involvement of the state, the market and kin or family systems, for example. They argue that voluntary civic activities can easily mobilise unpaid labour, produce services people can trust, engage residents in community welfare activities, raise empathy for and moral engagement with the less fortunate, and include marginal and vulnerable groups in collectives (cf. Van den Bos 2014: 20).

The Dutch Voluntary Policy Committee, established in 2001 by the Ministry of Health, Welfare and Sports to encourage municipalities and provinces to set up new voluntary policies, identifies the positive social impact of voluntary work as promoting participation, democracy, socialisation, integration, channelling, quality and solidarity, detection of problems and emancipation (Van den Bos 2006: 11). Langendijk (2006: 12) adds to this that volunteering contributes to building shared trust, social connectivity, stimulates participation in society and the development of shared values and conventions.

However, volunteering, apart from positively impacting volunteers, local community and the broader society, also has its drawbacks. The constant pressure to reach goals is sometimes felt to be a burden. The gradual exhaustion of cognitive resources, unclear role patterns or expectations, or a lack of voice within the initiative can even eventually lead to what has come to be known as a 'volunteer burnout' (Meerstra-de Haan 2019: 71-72). Moreover, not every community is able or willing to start a citizens' initiative because they lack the social capital needed, among other things. This unfortunately can result in growing disparities in levels of service delivery and eventually to uneven rural development. Furthermore, continuity in voluntary engagement concerning essential services is also a tricky aspect. Individuals can, for example, change their priorities while their assets are dearly needed to make the initiative a success. Also, initiatives can be exclusive, shutting people out, causing discord within the community. (ibid. 2019: 4). And finally, the relationship between governments and citizens' initiatives is very important because often there is a financial relationship between both parties. This implies that the volunteers in the initiative have to stand for their own targets and principles while in the meantime they need to keep in touch with the ideas and the policy of the local and regional governments; a delicate balance that, when things go awry, can cause lots of frustration and disappointment within the community (ibid. 2019: 4).

2.2 Social Capital theory and social networks

One of the most influential books within social capital theory is Robert Putnam's study *Bowling alone. The collapse and revival of American Community* published in 2000. In his book Putnam describes social capital and how it has changed over time. With *Bowling alone* we touch upon the field of social capital theory focussing on features of social life that enable collective action and constitute a part of social structure. Whereas physical capital refers to physical objects and human capital refers to the properties of individuals, social capital refers to connections among individuals – social networks and the norms of reciprocity and trustworthiness that arise from them […]. 'Social capital' calls attention to the fact that civic virtue is most powerful when embedded in a network of reciprocal social relations. "A society of many virtuous but isolated individuals is not necessarily rich in social capital" (Putnam 2000: 19).

Putnam (2000: 19-23) introduces two different types of social capital: 'bonding social capital' and 'bridging social capital'. Bonding social capital is seen as more exclusive, inward looking and reinforcing exclusive identities and homogenous groups (sometimes even creating strong out-group antagonism). Bridging social capital is positioned as more inclusive, encompassing people across diverse social cleavages. For example, in interaction around sports or cultural practices, trust grows. Because of this, people can bridge other dividing lines, such as those of religion, ethnicity, or education. This last type of social capital comes closest to the views of Fonseca et al. (2019: 246) on voluntary engagement, being an essential part of the process that binds people together and therefore an essential element in building and upkeeping social cohesion. Also, the benefits attributed to voluntary civic activities as mentioned above by Lorentzen and Dugstad, like raising empathy for and moral engagement with the less fortunate, and the inclusion of marginal and vulnerable groups, link to Putnam's bridging capital-concept (cf. Van den Bos 2014: 20). While Langendijk's (2006: 12) argument that voluntary engagement builds shared trust and social connectivity and stimulates the development of shared values and conventions also matches Putnam's concept of bridging social capital. The fact mentioned by Meerstra- de Haan that civic initiatives can also be exclusive in the sense that they are shutting people out (2019: 4), is more aligned with the concept of bonding social capital. However, both types of social capital are visible in the different citizens' initiatives studied by the scholars mentioned above.

Szreter and Woolcock (2004: 651) summarise some of the health effects that can empirically be linked to social capital as defined above. They mentioned among others child development, adolescent well-being, increased mental health, reduced mortality, lower susceptibility to depression and loneliness and higher perceptions of well-being and self-rated health. In addition, they introduced a third type of social capital, to wit 'linking social capital'. They defined linking social capital as:

> "... norms of respect and networks of trusting relationships between people who are interacting across explicit, formal or institutionalized power or authority gradients in society [...] just as health outcomes can be improved by expanding the quality and quantity of bonding social capital (among friends, family and neighbours) and bridging social capital (trusting relations between those from different demographic and special groups), so, too, is it crucial to facilitate the building of linking social capital across power differentials, especially to representatives of institutions responsible for delivering those key services that necessarily entail ongoing discretionary face-to-face interaction" (ibid. 2004: 655).

Using the above theories concerning voluntary engagement and the different types of social capital as a theoretical frame, we will now turn to small-scale community-based care initiatives in the Netherlands.

3. Small-scale community-based care initiatives in the Netherlands

In the 2010s, in the Netherlands a relatively new community-based care initiative developed. In this new initiative the network of family and kin was supplemented by a larger network of volunteers from outside the closer network of the person in need of care and a professional called the village support worker. This is in line with the argument of Jenny de Jong-Gierveld (2011: 43), who argues that people in need of care more and more will have to rely on an active involvement of networks, other than family and kin, or the 'convoy'.

However, before turning to two case studies centred around these village support workers, we will discuss small-scale care initiatives in the Netherlands in general. Even though their 'label' is the same, their structure, name and the way they are financing their activities varies hugely. After discussing these initiatives more generally, the last paragraphs of this chapter will focus on care initiatives that come closest to realising Szreter and Woolcock's linking social capital. Furthermore, the way care is organised in these case studies, in a more equal collaboration between relatives, volunteers, and professionals, is very similar to the way in which the care should be organized according to the call for action from the Dutch Council of Public Health and Society.

3.1 Community-based care initiatives in the Netherlands

Since 2012, a significant number of small-scale community-based care initiatives were launched by citizens in urban and rural areas in the Netherlands. The monitor *Zorgzame gemeenschappen ('caring communities')*, constructed in 2021, was able to trace no less than 1471 initiatives at that time. Based on data gathered from 323 of these initiatives Van Zoest et al. (2021) enable us to draw a picture of what those initiatives stand for and how they function. First, the listed initiatives all have, as already mentioned, different characteristics. Some are formally (80 per cent), others are informally (20 per cent) organised; they can be found in exclusively urban (36 per cent) or rural (45 per cent) areas; they sometimes focus more on specific target groups and sometimes link with professional care. Most of the time the initiatives combine different activities within care and welfare, as can be seen from the data in table 1.

Table 1: Distribution of activities among respondents

Activity (N=323)	%
Social cohesion	57
Welfare	47
Liveability	41
Loneliness	40
Participation	29
Care	19
Supported living	16
Health	10
Prevention	8

Source: Van Zoest et al. 2021

When focussing on groups in society that benefit from these initiatives, the monitor shows that 68 per cent of the initiatives focus on all residents while 32 per cent focus on specific groups like the elderly, youngsters, migrants, or residents with mental or physical challenges. Linking this to Putnam's theory on bonding and bridging social capital, we can conclude that most of these initiatives 'encompass people across diverse cleavages', are therefore socially inclusive and can therefore be categorised as 'bridging social capital'. However, as regards initiatives focussing exclusively on one target group, we need more information in order to be able to classify them as bonding or bridging social capital because they can (un)consciously 'reinforce exclusive identities and homogenous groups'.

When we take it one step further by screening the initiatives on the extent to which they may be linked to the concept of 'linking social capital', we find that 49 per cent of the initiatives has relations with a welfare institution; 7 per cent cooperates with a health insurance company; and 85 per cent has direct relations and 46 per cent indirect relations with a municipality. A minority of initiatives employs professionals; 16 per cent on payrolling and 14 per cent under direct contract. All other activities are executed by volunteers (Van Zoest et al. 2021). It appears from the above data that a considerable number of Dutch small-scale care initiatives involved in Van Zoest's monitor can be linked to the concept of 'bridging social capital' but can also be classified as 'linking social capital'. This appears to be in line with the observations of Szreter and Woolcock (2004: 651), who found that social capital stimulates child development, adolescent well-being, mental health, reduced mortality, lower susceptibility to depression and loneliness and higher perceptions of well-being and self-rated health. An argument that was reinforced by the research of Kristina Sundquist et al. (2014) which was focussed on the entire Swedish population aged 65 years and over, showing some of the positive effects of linking social capital. The research showed a significant negative correlation between the presence of linking social capital and all-cause mortality among people aged 65 years and over. Furthermore, Sundquist et al. (2014) show a clear positive correlation between the presence of linking social capital and the prevalence of cause-specific mortality in coronary heart disease, psychiatric disorders, cancer, stroke, chronic lower respiratory diseases, type 2 diabetes, and suicide.

Unfortunately, as so little information is uncovered on results for and impact on the people in need of care in the monitor, it is not possible to make a comparison with the above studies. However, the information that is available reveals that 65 per cent of the initiatives can fulfil their pre-set targets of which the top 5 targets are: 1. Social liveability, self-sustainability, well-being; 2. Reducing loneliness; 3. Empowering; 4. Healthy lifestyle; 5. Longer and better living at home. Even though different concepts are used, this list suggests that the initiatives at least set their targets in line with the effects grouped by Szreter and Woolcock (2004: 651) as: child development, adolescent well-being, increased mental health, reduced mortality, lower susceptibility to depression and loneliness and higher perceptions of well-being and self-rated health and some of the effects registered by Sundquist et al. (2014) listed as reducing all-cause mortality among people aged 65 years and over.

After this more general overview of community-based small-scale care initiatives in the Netherlands and their link with theories on volunteering, social cohesion and social capital, we now turn to two case-studies where the initiatives were supplemented by a professional, the village support worker.

3.2 Caring community Elsendorp

A forerunner in the Netherlands in the field of caring communities is the 'Small-scale village or district-oriented care-project' in the municipality of Gemert-Bakel. Starting in the village Elsendorp in 2007, it subsequently spread to other small villages within the municipality. The concept, centred around reciprocity, was developed bottom-up, together with the village council and other residents. It was targeted at empowering residents in need of care by giving them back control over their care and welfare situation and (re)connecting them with society. A local working group (informal) or cooperative (formal), consisting of volunteers and closely linked to the different village councils, was formed in each participating village. At the start of the project the working groups/cooperatives provided low-level care themselves without the involvement of or connection with professionals. Given its principle, to empower residents in need of care, and the interconnectivity of the residents directly or indirectly linked to these initiatives, the concept of binding and possibly bridging social capital seems to apply to this phase of the project.

In 2008 the project in Elsendorp entered a new phase; the 'village support worker' was introduced. She was the first professional of her kind installed in the Netherlands. The support worker there was, for a limited number of hours, formally employed by the municipal welfare organisation. The existing working group became her day-to-day supervisor. Her prime tasks were mediating between residents and health care professionals, helping with Wmo-applications, connecting residents, stimulating the residents' own strength, identifying problems, supporting caregivers and last but not least sometimes focussing on strengthening village liveability in general. In this phase the concept of linking social capital became also applicable to the Elsendorp-project.

After some years this small-scale care initiative was evaluated by Verbeek et al. (2014: 18) on behalf of the Trimbos Institute, the Dutch knowledge institute for mental health care, addiction care and social care. The study concluded that, even though no significant changes could be observed in respect of general well-being and cost effectiveness of total health costs, a significant drop in Social Support Act-related expenses over the same period for people aged 75-95 became clear. WMO-costs dropped by €134 per person per year in the period under research against a rise in Social Support Act -costs of €150 per person per year in a control village. These findings have to be set against a rise in care-related costs associated with the work of the village support worker by €40 per person per year Nevertheless, this means a positive result of €96 per person per year. Care and services provided did not significantly differ in both villages, nor did both populations during the period of research.

A more qualitative part of the research focussed more precisely on the role of the village support worker within the project and the results and impact of this expansion of the model observed. Residents and other stakeholders voiced that, among other things, the village supporter stimulated social cohesion in the village or district and empowered residents. Furthermore, she was able to identify problems at an early stage so other care and welfare professionals could be brought into action earlier while in doing so health gains could be realised. All this due to a low threshold. (Verbeek et al. 2014: 28-31). Unfortunately, no follow-up research has been done thus far.

3.3 Caring community Wedde

In 2014, the project *'Wedde dat 't lukt'* (*Bet that it works*) inspired by Elsdorp, started in the village Wedde. Similar as in Gemert- Bakel the concept in the following years spread to other villages in the municipality of Westerwolde. In total approximately 2,500 residents were connected to care and welfare services in this way. Unlike the project in Elsdorp, *Wedde dat 't lukt* was initiated by the general practitioner in cooperation with the village council and the residents of the village because he had noticed that his patients needed another type (and or intensity) of care than was offered. From an early start a village support worker, with a background in health care, was part of the project. Start-up costs were covered by the municipality (salary of the village support worker), the regional health insurance organisation (hours put in by the general practitioner), the province Groningen and LEADER. After the starting up period the municipality still covered the costs of the village support worker's salary.

Wieke Paulusma, project leader at the regional hospital, stated in an interview: "In my opinion, village supporters not only make a very valuable contribution to the quality of life in communities, but they are also the right people for any questions and concerns that we cannot (immediately) address in hospital. Questions and concerns related to loneliness, for example. In this way, we can complement each other if we, as a society, invest in quality of life. This also allows us to keep facilities, such as a hospital in the region, available to everyone" (cited in Smelik/Pijnenborg 2021: 8).

This statement again lays the foundation for the argument that care initiatives organised around a village support worker can be classified as 'linking social capital' with all acclaimed benefits. Furthermore, Paulusma, who is quite outspoken about the necessity of small-scale initiatives including a village support worker, adds another positive feature. She argues that this type of initiatives is vital when it comes to keeping up facilities like a regional hospital in more rural areas.

In 2020, the Aletta Jacobs School for Public Health published a white paper summarising the result of research on the village support worker in three Groningen villages. Richard Jong-A-Pin, the responsible researcher, among others, compared cost development of care provided by the general practitioner in the period 2015-2017 over time. Jong-A-Pin (2020) observed a significant drop in these costs during the period of research. His findings were supported by the analysis in one of the other villages involved in the case study. However, given the short research period, no relation with the health situation of villagers nor with higher perceptions of well-being and self-rated health could be established at that time. Two years later, Jong-A-Pin, together with students, revisited Wedde, trying to picture the societal impact of the project and the village support worker. The results of this more qualitative research are still under analysis. However, some preliminary results are already available. It is argued that the village support worker enables residents to remain longer in their own homes and feel less lonely. The village support worker's help with 'translating' the jargon from care and welfare professionals is explicitly mentioned as a positive effect. In his 2020-research Jong-A-Pin already mentioned that, in our increasingly digital world, a professional assisting older (single) villagers and individuals with low literacy is of great importance.

The results of this research also allow us to shed some light on the effects of the care initiative on voluntary caregivers. It shows that volunteers participating in the project take pride in their work and find they are doing something useful for their village and society. They are more involved in village life and meet new people. The feeling that social relations are strengthened as is the feeling of togetherness, is also mentioned. In this sense, the project can also be classified as bridging social capital while on the other hand, some of the advantages of voluntary engagement mentioned in chapter two are supported. Furthermore, family members and neighbours find relief and feel more relaxed because the support worker takes over some of the burden. The effects of the small-scale care initiatives including a community support worker are thus felt on different levels and in different ways in the village community and appear to be strengthening linking social capital.

4 Discussion

Demographic changes like the ageing of the population and changes in household structures erode the basis of the Dutch welfare system introduced in the 20th century. In the slipstream of the Big Society theory spreading through Europe, the government in the Netherlands introduced a set of laws in the 2010s stimulating citizens to participate in society to the best of their ability. For society to be able to cope with these developments in the care and welfare system, to continue to offer optimal care and support in the event of a rising demand for long-term care, the Dutch Council for Public Health and Society (Lenselink/Reerink 2021; Raad Volksgezondheid and Samenleving 2022: 11) advocated a fundamental review of the relationships between formal and informal care to provide a more equal collaboration between relatives, volunteers, and professionals.

In the meantime, a significant number of small-scale community-based care initiatives sprang up in urban and rural areas in the Netherlands. Given the accelerated ageing of the rural population and the thinning of social networks in those areas, these initiatives have now become vital for upholding the well-being and even the facilities in more peripheral regions. Only a small number of these Dutch small-scale care initiatives work with professionals who are sometimes targeting a special group, but who are most of the time trying to help the whole community solely based on voluntary engagement. Even though volunteering has many positive effects on an individual and community level like promoting participation, democracy, socialisation, integration, channelling, promoting quality and solidarity, identifying issues and emancipating (Van den Bos 2006: 11) it can also have serious drawbacks for volunteers, as is explained above.

Furthermore, volunteers are at liberty to change their priorities, move out of a community and, in doing so, leave their jobs in the organisation. This makes initiatives based on voluntary engagement and a care and welfare system that is built on them very vulnerable.

Social capital theory in which bonding, bridging, and linking social capital are presented can help us frame these initiatives. The data presented in this article, taken from different sources, enable us to throw some more light on the targets, organisation, effects, and impact of these initiatives. Based on available data we conclude that most of the small-scale community-based care initiatives in the Netherlands can be classified as 'bridging social capital' or even 'linking social capital'. Furthermore, the initiatives that include a professional village support worker, as the first point of contact for residents, volunteers, other professionals and care and welfare institutions, are able to strengthen linking social capital. Exchanging knowledge of and experiences with as well as further research on these community-based caring communities and their vulnerability in the light of cut downs will help us deal with developments occurring not only in the Netherlands but everywhere in Europe.

References

Bulder, Elles (forthcoming): Volunteering and social cohesion. A Dutch-German case study. In: Bartman, Sylke/Bulder, Elles/Gloy, M. Morten (Hrsg.) Soziale Kohäsion im ländlichten Raum. Eine deutsch-niederländische Perspektive, Leverkusen, Opladen: Barbara Budrich Verlag.

Bulder, Elles/Melis, Korrie (2021): Inwoners werken aan lokale leefbaarheid. Vrijwillige inzet in plattelandsgebieden in Noord- en Midden-Nederland tussen 2015 en 2021. In: Bulder, Elles/Molema, Marijn/Tassenaar, Vincent (Hrsg): Spitten in de economische, sociale en regionale geschiedenis, Hilversum: Verloren, pp. 153-168.

De Jong-Gierveld, Jenny (2011): Safeguarding the Convoy. A call to action from the Campaign to End Loneliness. Abingdon: Age UK.

European Commission (no year): Urbanisation. The Future of Cities. European Commission https://urban.jrc.ec.europa.eu/thefutureofcities/urbanisation#the-chapter

European Parliament (2010): Vraag met verzoek om schriftelijk antwoord E-5908/2010 aan de Commissie. EU Parlement, https://www.europarl.europa.eu/doceo/document/E-7-2010-5908_NL.html. [accessed January 5 2023]

EuroStat (2020): Ageing Europe – statistics on population development. https://ec.europa.eu/eurostat/statistics-explained/index.php?title=Ageing_Europe_-_statistics_on_population_developments#Older_people_.E2.80.94_population_overview. [accessed January 5, 2023]

EuroStat (2017): Archive: Bevolkingsstatistieken op regionaal niveau. https://ec.europa.eu/eurostat/statistics-explained/index.php?title=Archive:Bevolkingsstatistieken_op_regionaal_niveau&oldid=263777#EenpersoonEenpersoonsh. [accessed: Jnuary 5, 2023]

Fonseca, Xavier/Lukosch, Stephan/Brazier, Franzes (2019): Social cohesion revisited: a new definition and how to characterize it. In: Innovation: The European Journal of Social Science Research, 32, pp. 231-253.

HM Government UK (2010): Building Big Society. UK: HM Government. https://assets.publishing.service.gov.uk/government/uploads/system/uploads/attachment_data/file/78979/building-big-society_0.pdf. [accessed: August 10, 2022].

Hurenkamp, Menno/Tonkens, Evelien (2020): Ontwerpprincipes voor betere burgerparticipatie. In: Bestuurskunde, 29, pp. 54-63.

Jong-A-Pin, Richard (2020): Evaluatie van de dorpsondersteuner. Groningen: Aletta Jacobs School for Public Health.

Kiss, Monika/Lecerf, Marie/Atanassov, Nikolai/Margaras, Vasileios/Zamfir, Ionel/Sabbati, Giulio/Killmayer, Lucille (2021): Demographic outlook for the European Union 2021. Brussels: European Praliament. https://www.europarl.europa.eu/RegData/etudes/STUD/2021/690528/EPRS_STU(2021)690528_EN.pdf [accessed: August 16, 2022].

Koninklijk Huis (2013): Troonrede. Koninklijk Huis. https://www.koninklijkhuis.nl/documenten/toespraken/2013/09/17/troonrede-2013. [accessed: August 14, 2022]

Langendijk, Erwin (2006): Vrijwilligersbeleid nog in de kinderschoenen. Vrijwillige inzet onderzocht. Utrecht: Coviq.

Lenselink, Myrthe/Reerink, Antoinette (2021): Ons een zorg! Naar een vloeiende samenwerking tussen zorgverleners, naasten en vrijwilligers. Rapportage co-creatie onderzoek. https://www.captise.nl/Portals/1/Rapportage_co-creatie_onderzoek_samenwerken_in_de_zorg.pdf. [accessed: August 14, 2022]

Meerstra-de Haan, Erszi (2019): Citizens' initiatives in depopulating rural areas. Understanding success, failure, and continuity from multiple perspectives. Dissertation. Groningen: University of Groningen.

Putnam, Robert (2000): Bowling Alone: The Collapse and Revival of American Community. New York: Simon & Schuster.

Putters, Kim (2018): Een lokaal sociaal contract. Voorwaarden voor een inclusieve samenleving. Den Haag: Social Cultureel Planbureau. https://www.scp.nl/publicaties/publicaties/2018/03/15/een-lokaal-sociaal-contract. [accessed: August 10, 2022]

Raad Volksgezondheid en Samenleving (2022): Anders leven en zorgen. Naar een gelijkwaardig samenspel tussen naasten, vrijwilligers en beroepskrachten. The Hague: RVS.

Smelik, Jan/Pijnenborg Freya (Hrsg.) (2021): De dorpsondersteuner. Verbindende schakel van de gemeenschap. Oegstgeest/Buggenum: NLZVE and VKKL.

Sociaal Planbureau Groningen (no year): Bevolkingsontwikkeling in Groningen. Groningen: SCP. https://sociaalplanbureaugroningen.nl/brede-welvaart/bevolking/#aantal-huishoudens-neemt-toe-door-groei-alleenstaanden. [accessed: January 7, 2023]

Statline 1: Gezonde levensverwachting. Den Haag: Centaal Statstisch Planbureau. https://opendata.cbs.nl/statline/#/CBS/nl/dataset/71950ned/table?ts=1661706683754. [accessed: August 28, 2022]

Statline 2: Bevolking; kerncijfers. Den Haag: Centaal Statstisch Planbureau. https://opendata.cbs.nl/statline/#/CBS/nl/dataset/37296ned/table?ts=1661707273882. [accessed: August 28, 2022].

Statline 3: Particuliere huishoudens naar samenstelling en grootte. Den Haag: Centaal Statstisch Planbureau. https://opendata.cbs.nl/statline/#/CBS/nl/dataset/37975/table?ts=1661706915740. [accessed: August 28, 2022]

Statline 4: Regionale prognose 2023-2050, Centraal Statistisch Planbureau, https://opendata.cbs.nl/#/CBS/nl/dataset/85171NED/table?searchKeywords=prognose%20regio. [accessed: August 28, 2022]

Stuifenberg, Maria/Van Delden, Johannes/Dykstra, Pearl (2008): The implications of today's family structures for support giving to older parents. In: Ageing & Society, 28, pp. 413-434.

Sundquist, Kristina/Hamano, Tsuyoshi/Naomi Kawakami, Xinju Li,/Kuninori, Shiwaku/Sundquist, Jan (2014): Linking social capital and mortality in the elderly: A Swedish ational cohort study. In: Experimental Gerontology, 55, pp. 29-36.

Szreter, Simon/Woolcock, Michaeal (2004): Health by association? Social capital, social theory, and the political economy of public health. In: International Journal of Epidemiology, 33, pp. 650-667.

Ubels, Hiska/Bock, Bettina/Haartsen, Tialda (2019): The Dynamics of Self-Governance Capacity: The Dutch Rural Civic Initiative 'Project Ulrum 2034'. In: Sociologia Ruralis, 59. pp. 763-788.

Van der Knaap, Thijs/Smelik, Jan/De Jong, Floor/Spreeuwenberg, Peter/Groenewegen, Peter (2019): Citizens' initiatives for care and welfare in the Netherlands: an ecological analysis. In: BMC Public Health, 19, 1334, pp. 2-12.

Van den Bos, Cees (2006): Vrijwilligersbeleid nog in de kinderschoenen. In: Boss, E./Hetem, R. Vrijwillige inzet onderzocht. Utrecht: Movisie, pp. 6.17.

Van den Bos, Cees (2014): Using volunteering infrastructure to build civil society. Arnhem: Stichting Rijnstad.

Van Gaalen, Ruben/Van Poppel, Frans (2007): Kinderen en de veranderingen in de gezinsstructuur in de afgelopen anderhalve eeuw. In: Van der Lippe, Tanja/Dykstra, Pearl/Kraaykamp, Gerbert./Schippers, Jos (Hsrg.): De maakbaarheid van de levensloop. Van Gorcum: Netherlands Interdisciplinary Demographic Institute (NIDI), pp. 21-42.

Verbeek Marjolein/Van der Velden,Claudia/Lokkerbol, Joran/Willemse, Bernadette/Pot, Anne Margriet (2014): Kleinschalige wijkgerichte zorg in Gemert-Bakel. Een studie naar kosteneffectiviteit en succesfactoren. Utrecht: Trimbos-instituut.

Van Zoest, Frans/Stouthard, Lian/Van Schaijk, Roos/Sok, Karin/Van der Heijden, Nanneke/Smelik, Jan (2021): Monitor zorgzame gemeenschappen 2020. Utrecht: Movisie. https://www.nlzorgtvoorelkaar.nl/kennisbank_themas/landelijkebeweging_overzicht/landelijkebeweging_kennisvragen/2204009. Aspx [accessed: August 25, 2022]

Strengthening the vitality of neighbourhoods: Countercultures and self-evident meeting places

Arnold Reijndorp

In this chapter, the role of informal networks and common goods initiatives in redefining the commons for social inclusion on the local level, will be explored by focusing on the socio-spatial practices of both residents and organisations in the city district Brugse Poort in Ghent (Flanders) which were empirically investigated in a research project. The research project arose from the goal of the city of Ghent to further strengthen the district's vitality, a district where it is good to reside, work and live. The Brugse Poort, built as a working-class district at the end of the 19th century, nowadays has an enormous diversity of residents and some facilities of urban importance, and as such it is already an urbanised city district. The real ambition appears in the addition 'vital'. A neighbourhood in which it is good to reside, work and live can also be called a pleasant or an attractive urban district. Vitality sounds like more than that, but what exactly? And: what is the role of participation of different groups of residents in this regard? And participation in what and in which way? However implicitly, on the part of the city department of urban development and participation, social exclusion and inclusion of vulnerable residents or members of so-called minority groups played an important role in the assignment of the research project and the notion of vitality. Worries were expressed about the participation of different groups, varying from poor people to new immigrants, and a feeling they cannot be reached with the projects and programs organised by the city.

1. Vitality, inclusion, and participation

In the assignment, the city department stated that the vitality of a neighbourhood 'depends of enough resilience to adapt to changing circumstances, both on an individual and a collective level.' The aim of the research and the central research question are based on this statement: 'This requires insight into the existing social dynamics. What is the level of vitality of the neighbourhood already and what does resilience look like on an individual and collective level?' The last question looks like a clear one, but on closer inspection, the two concepts, vitality and resilience, seem nearly synonymous, which makes the question almost tautological. Recently, both concepts have also acquired the character of a policy slogan, in Flanders as well as in the Netherlands.

Some years ago, resilience usually referred to the ability to withstand natural disasters and to overcome the damage caused (Kilper 2012). This relates to the physical domain, but it has also social dimensions. Resilience shows the vitality of a community, especially in extreme circumstances. Perhaps the relationship between resilience and vitality is therefore exactly the opposite way around to the way it is stated in the proposed research question. Not: the vitality of a neighbourhood depends on enough resilience to adapt to changing circumstances, but: to be able to respond resiliently to those changes, a neighbourhood must have enough vitality. Vitality then indicates the capacities and skills to look at changes differently, less defensively, and to embark upon new paths. The emergence of new initiatives, places, and partnerships, which are provoked but also made possible and given space precisely by these changes, characterise the vitality of a neighbourhood. Although this answers the question of what constitutes the vitality of a neighbourhood, it by no means explains how this works.

Recently the answer to this question was sought, in the Netherlands and Flanders, in the proportion of highly educated people, leading to policies called 'neighbourhoods in balance'. The idea behind this was that higher educated people would provide 'strong shoulders', helping 'vulnerable' groups to take part in bettering living circumstances in the neighbourhood, but resulted in what is known as 'state led gentrification' (Lees 2008, Hochstenbach 2017). Sociological research shows that the ability of residents to jointly do something about the physical and social quality of their neighbourhood is not directly related to the number of residents with a high degree of economic, social, or cultural capital, but to the socio-spatial fabric of the neighbourhood (Sampson et al. 2005; Diani 2015). This socio-spatial fabric or infrastructure could easily be (mis)understood as a collaboration of organisations and municipal departments active in the neighbourhood, the so-called integrated approach. For the vitality of a neighbourhood, however, the informal connections within the network of people who are active as professionals in those organisations in connection with volunteers, residents, and participants are far more important. Not the level but the diversity of social and cultural capital is what matters here. By finding each other to solve daily problems and for support, a breeding ground for new ideas and initiatives is created at the same time. But where do they find each other?

In times of mobile phones, internet, email, Facebook, Instagram and WhatsApp, physical encounters seem less and less necessary. For the demand for inclusiveness, however, the openness of the social infrastructure for newcomers is essential in order for them to become participants and initiators. This requires physical places where activities take place and encounters can occur. There, the vitality of the neighbourhood becomes visible and that in turn invites

Strengthening the vitality of neighbourhoods

participation. Newcomers often join in unnoticed, but never without their own motives and aspirations. They bring their own perspectives and ideas and add something different. The subtle balance between the capacity to let people fit in and the space given to add something makes a neighbourhood vital and open to solutions for new problems, and new solutions for stubborn old ones.

Neighbourhoods not only have a history, but also a memory, a collective memory, that plays an important role in the question of inclusiveness or exclusivity, in both social policies and social practices. Collective memory should contain memories and stories associated with different periods, generations, groups, and stages of life. If one story becomes too dominant, it suppresses other stories and excludes the groups that feel connected to those. Parts of the collective memory play up and are sometimes used selectively in actions for or against certain initiatives and interventions in the neighbourhood. The collective memory of a neighbourhood is strongly connected with the spatial structure of it, the streets, squares, parks and buildings, and its changes over time (Hebbert 2005).

In summary, the vitality of a neighbourhood is not the result of the highest possible amount of self-reliant residents, but a neighbourhood with a vigorous socio-spatial fabric consisting of an extensive and innovative network of residents, participants and professionals from informal and formal social organisations that develops initiatives, creates new organisational forms and meeting places in response to social changes and new challenges, building on a rich history stored in a multiple collective memory, open to newcomers and curious about other stories, ideas, and approaches.

2. Four perspectives

To answer the question of whether the Brugse Poort is such a district, I was less interested in opinions than in the socio-spatial practices of both residents and professionals. Therefore, a participatory and observational study was proposed. I lived in the neighbourhood for a year and participated in everyday life, as well as in special events and not to forget in programs, projects and studies carried out by community workers, other professionals, and activists. The research was structured by looking at the district from four perspectives. Firstly, as a society, the lived city, or the city of everyday life. Secondly, as a domain of social and physical interventions, the planned city. Thirdly, neighbourhoods like the Brugse Poort appear to be laboratories of social innovations, the creative city. Finally – and often neglected in social analyses – a neighbourhood is a physical-spatial environment with specific qualities in terms of housing and other building stock, property relations, and a specific urbanistic layout, with private, collective, and public space, that is constantly in transition, the built city. Over time, these four perspectives determine the developments in a neighbourhood, but in varying ways and extents.

In the case of the Brugse Poort, the 1990s are characterised by innovations, partly as a liberation from the intervention frameworks of the church and social democrats, partly because of the settlement of new groups, families of Turkish and Moroccan origin and young graduates. The first steps were already taken two decennia before. The El Faitha Mosque, one of the first in Flanders, opened in 1973. At the same time, young graduates and students took the initiative to develop a first 'secular' (non-religious, non-political) community centre, and a playground according to the Dutch model that neighbourhood activists found in The Hague. But it wasn't until the 1990s that these fledgling initiatives came to fruition through a colourful coalition of the new settlers of different origins, second generation immigrants, artists, squatters, critical professionals, and people working for welfare institutions and the city. This not only resulted in many different innovative facilities, from a youth centre for immigrant children to an alternative theatre, a thrift shop, and a food bank. It also led to an urban renewal operation called 'Oxygen for the Brugse Poort' in which still existing slums were demolished (much to the fury of the squatters, incidentally) to make place for social housing, public space, and small parks or public gardens. In the following period, a certain institutionalisation occurred again, which was only one, but an important, cause of a conflict arising in 2020. Young men of Moroccan and Turkish origin, born and raised in the neighbourhood, acted against the drug dealing in the central square and shopping street by what was said to be Tunisian youngsters who travelled to Europe on spec. This conflict sharpened the grown contradictions in the Brugse Poort, but also opened the prospect of new opportunities (Verloo/Davis 2021).

In the daily press coverage of 'the incident', the discussions this in turn provoked, the political reactions, and subsequent measures that were taken, mainly 'us versus them' contradictions came to the fore. Often it was not clear who exactly was referred to as 'we' or 'them'. On the one hand, the age-old contrast between immigrants and natives was expressed, which also translated into the government and the police versus 'we immigrants' who still do not belong to 'we Ghent residents'. On the other hand, the gap was emphasised between 'we immigrants' and older Flemish residents versus the higher educated newcomers originating from the West-Flemish countryside with their 'living streets' (Leefstraten), small gardens against facades and allotment gardens and cultural hotspots. Residents of Moroccan and Turkish origin, together with the original Ghenters and Brugse Poorters, therefore emerged as the established compared to the highly educated gentrifiers as newcomers. Newcomers who, at least that is the suggestion, can rejoice in the warm interest of the city council. So, referring to the classical distinction made by Elias and Scotson (1965), who actually are the established here and who the outsiders? Apparently, the newcomers are in a way already self-settled, just coming to take up,

Strengthening the vitality of neighbourhoods

as it were, the place assigned to them by the city council. Which in turn transforms the longer established residents into outsiders. 'Us versus them' also applies to poverty. The poor are given their place in the differentiated, unheard 'we' versus the unambiguous and dominant 'them' of the newcomers, the government, and the institutions.

Another matter of discontent that was revealed by the 'incident', was the dissatisfaction with the decrease and formalisation or bureaucratisation of neighbourhood activities. Less youth work, less homework supervision, fewer opportunities to ask for help, less space for hanging around and relaxing. But also, fewer possibilities for active participation and partaking of youngsters in the organisation of these activities, and less well-known and involved employees, both caused by the limitation of the autonomy with which workers and participants used to jointly determine the work in the decade before. This seemed to apply not only to youth work, but also to other areas of community work and social activities. In this way, a tension has been growing between intervention and innovation.

The 'incident' led to rapid political attention, with politicians visiting the neighbourhood to discuss the situation with residents and professionals, resulting in a decisive approach. The neighbourhood budgets were brought forward, street workers were appointed, and an open call for initiatives and creative solutions was launched. This resulted in four proposals from which the Brugse Puurte University was chosen, a joint initiative of four organisations already active in the district. In addition to money, an empty space would be made available for the youth activities of Averroes, an organisation of second-generation immigrants, working for and with youngsters of different immigration backgrounds. In 2021, the so-called Beehive (Bijenkorf) opened for boys from the neighbourhood, shortly followed by activities for girls.

It is amazing that all this was arranged so rapidly. However, that also raises questions. Something was added to the existing socio-spatial infrastructure, but its functioning was not questioned. An important question is therefore what this addition causes in the tension between intervention and innovation in that socio-spatial fabric. The same question arises for the functioning of different existing places, all the result of the above-mentioned innovative phase of former years. How can they develop as a truly public domain, as places of social and cultural exchange between different groups in the neighbourhood?

3. Growing diversity

In the 'us' versus 'them' perspective that comes to the fore in the aftermath of the incidents, three social developments are expressed: continuing immigration, ongoing gentrification, and persistent poverty. These developments are not new, but their character has changed considerably in recent years. Concerning immigration, the simple distinction between native and non-native has long since ceased to apply. Old and new groups of migrants together now form half or most of the population in neighbourhoods in Ghent such as the Brugse Poort, but that is a 'majority of minorities' (Verhaeghe 2013). The diversity of a few large migrant groups has changed into a still growing diversity of very many small ones. And that change is still ongoing. In some respects, the same applies to gentrification and poverty; adding up to a superdiversity that transcends the one-sided use of the term for immigrants only (see also: Çaglar 2016).

In various neighbourhoods, the growing diversity leads to a situation that is unstable, always unfinished, and unpredictable (Blommaert 2013). Yet there is a certain form of order or logic in the way in which superdiversity is precipitated in neighbourhoods like the Brugse Poort. Different forms of infrastructure are emerging, tailored to the needs and interests of the different groups and their immigration and settlement trajectories. Facilities of a social nature, such as religious denominations, mosques, organisations that represent their interests, provide help and space for socialising, in addition to shops, cafes, coffee houses and eateries. Here is an important link to what has been said above about the socio-spatial fabric and the importance of places for the vitality of the neighbourhood.

In many respects, gentrification seems to be a completely different development, but here too we see substantial differences between the gentrifiers who settled in the Brugse Poort in successive periods. The pioneers of the 1970s, 1980s and 1990s, however few, increasingly left their mark on the neighbourhood through cultural initiatives and actions. In this way, they not only created connections with the established residents and with other newcomers, but from the 1990s on, also paved the way for the next group of highly educated parents with young children. These were already more focused on each other and made their voices heard in the urban renewal operation. Partly because of this, they play such an important role in the us-them contradictions. The most recent group seems to have less interest in the neighbourhood as such than as an expression of their urban lifestyle.

On closer inspection, poverty also turns out to be not as unambiguous as it appears at first sight. My limited study at the 'Open Plaats' food bank shows how diverse this group is. These differences often relate to the circumstances that lead people into poverty and the possibilities they see of getting out of it, or at least achieving a better life. It also shows that poverty can happen to anyone. As a result, this group overlaps to a certain extent with the other two. Many poor people are immigrants, or vice versa, but the image of low education and therefore poor is also incorrect for these two groups. There are too many highly educated immigrants for such an oversimplification, who are nevertheless dependent on food aid. The same goes for native Belgians who can easily pass for gentrifiers in terms of education and/or appearance. Anyone can end up in a situation of poverty, but not everyone has equal opportunities to get out of it.

According to Blommaert (2013), superdiversity forces us to distance ourselves from the established modernist images of society and social processes and to develop new instruments to deal with the grown diversity and permanently changing circumstances. Social cohesion no longer seems to be an option. Nor does bridging the gaps between groups, as American sociologist Putnam (2000) proposed. We will have to look at new forms of living together, and at participation as these developed in neighbourhoods like the Brugse Poort over the last decades. In this quest two concepts can be helpful: conviviality and counterpublics.

4. Conviviality instead of social cohesion

Twenty years ago, American sociologist Robert Putnam (2000) introduced the distinction between bonding and bridging. He increasingly saw bonding within groups. He saw less and less building of bridges with other groups. But how can we envisage this bridging? Doesn't it only happen when individuals belonging to different groups are in contact with each other (Glick Schiller/Schmidt 2016)? Actually, the idea of bonding and bridging seems to be a remnant of a situation that was still manageable and not yet superdiverse. To begin with, we could take a better look at how people live together day after day, in their street and in their neighbourhood. At the small contacts they have with neighbours, with other parents at school, and with shopkeepers, who belong to groups other than they themselves do. This kind of living together, or conviviality (derived from the French. 'convivre'), in everyday practice questions the ideological concept of social cohesion.

Due to the mix of owner-occupied homes, rental homes, apartments, and social housing, everyone in the Brugse Poort lives amidst members of different groups. This stimulates small contacts, but it also necessitates keeping a distance. In almost all cases, people have not chosen their neighbours, but they are there, and you must deal with them anyway (Mayol 1998). This is not the case for the places where neighbours who live next to each other continue to organise their lives, the places where they work, study, take the children to school, go shopping, go out, go to a café, restaurant, or coffee bar, play sports and so on. There they have a choice and, unlike in the immediate living situation, segregation does occur there. It has grown strongly in recent decades, partly because of the increased expression of differences in lifestyles and cultural preferences (Lofland 1989, Zukin 1995).

The living worlds of some groups are expanding. They appropriate certain places and increasingly leave their mark on the neighbourhood. Other groups see their living environment shrink. Their familiar places are taken over or disappear, making their way of life less visible. The expansion and contraction of living worlds, the growing dominance of some groups and the disappearance of others does not go without a struggle, figuratively and sometimes literally, as it turned out in May 2020. The question then is, where do they encounter each other outside their own street? Where are (potentially) new public domains developing as places of natural encounter and cultural exchange (Hajer/Reijndorp 2001)? These are the places that play a crucial role, not only in the functioning of the networks that make the neighbourhood a vital neighbourhood, but also in the forming of networks of poor people to survive and get ahead (Small/Gose 2020).

5. Counterpublics and natural meeting places

As a reaction to but also as a mirror of the existing dominant public and semi-public facilities, older immigrant groups such as Turks and Moroccans formed their own alternative sphere of facilities. In this way they created, in the terms of Nancy Fraser (1990), 'subaltern counterpublics', forms of a culture of counterbalance or contradiction. In contrast with what terms like inclusive and public domain suggest, participation in public matters and debate is not a given for everybody, as Fraser already showed 30 years ago. You need to be familiar with the social conventions and the right words in order to be heard. Using the women's movement of the 1970s and 1980s as an example, she argued that 'subaltern' groups only succeed in participation through the creation of counterpublics, broader movements in which activists, writers, academics, artists, professionals, and politicians come together. Figuratively but also literally, by meeting in more or less exclusive localities like women's bookshops, gay cafes, or immigrants' mosques or tea houses. Defined in this way, there will always be a tension between inclusion as a general term, welcoming all people without concern for specific characteristics like origin, ethnicity, faith, class, education, gender, and physical, mental, or other disabilities and the way the ability to partake must be repeatedly fought for by those different groups. On the other hand, places where different groups meet are crucial for the vitality of a neighbourhood, the social networks, and the possibilities of residents to make ends meet and make progress.

Cities offer the opportunity for an alternative public sphere. Firstly, because of the scale or size of migrant groups there, secondly, because social contradictions fuel the formation of their own 'counter' identity, and thirdly, because they have opposition networks and alternative institutions that can

Strengthening the vitality of neighbourhoods 89

serve as an example and support (Nicholls/Uitermark 2016). Ghent offers an outstanding example of the rise of this kind of subaltern counterpublics of immigrants from the 1970s on. In the Brugse Poort, the El Fath mosque, a group of youngsters called the Rif boys, social and cultural organisations such as Averroes and Al Istiquama are examples of the formation of such an immigrant counterculture, the initiators of which (meanwhile) no longer live in the district but are still active within it.

However, a development of this kind of counterculture no longer seem to be the case for the new migrant groups, if only because of their much smaller size, certainly at district level. In recent years, in addition to many smaller migrant groups, including refugees from Afghanistan, Eritrea and Syria, for example, more and more Bulgarian and Slovak migrants have come to live in the Brugse Poort. They are clearly present in the street scene, but only make up a small part of the population. The 'Turkish' Bulgarians use the existing Turkish infrastructure for work, housing and partly by taking over shops and other businesses and can therefore apparently find their way around more easily than the Slovaks, who do not have such anchor points in the city and need to find out more for themselves.

Municipal actors of the city of Ghent conclude that it is difficult for them to connect with these new groups. However, the difficulty of connecting with new groups of immigrants should be put into perspective. The city and other institutions operating in the neighbourhood may not find the connection with the Slovaks, but although the Slovaks keep to themselves, they have certainly found the connection with the city and these institutions. This is much less true for the Bulgarians. Both groups may not participate in Neighbour Day or other participatory activities, but their children are in school, sometimes the same one they went to when they arrived as a child of 8 or 10 years old. Their children also go to youth centres in the neighbourhood. The parents have found their way to the centres for help and advice with problems around bad housing, to the food banks, and other places. The real problem is perhaps that as individuals they are connected, but as a group they are not. These new groups do not organise themselves, as the old migrant groups did, in counterpublics. The same seems to be true for the poor in general. Therefore, they are not visible in the public arena and not able to let their voice be heard to improve their situation and realise their ambitions.

The problem, however, is not entirely due to the lack of organisation of the new groups. From the 1990s on, we have seen the 'individualisation of the social' (Ferge 1997), a growing tendency towards individualisation of social problems and their solutions. The retreating government, the promotion of market forces in civil society and the emphasis on citizens' self-reliance might have – perhaps more often forced than voluntarily – created space for small-scale citizens' initiative. On the same time, these policies seriously undermined the idea of collective action. So, if it is true, as Nicholls and Uitermark (2016) observe, that cities offer the opportunity for an alternative public sphere, partly because existing opposition networks and alternative institutions can serve as an example and support, then the reverse could also apply, namely that the more recent small-scale citizens' initiatives fulfil that exemplary and supportive function to a much lesser degree (at least not by themselves).

6. Conclusion

When we look at the counterpublics of the 1970s, 1980s and 1990s and the way they were created, we see a combination of culture, advocacy, and politics. Today, especially the last two are much less developed. From the viewpoint of a vital neighbourhood as a socio-spatial fabric consisting of an innovative network as well as meeting places, these initiatives must deliberately develop into natural or self-evident meeting places, places where social and cultural exchange takes place between members of different groups. Thanks to the social interaction of different groups of residents as well as professionals and volunteers, these places may develop into breeding grounds for social initiatives, presenting alternatives to official policies. From this perspective, inclusion and participation are understood as partaking not only in activities but also in the way social problems are defined and solutions dreamed up. In this sense, participation means being part of something, especially through sharing knowledge and experience, and moreover a feeling of belonging, of being connected to a cause and therefore to each other.

Places where a kind of public familiarity may develop are often not the places designated for this purpose by urban design. Nor are they simply the self-evident result of interventions and innovations in response to changes in the composition of the population. Public familiarity "can hardly be achieved, if at all, by a merry-go-round of projects for which people deliberately have to leave the house," states urban sociologist Talja Blokland, but are "rather an unintended side effect of the daily, self-evident use of facilities, which consequently become a self-evident meeting place" (Blokland 2009: 255). Self-evident or natural meeting places include both outdoor and indoor spaces, squares and parks, and facilities such as a library, school, shop, or women's centre; not to forget the relationship between the two, facilities in a square or in a park, the shopping street, and the café terrace.

What is the daily, natural, self-evident use of places? This is clear in a shop, and in a library. But what is the natural use of, for example, the newly planned Women's Centre, or the food bank if it wants to be more than just a place for food aid, or a cultural facility if it wants to attract a more diverse audience? The point – and the comparison with the project carousel makes this clear – is that you don't necessarily have to participate in a planned activity.

Strengthening the vitality of neighbourhoods

You can look around, browse, crib and copy, listen and eavesdrop, but you don't have to do anything with others or necessarily make contact. Natural meeting places offer familiarity, but do not force it; looking does not oblige anyone to buy, or to chat, so to speak. On these points the new informal youth centre De Bijenkorf can offer inspiration, despite its short existence. Boys have quickly found their way, they like to walk in, they can play games or do other things, do their homework, but also ask questions and exchange experiences with each other. On the day many boys went to secondary school for the first time, they immediately came to the Bijenkorf after school to share their experiences with each other and with the 'hostess' and ask her, like an older sister, how things work exactly at such a new school. Girls now also have their place there.

What can, in short, be learned from the research into the Brugse Poort district about the role of informal networks and common goods initiatives in redefining the commons for social inclusion on the local level? First, that informal networks of residents, professionals, volunteers, and other participants are essential for the vitality of a neighbourhood, both on a collective and an individual level. Social inclusion and openness to newcomers is a *conditio sine qua non* to address new problems or create new solutions for stubborn old ones. This requires physical places where activities take place, encounters can occur, and the vitality becomes visible which invite participation. Second, that the growing diversity forces us to say goodbye to the modernist conceptions of society and look for new tools to deal with diversity. Two of these tools come to the fore but seem contradictory at first glance: the development of counterpublics and the creation of natural meeting places. The first one is essential for the participation of subaltern groups and requires the possibility of creating more or less exclusive places. The second one is crucial for the cultural exchange between members of different groups, no matter how this is. defined. When inclusion and participation is understood not only as partaking in activities, but also in the way social problems are defined and solutions are dreamed up, both are necessary. In this way, the four perspectives as developed above come together, with a special concern for intervention and innovation. The challenge is to make them complementary to create a sense of participation as 'being part of' and 'belonging', especially by sharing knowledge and experience.

References

Blokland, Talja (2009): Oog voor elkaar. Veiligheidsbeleving en sociale controle in de grote stad. Amsterdam: Amsterdam University Press.

Blommaert, Jan (2013): Ethnography, Superdiversity and Linguistic Landscapes. Chronicles of Complexity. Bristol/Buffalo/Toronto: Multilingual Matters.

Çaglar, Ayse (2016): Still 'migrants' after all those years: foundational mobilities, temporal frames and emplacement of migrants. In: Journal of Ethnic and Migration Studies, 2016, 45, pp. 952-969.

Diani, Mario (2015): The Cement of Civil Society. Studying Networks in Localities. Cambridge (UK): Cambridge University Press.

Elias, Norbert/Scotson, John L. (1965): The Established and the Outsiders. London: Frank Cass and Co.

Ferge, Zsuzsa (1997): The changed welfare paradigm: the individualization of the social. In: Social Policy and Administration, 1997, 31, 1, pp. 20-44.

Fraser, Nancy (1990): Rethinking the Public Sphere: A Contribution to the Critique of Actually Existing Democracy. In: Social Text, 1990, 25/26, pp. 56-80.

Glick Schiller, Nina/Schmidt, Garbi (2016): Envisioning place: urban sociabilities within time, space and multiscalar power. In: Identities. Global Studies in Culture and Power, 2016, 23, 1, pp. 1-16.

Hajer, Maarten/Reijndorp, Arnold (2001): In Search of New Public Domain. Analysis and Strategy. Rotterdam: NAi Publishers.

Hebbert, Michael (2005): The street as locus of collective memory. In:Environment and Planning D: Society and Space, 2005, 23, pp. 581-596.

Hochstenbach, Cody (2017): State-led Gentrification and the Changing Geography of Market-oriented Housing Policy. In: Housing, Theory and Society, 2017, 34, 4, pp. 399-419.

Kilper, Heiderose (2012): Vulnerability and Resilience. In: Raumforschung und Raumordnung. 2012, 70, pp. 257-258.

Lees, Loretta (2008): Gentrification and Social Mixing: Towards an urban renaissance? In: Urban Studies, 2008, 45, pp. 2449-2470.

Lofland, Lyn (1989): Private Lifestyles, Changing Neighborhoods, and Public Life: a Problem in Organized Complexity. In: Tijdschrift voor Economische en Sociale Geografie, 1989, 80, 2, pp. 89-96

Mayol, Pierre (1998): Living. Volume 2, Living and Cooking. In: De Certeau, Michel/ Giard, Luce/Mayol, Pierre (eds.): The Practice of Everyday Life. Minneapolis: University of Minnesota Press, pp. 5-131.

Nicholls, Walter J./Uitermark, Justus (2016): Migrant cities: place, power, and voice in the era of super diversity. In: Journal of Ethnic and Migration Studies, 2016, 42, pp. 877-892.

Putnam, Robert D. (2000): Bowling Alone: the collapse and revival of American community. New York: Simon and Schuster Paperbacks.

Sampson, Robert J./McAdam, Doug/MacIndoe, Heather/Weffer-Elizondo, Simón (2005): Civil Society Reconsidered: The Durable Nature and Community Structure of Collective Civic Action. In: American Journal of Sociology, 2005, 111, pp. 673-714.

Small, Mario L./Gose, Leah E. (2020): How Do Low-Income People Form Survival Networks? Routine Organizations as Brokers. In: Annals AAPSS, 2020, 689, pp. 89-109.
Verhaeghe, Pieter Paul (2013): Ruimtelijke segregatie van 'oude' en 'nieuwe' migrantengroepen in Gent. In: Ruimte and Maatschappij, 2013, 4, 4, pp. 7-35.
Verloo, Nanke/Davis, Diana (2021): Learning from Conflict. In: Built Environment, 2021, 47, pp. 5-12.
Zukin, Sharon (1995): The Cultures of Cities. Cambridge (Mass.): Blackwell Publishers.

Lessons (not) learned from pandemic times. Individual, socio-spatial and organisational aspects of digital transformation in the disability field

Martin F. Reichstein

Introduction

The COVID-19 pandemic was and still is a shared global and social experience. However, different groups are "both in terms of the actual illness and public health measures put in place to curb its spread, [...] affected [...] to varying degrees" (Whitley et al. 2021: 1693). From a social work perspective, it is important to ask how this has affected marginalised groups in society such as persons with disabilities.

In recent times, no new technology has influenced social life to the same extent as digital technologies in general and the Internet in particular (cf. van Eimeren/Frees 2014: 379). In Germany, the proportion of Internet users among the German-speaking population increased by 5 percent compared with the previous year to 94 percent in 2020 (cf. Beisch/Koch 2021: 489). Not least, the use of digital communication tools has increased considerably (cf. ibid.: 464; Hacker et al. 2020: 564). Both phenomena – the further increase in Internet usage and the growth in the use of digital communication tools (not only) in Germany – are likely to be side effects of COVID-19 pandemic control measures starting in 2020. During the pandemic, significant parts of social life have been shifted ad hoc into the digital space in an unprecedented way (cf. Dobransky/Hargittai 2021: 1699). This aspect of the pandemic is addressed in this paper, focusing on both individual and organisational aspects of the topic and referring to the living conditions of persons with disabilities.

In this paper, individual and spatial aspects are addressed with reference to the socio-spatial theory of social work (cf. Früchtel et al. 2013). In this context, the individual 'social space' consists of personal networks that are understood as a source of reciprocal informal support. This understanding opens the possibility of individual social spaces being digitally enhanced and enlarged by adding a 'digital social space'.

The group of persons in question depends on a variety of support services that are organised differently from country to country. Beyond all national differences, what these services have in common is that they can have a great influence on the living conditions of their addressees through the way they are organised and designed. This applies in particular to housing-related services (cf. Reichstein 2021: 29–30). Therefore, the topic addressed in this paper needs to have an analytical basis that can be applied to organisational frameworks and routines. The author here refers to neo-institutionalist approaches in organisational theory (cf. DiMaggio/Powell 1983; Schädler 2003).

Following this introduction, the theoretical background of this paper will be outlined. In this context, the living conditions of persons with disabilities as well as their use of digital applications will be discussed. A central component of this paper are selected findings from the international literature on the effects of the ad hoc digitalisation that took place during the COVID-19 pandemic for the group of persons in question. Building on this, the paper concludes with theses on the digital transformation of social services in the context of services for persons with disabilities.

1. The 'disability field', persons with disabilities and digital applications

Reflecting the German example against the backdrop of neo-institutionalist theory, Schädler (ibid.: 27) identifies local disability support systems as organisational fields. These are defined by DiMaggio/Powell (1983: 148) as "those organizations that, in the aggregate, constitute a recognized area of institutional life: key suppliers, resource and product consumers, regulatory agencies, and other organizations that produce similar services or products". For local 'disability fields', this means that they not only include support services, funding agencies and supervisory authorities but also individual persons with disabilities and their relatives.

Neo-institutionalist organisational theory has a high explanatory potential when it comes to institutionalised forms of organisational life (cf. Reichstein 2021: 29–30) as well as to institutionalised routines within organisations (cf. Klatetzki 2003: 95; Schädler/Reichstein 2019: 835). Within the framework, these effects are explained through mechanisms of organisational isomorphy that lead to increasingly dense sets of rules (institutions) that determine organisational action.

Drawing on neo-institutionalist theory, Schädler (2003: 29) and Muche (2017: 31) elaborate that support systems for persons with disabilities show a high degree of persistence. Although these authors refer to the situation in Germany, it can be assumed that the phenomenon also occurs in other (Western) societies. In Germany, the persistence described above is reflected not least in the continuing importance of institutionalised forms of housing for the support of persons with so-called intellectual disabilities (cf. Reichstein 2022: 140; Thimm et al. 2018: 28).

Arguing from the perspective of path dependence theory, Schreyögg (2003: 286) states that organisational change (as well as change in organisational fields) is generally possible but works best as a sequence of incremental steps. In this context, a momentum (cf. ibid.) is helpful to overcome institutionalised routines and organisational patterns. Trescher and Nothbaum (2022: 138–139) argue that the COVID-19 pandemic and, in particular, its impact on institutional living has disrupted institutionalised routines resulting in a possible momentum for change. However, it should be noted that the group of persons in question was particularly affected by the pandemic in general as well as by (unintended) side effects of the countermeasures (cf. Dobransky/Hargittai 2021: 1700; Embregts et al. 2022: 581; Landes et al. 2020: 3; Trescher/Nothbaum 2022: 140–143).

In general, the living conditions of most persons with disabilities in Western societies are characterised by a low socio-economic status (cf. Dobransky/Hargittai 2016: 18; 2021: 1699–1700). This affects not least persons with high or complex individual support needs (cf. Bundesministerium für Arbeit und Soziales 2016: 206; World Health Organization/World Bank 2011: 172).

In the literature, the group of persons in question here is assumed to have comparably small personal networks (cf. Kamstra et al. 2015: 253–255; Seifert 2006: 385) respectively 'social spaces' that could – in theory – be enhanced by using digital applications in general and digital communication tools in particular. This potential is assumed for the time being, even though the quality of digitally mediated communication is also critically questioned in the literature (cf. Turkle 2017: 83). Besides this aspect, Schädler et al. (2021: 14) see a generally high potential of digital applications for addressees of social services but admit a 'digital divide' in society (cf. Rudolph 2019: 109) that already existed before the pandemic.

It can be assumed that the group of persons in question still uses digital applications to a significantly lesser extent than the general population (cf. Lebenshilfe Berlin 2021: 7; 33). Poor socio-economic conditions (cf. Dobransky/Hargittai 2016: 18) and (discriminatory) practices in institutionalised forms of support (cf. Düber/Göthling 2013: 27) are not least responsible for this. Against the backdrop outlined above, it is worth asking how the ad hoc digitalisation during the COVID-19 pandemic a) affected institutional routines in services for persons with disabilities and b) affected their individual 'social spaces'.

2. Digital transformation in pandemic times and its implications for persons with disabilities and the services they use

Since the COVID-19 pandemic is not over yet, the following reflections can only be preliminary. The reflections conducted here refer to both individual aspects and aspects notably for the disability (service) field. In this context, it might be possible that existing 'digital divides' in society have deepened during the pandemic. This might not be a contradiction to the idea of a catalytic effect regarding the digital transformation of mainstream society.

Digital applications and media were already widely used in (Western) societies before COVID-19. Presenting data on Internet usage in Germany, Beisch and Koch (2021: 489) state that rates have risen more or less continuously since 1997. According to the authors, in 2015 the Internet was already used by 80 percent of the population. Three years later, the share was already 90 percent. As stated before, in 2020 94 percent of the German population used the Internet. Due to the already high percentage of Internet users in Germany in pre-pandemic times, it is not possible to speak of a dynamic development here. However, it seems likely that the recent development is a side effect of the countermeasures.

Demographic differences, identified by van Deursen and van Dijk (2014: 511) as a key factor when it came to differences in Internet usage in pre-pandemic times, have been significantly reduced since COVID-19 (cf. Beisch/Koch 2021: 489). The development shown by Beisch and Koch (ibid.) makes it very likely that this effect will be sustained after the pandemic has ended. If so, the pandemic would have acted as a catalyst for digitalisation at least in parts of the mainstream society. Nevertheless, this may not be a contradiction to the idea of a deepening digital divide.

2.1 Individual and socio-spatial aspects

To avoid loneliness among their residents and to enable them to stay in contact with relatives, friends, etc. under the given restrictions, residential services in Germany have made increasing use of digital means of communication since spring 2020. In the area of workshops for persons with disabilities, digital communication tools were used in some cases to stay in contact with the persons with disabilities employed there. The importance of digital participation for persons with disabilities – during and after the pandemic – is pointed out, for example, by the Bundesvereinigung Lebenshilfe (2020: 7). Internationally, for example, Armitage and Nellums (2020: 257) pointed to the need for inclusion-oriented responses to the pandemic at quite an early stage. However, in both cases the remarks remain rather unspecific and refer more to the digital divide in general than to concrete applications.

Goggin and Ellis (2020: 168–169) note that digital means of communication were already of great relevance, especially for persons with physical impairments, before the COVID-19 pandemic. This is consistent with the assumption of fundamental potentials of digital tools described earlier. In analogy to the considerations made here, the authors point to the fundamental problem of general access in individual cases – i.e., the digital divide in the context of disability caused by low socio-economic status, living in institutions or other 'upstream barriers' (cf. Reichstein 2016: 83).

Caton et al. (2022: 20) see a "largely positive experience of Internet use [by adults with intellectual disabilities; M. R.] during the COVID-19 pandemic" with "the most commonly identified uses and benefits" being social (e.g., reduction of loneliness during the pandemic; cf. ibid.: 18). Taking a more general look at loneliness in society, Patulny and Bower (2022: 1) state that "longer-term effects and inequities of COVID-19 on social interaction and loneliness as the pandemic recedes are unclear". In contrast to the quite positive assessments of Caton et al. (2022: 20), these authors see "both higher levels of loneliness in lockdown and persistent loneliness post-lockdown" for "those with a physical disability, low income or who lacked multiple strong ties pre-COVID". As stated before, low income and a lack of strong social networks are again more likely to affect persons with disabilities than persons without. The quite different conclusions arrived at by Patulny and Bower and Caton et al. can possibly be explained by the structure of the survey conducted by Caton et al. (2022: 5), which included mainly persons with intellectual disabilities who lived with their families, alone or with a partner. As stated above, this is not the case for a significant number of persons with intellectual disabilities at least in Germany. A positive effect on individual contacts and thereby personal networks and 'social spaces' is therefore generally possible but whether it becomes realised depends on further variables.

2.2 Social service delivery

The countermeasures against the COVID-19 pandemic affected persons with disabilities not only as individuals but also as service users. During the pandemic, some support services were forced to adapt institutionalised routines (cf. Trescher/Nothbaum 2022: 138–139), to cancel their activities or to substitute them in digital form. In this context, Looi and Pring (2020: 511) as well as Nguyen (2021: 2) also identify a generally positive potential of digital applications. This is in line with the argumentations of Embregts et al. (2022: 581) as well as Jumreornvong et al. (2020: 1684). At the same time, these authors clearly point out that digitally substituted services for persons with disabilities are not always sufficient to suit individual support needs. This corresponds to the findings of Park (2022: 7) who concludes that the persons with disabilities in the respective sample found digital substitutes for face-to-face services installed during the pandemic "less useful than the non-disabled population". He therefore states a "necessity to develop technologies […] that address the diverse needs of people with different types of disabilities. Moreover, relevant policies that fulfil the unique needs of different vulnerable groups need to be formed and implemented" (ibid.).

Embregts et al. (2021: 486–487) identify a high degree of creativity in the development of "alternative ways of meeting and arranging day programs" among professional supporters they interviewed, but at the same time point out that digital means of communication are sometimes perceived as inefficient by the professionals. This applies in particular to agreements among professionals, which "were often ineffectual due to the fact that people either talked at the same time or failed to add anything of substance to the meeting" (ibid.: 488). This is not only consistent with Turkle's (2017: 83) critical remarks on digitally mediated communication but is also very likely to refer to institutionalised routines of support staff (cf. Schädler/Reichstein 2019: 835) that have been questioned (cf. Trescher/Nothbaum 2022: 138–139) but not overcome during the pandemic. Specifically, the use of digital communication still does not seem to be part of these routines.

Pinto et al. (2020: 10) emphasise again the general potential of digital services for the group of persons in question but consider these services to be insufficient in themselves when it comes to substitution of face-to-face contacts. This finding – in conjunction with the at least partially critical voices mentioned above – points to aspects that can be learned from the current situation for the time after the pandemic.

3. Beyond the pandemic: Concluding remarks and needs for future research and discourse

Research literature on how the pandemic has affected persons with disabilities in the context of digital media usage has so far referred more or less consistently to a generally positive potential when it comes to the enhancement of individual social networks or social spaces. However, the corresponding effect is highly linked to other circumstances. Aspects that hindered digital participation during the pandemic are again institutionalised support, institutionalised routines in service delivery and low socio-economic status. These seem to remain 'upstream barriers' even under the conditions of the global pandemic.

The 'digital divide' is likely to have closed in regard to older people during the pandemic. It is also likely that this change will be sustained even after the pandemic has ended. When it comes to the digitalisation of social services and to tackling the digital divide for persons relying on those services, the aspects outlined above point to a need for broader approaches to maintain a sustainable and appropriate digital transformation (cf. Schädler et al. 2021: 15–16) beyond what was implemented ad hoc during the COVID-19 pandemic. It is not likely that full digital substitutes will work to the same extent as face-to-face services. Schädler and Reichstein (2019: 830) in this context call for a link back to the physical and socio-spatial living environment of service users. In this perspective, social service provision in the digital sphere does not lead to a whole new form of service but to digital enhancements of present-day services and (hybrid) support arrangements with digital and analogue components based on the wishes and requirements in each individual case.

The enormous persistence of established organisational forms and routines, in this case in the field of services for persons with disabilities, makes a sustainable digital transformation based on the experiences from the pandemic unlikely. Rather, further efforts in research and organisational development are needed to find solutions both adequate for services and their users. The implementation of adequate practices and routines in social services associated with such requirements therefore does not automatically arise from experiences made during the pandemic. However, it could contribute to making social services more resilient in future crises.

The remarks in this article show that digital applications and communication are still not accessible to persons with intellectual disabilities to the same extent as they are to other people. The development of "inclusive localities" would presuppose this, however, since an additional level of space has apparently been constituted in the digital. In principle, this digital space offers the opportunity to expand one's own social space in the sense of a network using digital means of communication. This appears to be particularly relevant for a group of persons with comparatively small social networks.

In terms of social work practices, the existence of a digital level of space opens up an additional level of action. At the same time, however, there is also a need to address the problem of unequally distributed access. Both aspects might be a challenge for a field that is said to be sceptical when it comes to the implementation of new technologies (cf. Mayerle 2015: 9). It is important to emphasise here that, in the context of digitalisation and social work, the aim must not be to prevent addressees from accessing digital media. Rather, social work as a profession that is not least based in human rights (cf. Ife et al. 2022: 6) is called upon to help realise the right to digital participation of all persons (cf. Art. 9 UN CRPD) as formulated in the United Nations Convention on the Rights of Persons with Disabilities (UN CRPD). At the societal level, this also means that social work needs to address existing 'upstream barriers' – not only for persons with disabilities. In conclusion, this means that tackling the digital divide is a central task for (future) social work. However, succeeding in this endeavour implies formulating own requirements for ongoing digitalisation processes, and a critical reflection on these processes from a social work perspective. Here again, further research but also professional discourse is required.

References

Armitage, Richard/Nellums, Laura B. (2020): The COVID-19 response must be disability inclusive. In: The Lancet Public Health 5, p. 257. Doi:10.1016/S2468-2667(20)30076-1.
Beisch, Natalie/Koch, Wolfgang (2021): 25 Jahre ARD/ZDF-Onlinestudie. Unterwegsnutzung steigt wieder und Streaming/Mediatheken sind weiterhin Treiber des medialen Internets. In: Media Perspektiven 10, pp. 486–503.
Bundesministerium für Arbeit und Soziales (Ed.) (2016): Zweiter Teilhabebericht der Bundesregierung über die Lebenslagen von Menschen mit Beeinträchtigungen. Bonn: Bundesministerium für Arbeit und Soziales.
Bundesvereinigung Lebenshilfe (Ed.) (2020): Welche Lehren ziehen Menschen mit Behinderung und ihre Angehörigen aus der Corona-Pandemie? Positionspapier der Bundesvereinigung Lebenshilfe e. V. Marburg: Bundesvereinigung Lebenshilfe.
Caton, Sue/Hatton, Chris/Gillooly, Amanda/Oloidi, Edward/Clarke, Libby/Bradshaw, Jill/Flynn, Samantha/Taggart, Laurence/Mulhall, Peter/Jahoda, Andrew/Maguire, Roseann/Marriott, Anna/Todd, Stuart/Abbott, David/Beyer, Stephen/Gore, Nick/Heslop, Pauline/Scior, Katrina/Hastings, Richard P. (2022): Online social connections and Internet use among people with intellectual disabilities in the United Kingdom during the COVID-19 pandemic. In: New Media & Society, pp. 1–25. doi:10.1177/14614448221093762.
Deursen, Alexander van/Dijk, Jan van (2014): The digital divide shifts to differences in usage. In: New Media & Society 16/3, pp. 507–526. doi:10.1177/1461444813487959.
DiMaggio, Paul J./Powell, Walter W. (1983): The iron cage revisited. Institutional isomorphism and collective rationality in organizational fields. In: American Sociological Review 48, 2, pp. 147–160.
Dobransky, Kerry/Hargittai, Eszter (2016): Unrealized potential. Exploring the digital disability divide. In: Poetics 58, pp. 18–28. doi:10.1016/j.poetic.2016.08.003.
Dobransky, Kerry/Hargittai, Eszter (2021): Piercing the pandemic social bubble. Disability and social media use about COVID-19. In: American Behavioral Scientist 65/12, pp. 1698–1720. doi:10.1177/00027642211003146.

Düber, Miriam/Göthling, Stefan (2013): Barrieren im Internet für Menschen mit Lernschwierigkeiten. In: SIEGEN:SOZIAL 18, 1, pp. 24–29.

Eimeren, Birgit van/Frees, Beate (2014): 79 Prozent der Deutschen online. Zuwachs bei mobiler Internetnutzung und Bewegtbild. In: Media Perspektiven 7–8, pp. 378–396.

Embregts, Petri/Bogaard, Kim van den/Frielink, Noud/Voermans, Moniek/Thalen, Marloes/Jahoda, Andrew (2022): A thematic analysis into the experiences of people with a mild intellectual disability during the COVID-19 lockdown period. In: International Journal of Developmental Disabilities 68, 4, pp. 578–582. doi:10.1080/20473869.2020.1827214.

Embregts, Petri/Tournier, Tess/Frielink, Noud (2021): Experiences and needs of direct support staff working with people with intellectual disabilities during the COVID-19 pandemic. A thematic analysis. In: Journal of Applied Research in Intellectual Disabilities 34, 2, pp. 480–490. doi:10.1111/jar.12812.

Früchtel, Frank/Cyprian, Gudrun/Budde, Wolfgang (2013): Sozialer Raum und soziale Arbeit. Textbook. Theoretische Grundlagen. Wiesbaden: Springer VS Verlag.

Goggin, Gerard/Ellis, Katie (2020): Disability, communication, and life itself in the COVID-19 pandemic. In: Health Sociology Review 29, 2, pp. 168–176. doi:10.1080/14461242.2020.1784020.

Hacker, Janine/Brocke, Jan vom/Handali, Joshua/Otto, Markus/Schneider, Johannes (2020): Virtually in this together. How web-conferencing systems enabled a new virtual togetherness during the COVID-19 crisis. In: European Journal of Information Systems 29, 5, pp. 563–584.

Ife, Jim/Soldatić, Karen/Briskman, Linda (2022): Human rights and social work. Towards rights-based practice. Cambridge: Cambridge University Press.

Jumreornvong, Oranicha/Tabacof, Laura/Cortes, Mar/Tosto, Jenna/Kellner, Christopher P./Herrera, Joseph E./Putrino, David (2020): Ensuring equity for people living with disabilities in the age of COVID-19. In: Disability & Society 35, 10, pp. 1682–1687. doi:10.1080/09687599.2020.1809350.

Kamstra, Aafke/Putten, Annette van der/Vlaskamp, Carla (2015): The Structure of Informal Social Networks of Persons with Profound Intellectual and Multiple Disabilities. In: Journal of Applied Research in Intellectual Disabilities 28, 3, pp. 249–256.

Klatetzki, Thomas (2003): Skripts in Organisationen. Ein praxistheoretischer Bezugsrahmen für die Artikulation des kulturellen Repertoires sozialer Einrichtungen und Dienste. In: Schweppe, Cornelia (Hrsg.): Qualitative Forschung in der Sozialpädagogik. Opladen: Leske und Budrich, pp. 93–118.

Landes, Scott D./Turk, Margaret A./Formica, Margaret K./McDonald, Katherine E./Stevens, J. Dalton (2020): COVID-19 outcomes among people with intellectual and developmental disability living in residential group homes in New York State. In: Disability and Health Journal 13, 4, pp. 1–5. doi:10.1016/j.dhjo.2020.100969.

Lebenshilfe Berlin (Hrsg.) (2021): Ergebnisbericht für das Projekt Digitale Teilhabe von Menschen mit geistiger Beeinträchtigung. Eine aktuelle Nutzungs-Umfrage im Peer-Prinzip zur digitalen Teilhabe in Berlin. Lebenshilfe Berlin.

Looi, Jeffrey/Pring, William (2020): To tele- or not to telehealth? Ongoing COVID-19 challenges for private psychiatry in Australia. In: Australasian Psychiatry 28, 5, pp. 511–513. doi:10.1177/1039856220950081.

Mayerle, Michael (2015): "Woher hat er die Idee?" Selbstbestimmte Teilhabe von Menschen mit Lernschwierigkeiten durch Mediennutzung. Siegen: Universi.

Muche, Claudia (2017): Organisationale Identitäten als Behinderung? Entwicklungsdynamiken im Feld der Behindertenhilfe. Weinheim Basel: Beltz Juventa.

Nguyen, Dennis (2021): Mediatisation and datafication in the global COVID-19 pandemic: on the urgency of data literacy. In: Media International Australia 178, 1, pp. 210–214. doi:10.1177/1329878X20947563.

Park, Eun-Young (2022): Effect of COVID-19 on internet usage of people with disabilities. A secondary data analysis. In: International Journal of Environmental Research and Public Health 19/13, pp. 1–8. doi:10.3390/ijerph19137813.

Patulny, Roger/Bower, Marlee (2022): Beware the "loneliness gap"? Examining emerging inequalities and long-term risks of loneliness and isolation emerging from COVID-19. In: Australian Journal of Social Issues, pp. 1–22. doi:10.1002/ajs4.223.

Pinto, Monica/Gimigliano, Francesca/De Simone, Stefania/Costa, Massimo/Bianchi, Attilio/Iolascon, Giovanni (2020): Post-acute COVID-19 rehabilitation network proposal. From intensive to extensive and home-based it supported services. In: International Journal of Environmental Research and Public Health 17, 24, pp. 1–14. doi:10.3390/ijerph17249335.

Reichstein, Martin F. (2016): Teilhabe an der digitalen Gesellschaft? In: Teilhabe 55, 2, pp. 80–85.

Reichstein, Martin F. (2021): Leben in Exklusionssphären. Perspektiven auf Wohnangebote für Menschen mit komplexem Unterstützungsbedarf. Wiesbaden: Springer VS Verlag.

Reichstein, Martin F. (2022): Exklusionssphären und (k)ein Ende. Nebenfolgen und Perspektiven wohnbezogener Hilfen für Menschen mit sogenannter geistiger Behinderung und komplexem Unterstützungsbedarf. In: Behindertenpädagogik 61, 2, pp. 158–179.

Rudolph, Steffen (2019): Digitale Medien, Partizipation und Ungleichheit. Eine Studie zum sozialen Gebrauch des Internets. Wiesbaden: Springer Fachmedien.

Schädler, Johannes (2003): Stagnation oder Entwicklung in der Behindertenhilfe? Chancen eines Paradigmenwechsels unter Bedingungen institutioneller Beharrlichkeit. Hamburg: Kovač.

Schädler, Johannes/Reichstein, Martin F. (2019): Sektoralisierung Sozialer Dienste als kommunales Koordinationsproblem. Empirische Befunde am Beispiel der Behindertenhilfe, Pflege und Sozialpsychiatrie. In: Sozialer Fortschritt 68, 10, pp. 819–838.

Schädler, Johannes/Reichstein, Martin F./Strünck, Christoph/Wieching, Rainer/Wulf, Volker (2021): Soziale Dienste in digitalen Transformationsprozessen. Interdisziplinäre Perspektiven für Forschung und Lehre an der Schnittstelle von Sozialer Arbeit, Sozioinformatik und Versorgungsforschung. In: SI:SO 26, 1, pp. 12–21.

Schreyögg, Georg/Sydow, Jörg/Koch, Jochen (2003): Organisatorische Pfade. Von der Pfadabhängigkeit zur Pfadkreation? In: Managementforschung, 13, pp. 257–294.

Seifert, Monika (2006): Pädagogik im Bereich des Wohnens. In: Wüllenweber, Ernst/Theunissen, Georg/Mühl, Heinz (Hrsg.): Pädagogik bei geistigen Behinderungen. Ein Handbuch für Studium und Praxis. Stuttgart: Kohlhammer, pp. 376–425.

Thimm, Antonia/Rodekohr, Bianca/Dieckmann, Friedrich/Haßler, Theresia (2018): Wohnsituation Erwachsener mit geistiger Behinderung in Westfalen-Lippe und Umzüge im Alter. Münster: Katholische Hochschule NRW.
Trescher, Hendrik/Nothbaum, Peter (2022): Institutionalisierte Lebenslagen von Menschen mit geistiger Behinderung und Perspektiven pädagogischen Handelns während der COVID-19-Pandemie. In: Behindertenpädagogik 61, 2, pp. 137–157.
Turkle, Sherry (2017): Wir vergessen, was uns ausmacht. In: Schweizer Monat 97, 1050, pp. 80–83.
World Health Organization/World Bank (Eds.) (2011): World report on disability 2011. Geneva: World Health Organization. https://www.who.int/teams/noncommunicable-diseases/sensory-functions-disability-and-rehabilitation/world-report-on-disability
Whitley, Jess/Beauchamp, Miriam H./Brown, Curtis (2021): The impact of COVID-19 on the learning and achievement of vulnerable Canadian children and youth. In: FACETS 6, pp. 1693–1713. doi:10.1139/facets-2021-0096.

Inclusion – Governance – Participation

Participation of persons with disabilities in local political decision-making: Insights from the Second International Disability Alliance Global Survey on Organisations of Persons with Disabilities' participation in policies and programmes

Rebecca Daniel

1. OPD participation in local governance

1.1 Local political decision-making

Local governance is part of and influenced by decisions made on national or higher levels, such as world-regional or even international decisions and citizen-state relationships. At the same time, it can also contribute to such higher-level decisions (cf. Schädler/Wissenbach 2021: 317, 322).

Political decision-making at the local level can be on questions of overall development of the municipality or community, or sectoral decisions, e.g., in the area of housing, water, health, education, etc. It can also be related to field-specific decisions within sectors, e.g., regarding cross-cutting issues such as inclusion of marginalised groups, or sector-specific thematic sub-topics (cf. Schädler/Wissenbach 2021: 319). In this respect, all the Sustainable Development Goals (SDGs) are relevant for the local level – specifically SDG 11 on inclusive, safe, resilient and sustainable cities and human settlements (cf. UN 2015). Inclusion of persons with disabilities in all of these levels of local planning is, in consequence, a cross-cutting issue that is to be mainstreamed throughout local decision-making (cf. Wissenbach 2019: 12f.). Further areas of joint work of local, national and international decision-makers are also referred to by the United Nations (UN) Convention on the Rights of Persons with Disabilities (CRPD) (cf. UN 2006): disaster risk management (article 11), housing and community life (article 19, 28), education (article 24), health (article 25), or participation in political and public life (article 29). These provisions made by the CRPD are also addressed by the 2030 Agenda for Sustainable development (cf. UN 2015), and by UN HABITAT II New Urban Agenda (cf. UN 2016), to mention but a few.

Local governance involves a variety of different actors and processes (cf. Wissenbach 2019: 8), including local political institutions (such as local governments and local parliaments) and other bodies – such as administrative bodies, welfare agencies or service providers, as well as, not least, Civil Society Organisations (CSOs) such as Organisations of Persons with Disabilities (OPDs).

Relationships, interests and ways of life at local level are diverse and relations are not always reciprocal, based on equal access to rights and interests (cf. Wissenbach 2019: 8). Processes of regime building and agenda setting can be highly competitive, involve different interests, and result from joint learning processes. Depending on the context (e.g., state-society relationships and local concepts of citizenship), such processes can be more or less hierarchical, democratic, participatory and collaborative (cf. Schädler/Wissenbach 2021: 322) – thus promoting or limiting meaningful citizen participation to a varying extent (cf. e.g., NDA 2021; Shah 2006). Macropsychological views on power relations and advocacy can help to understand such power relations and necessary preconditions for structural change (cf. Wescott et al. 2021: 175ff.) – also at local level, where effective participation in decision-making requires engaging with partners who have different levels of power and resources (cf. Wescott/MacLachlan 2021).

1.2 Citizen participation at local level

In the sense of authors from critical theory, as well as deliberative and participatory democracy (cf. e.g., Habermas 1998: 7; Niesen 2007: 10, 23ff.; Cunningham 2002: 133), decision-making processes can and should be considered as a collaborative task for decision-makers and citizens – including voices from most affected communities.

CSOs play a range of many different (adversarial, supplementary, or complementary) roles in relationship with governments (Cote 2020: 16f.). OPDs, as one type of CSOs, are important actors in public decision-making overall and local governance in particular as they represent the diversity of disability constituencies and as they function as intermediary bodies between policymakers and persons with disabilities (Cote 2020: 18; IDA 2020: 14; UN 2018: 2f.).

Different typologies of political participation exist, and their origin reaches from theories based on human rights and political science to psychological theories. The democratic right to political participation is, in this paper, at minimum, seen as "citizens' activities to influence politics" (cf. van Deth 2016), at

Participation of persons with disabilities 111

best as "control by citizens of their own affairs" (cf. Cunningham 2002: 126). Participation (the input, i.e., the process) can lead to a two-fold output (cf. Pateman 1970: 43): It helps develop (1) policies or decisions in line with the interests of participants, and (2) social and political capacities of those participating. Local decision-makers have direct interaction with civil society, which bears the potential of "solving social, spatial and economic inequalities and enhancing social cohesion" (cf. Wissenbach 2019: 8f.). The involvement of civil society actors such as persons with disabilities and their organisations in local decision-making processes can, therefore, help to develop more inclusive societies and municipalities (cf. Schädler/Wissenbach 2021: 315, 320; Siska/Beadle-Brown 2021: 162-171). It should, however, also be noted that while participatory processes can – under meaningful conditions – contribute to positive changes for all members of society, it does not lead to accountability for all groups and to more legitimate results of decision-making processes per se. In fact, "participation can also be used to legitimize policies and processes that preserve the status quo or perpetuate inequalities" (cf. Cote 2020: 7).

1.3 Political participation in local governance as a human right

In line with the concept of local governance applied here, political participation as a human right and respect for the law and human rights in general are key elements of local political decision-making.

The human right to participation of persons with disabilities through their representative organisations in decision-making processes is, not least, declared in the CRPD. Amongst others, mainly articles 4.3 (on participation of OPDs in the implementation of the CRPD), 19 (on being included in the community), 29 (on participation in political and public life) and 33 (on participation of OPDs in national implementation and monitoring), as well as General Comment 7 on article 33 specify this right (cf. UN 2006). In addition to the CRPD, a range of non-binding international policy documents emphasize the right of persons with disabilities and their organisations to participate in decision-making[1].

The CRPD (cf. UN: 2006) and General Comment 7 (cf. UN 2018) describe what OPDs as well as the right to meaningful participation are. The General Comment also explains governments' duties in relation to OPD participation

---

1 Such as the 1975 UN Declaration on the Rights of Disabled Persons, the UN Standard Rules on the Equalization of Opportunities for Persons with Disabilities (UN, 1993, point 14, as well as rule 14, 15 and 18), or the UN Disability Inclusion Strategy (UN, 2020, indicator 5).

and it sets standards for what needs to be considered when it comes to meaningful participation, such as safe and free space and process for participation, the elimination of barriers to participation, the inclusion of the most marginalised, or equal access to information in accessible formats (cf. UN 2018; Cote 2020: 11).

1.4 Barriers to meaningful local OPD participation

While progress has been observed when it comes to OPD participation in decision-making, research and further analysis carried out so far suggests that OPD participation at different levels of public decision-making is not yet meaningful with regard to the standards set by the CRPD (cf. Cote 2020: 5; IDA 2020; NDA 2021; Kanova et al. 2021: 313ff.; UN 2018: 2; van Deth 2015).

Conditions for citizen participation in decisions on local policies, plans, projects, and programmes vary widely worldwide – given the continuously shrinking civic space and the diversity of countries with environments which are, to varying extents, constraining or enabling (cf. CIVICUS 2021). Governance processes are not always easily accessible for civil society, as they are often carried out 'in-camera' without (official) opportunity for civil society to participate. As studies have shown e.g., for Latin American countries, existing legal frameworks for participation often do not translate into high levels of participation on the municipal level, where civil society is mainly consulted without decision-making power (cf. Gaventa/Valderrama 1999: 9).

Power relations between citizens and local authorities have been identified as one of the main barriers for citizen participation on the local level overall in many different countries worldwide (cf. ib.: 7). But civil society itself can also be seen as an arena of exclusion of certain groups (e.g., persons from the Global South), due to internal power structures (cf. Brühl 2010: 193ff.).

What is more, participation requires a wide range of financial and personal resources (e.g., knowledge, technology, infrastructure, language, etc.), which are often not available to civil society. Nancy Fraser (cf. 2007: 21, 224ff.) argues from a theory of justice perspective that especially smaller or minority groups do not have the same access to means or resources necessary for equal participation and cannot put their arguments on the agenda in the way large groups do – for lack of (material) resources, rhetorical ability or because of existing biases on the part of the other participants within the discourse. Given the different circumstances of participating groups, existing opportunities to participate in local governance do therefore not automatically lead to meaningful participation of all groups. Often financial resources for local participation provided by authorities are also insufficient – e.g., because local governments are unable to access existing revenues, or because central revenues are not allocated appropriately (cf. Gaventa/Valderrama 1999: 9). But also a lack of 'participatory skills' on the part of local authorities, i.e., the "inability of local government officials to translate local needs into technical proposals of a high-quality standard" can limit the extent to which citizens' input is taken into consideration by national level administration (cf. ib. 1999: 7).

Barriers within decision-making processes, which hinder the participation of persons with disabilities specifically, can come in many forms – inaccessible information on decisions, lack of accessible meeting venues, lack of funding and provisions for assistance persons or other reasonable accommodation needs during political consultations being just a few (cf. IDA 2020; UN 2006: article 9; UN 2012). The following chapter summarises findings on such specific barriers as revealed by the study on OPD participation presented here.

2. Findings from the second IDA Global Survey on OPD participation in local decision-making

2.1 The first and second IDA Global Survey

Against the background described above on rights and obstacles to meaningful participation of persons with disabilities in public decision-making, the International Disability Alliance (IDA), an international alliance of global and regional OPDs, wanted to collect empirical evidence on the matter. It therefore launched the first IDA Global Survey on OPD participation in 2018 (IDA, 2020) and in partnership with the Assisting Living & Learning (ALL) Institute, Maynooth University, Ireland. Inspired by General Comment 7 on the CRPD, this was a first attempt to review the global perception of OPDs themselves of their own political participation in policies and programmes, plans and projects with (local/national) governments, regional[2] organisations, funding agencies and the United Nations (UN). The second IDA Global Survey was then completed by this partnership in 2021 to monitor the change of perceptions over the years (cf. IDA 2022).

The first and second Global Survey were developed jointly with members of IDA, i.e., different constituencies of persons with disabilities. These were involved at different stages of the process, commenting on accessibility of survey tools, inclusive content and language versions provided (cf. IDA 2020; Mc Veigh et al. 2021: 205ff.). A wide range of activities was undertaken to come

---

2 With this terminology ("region") the Global Survey refers to world regions, such as Africa, Asia, Europe, Latin America etc.

up with a more inclusive and accessible second IDA Global Survey in 2021[3]. The IDA Global Survey follows a human rights-based research approach, involving participatory research methods (cf. Arstein-Kerslake et al. 2020).

2.2 Participants of the second IDA Global Survey

845 OPD representatives (e.g., members, staff or volunteers) took part in the second IDA Global Survey. The average age of the respondents was 41 and with 48 % women and 50 % men, a near even gender split was achieved.

OPD respondents to the second IDA Global Survey mainly work at local (43 %) and national level (43 %), followed by OPDs working at international (9 %) or world-regional level (5 %). In comparison to the first IDA Global Survey, 11 % more OPD respondents to the second IDA Global Survey work at local level. This might be due to improved outreach strategies at local level, including local level in-person workshops and the improved survey tool that also works in areas with low internet connectivity. The responding OPDs work in different regions and countries all over the world, as presented in more detail below.

2.3 What the second Global Survey says on OPD participation at local level[4]

In the following, this paper presents key findings and recommendations from the 43 % (i.e., 369) respondents to the second IDA Global Survey who mainly work at local level. Results are clustered at outcome and process level, and contain:

> on outcome level: findings on the satisfaction of OPDs with their participation in local decision-making, and on their influence and impact in joint work with local governments.

---

[3] For a full outline on improvements for an inclusive and accessible survey methodology please refer to the report of the second IDA Global Survey (IDA, 2022).

[4] The IDA Global Survey neither aims to provide representative data for OPDs in the participating countries, nor to extrapolate the results to the overall view of OPDs worldwide. The results presented here therefore reflect the view of the participating sample only.

Participation of persons with disabilities

on process level: findings on OPDs' perceptions of the participating groups, levels of involvement, issues of joint work, and preconditions for participation in local decision-making processes.

The global findings (for OPDs working on all, i.e., also national, regional and international levels) can be found in the report on the 2nd Global Survey "Not Just Ticking the Disability Box? Meaningful OPD Participation and the Risk of Tokenism" (IDA 2022).

Countries and regions – OPD respondents to the second IDA Global Survey, who are mainly involved at the local level, work in 75 countries worldwide – with India, Kenya and Bangladesh being the countries with the most participants in the survey, as well as Asia (36 %), Africa (25 %) and Latin America (24 %) being the world regions with the highest numbers of survey participants (see figures 1 and 2). This is most probably thanks to the strong outreach effort by IDA and its members in countries of the Global South, including in-country workshops and other strong networks with IDA in some of these countries (e.g., India, Ireland, Uganda).

Table 1: Countries with the highest number of respondents (table)

Countries with highest number of respondents	Number	%
India	58	16
Kenya	20	5
Bangladesh	16	4
Colombia	13	4
Uganda	12	3
Ireland	9	2
Bolivia (Plurinational State of)	7	2
Venezuela (Bolivarian Republic of)	5	1

Satisfaction – OPD respondents report relatively low levels of satisfaction with the work with local governments, with the majority of respondents saying they are quite or very unhappy (56 %), and the others being quite or very happy (34 %), or neither happy nor unhappy (11 %). As reasons for their lack of satisfaction, respondents give examples in open questions, such as the low levels of OPD involvement or lack of preconditions for participation, as the following quotation from a respondent from Kenya exemplarily illustrates: *"[We are not satisfied at all in any way] because of lack of involvement, because of support, information and advice not being included in planning or implementation."*

Influence and impact – On a more positive note, 90 % of the OPD respondents report that they influence the work with local governments in some ways (74 %) or even fully (16 %), and 62 % say that they have an impact on the joint work of their local governments. What is more, 63 % of the OPDs say that their influence on local government work has improved in comparison to two years ago.

Figure 1: Distribution of responses by regions, in % (bar chart)

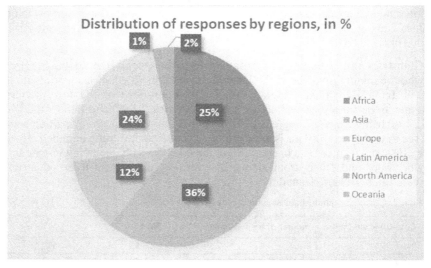

Groups participating – OPD respondents were asked how they can participate in work with their governments, as compared to other civil society groups. The findings might suggest a shift in comparison to 2018, with 58 % of OPD respondents reporting equal opportunities for OPDs to take part in work with their local governments – as compared to 2018 when only 21 % of respondents said that they can take part equally with other civil society groups in decision-making[5].

However, challenges are still reported, e.g., when it comes to the question of who represents whom, with many OPDs criticising that persons with disabilities are still too often represented by non-disabled experts, non-representative organisations or parents. This is exemplarily summarised by a respondent from Germany, saying that *"too few experts take part on their own behalf."*

---

5   As this question was not asked specifically regarding the participation in local governance in 2018, but with respect to participation with decision makers overall, the results cannot be directly compared. However, a significant shift was also observed when looking at fully comparable data from the first and second IDA Global Survey on work with all decision makers: with 57 % of respondents reporting in 2021 that they have equal opportunities to participate in work with all decision makers (as compared to 21 % in 2018).

Constituencies and intersectionality – As the first IDA Global Survey has already revealed, and the second IDA Global Survey shows again, many groups of persons with disabilities are still left behind. Groups most involved with local political decision-makers are persons with physical impairments (58 %), persons who are blind or partially sighted (43 %), deaf persons (37 %) and women with disabilities (34 %). Groups least represented are persons with disabilities who are also indigenous and/or from a minority (12 %), as well as persons with invisible or rare diseases. In an open question, a respondent from Nigeria summarises the danger of leaving behind certain groups in decision-making processes as follows: *"The limited number of groups participating [...] means that the objectives of the involvement cannot be fully realized as different group[s] have different needs."*

Level of involvement – The second IDA Global Survey also reveals that participation, while becoming more formalised overall, still remains limited with regard to the frequency of involvement and OPDs' roles in shared decision-making work. OPDs seldom enjoy fully influential and meaningful roles in joint work with their local governments, with only a minority of OPDs reporting that they are consulted, let alone able to co-decide during work with their local governments. Most OPDs are informed about which local government work is going on, but they are not involved in it directly (see figure 3).

Table 2: OPDs' roles in work with local governments in % (table)

OPDs' roles in work with local governments in %	Planning	Budgeting	Carrying out work	Data collection	Monitoring
We know nothing about it	6	12	7	8	8
We know it is happening but are not directly told about it	25	25	27	18	22
We are told what is happening	28	28	27	26	31
We are consulted	24	17	23	26	20
We decide together	12	12	12	17	12

When it comes to the average frequency of involvement, OPDs report that they are only sometimes involved in work with their local governments – regardless of the stage of decision-making, such as planning of local work, carrying out local work, data collection at local level, or monitoring and evaluation of local decision-making work. The least frequent involvement on local levels is reported in budgeting, with the majority of respondents saying that their OPD is rarely (21 %) or never (34 %) involved in local budgeting. Moreover, the frequency of involvement has declined slightly for almost all areas of joint work with local governments since 2018 (see figure 4).

Figure 2: Evolution of OPD involvement in work of local governments, on average

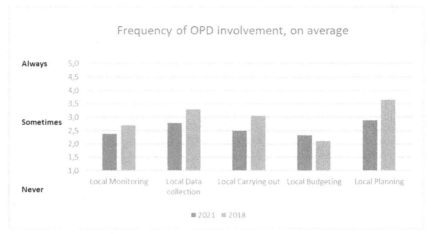

Issues – Overall, the second IDA Global Survey shows that OPDs are consulted on a wider range of issues than before: While the first Global Survey showed that they are mainly consulted on disability-specific issues, they are increasingly involved by all (also local) decision-makers on all issues which concern their lives, e.g., on housing, health, employment, environment and climate change etc.

What is more, the issues which they work on together with governments are usually in line with their own priorities. The latter positive trend is, however, only true in part when it comes to local level work, as OPDs report much lower levels of joint work on their priority issues with local governments than with other decision-makers, e.g., on national or regional levels (see figure 5).

Figure 3: Priority issues of OPDs vs. their involvement in work with decision-makers – comparison between local and all levels, in %

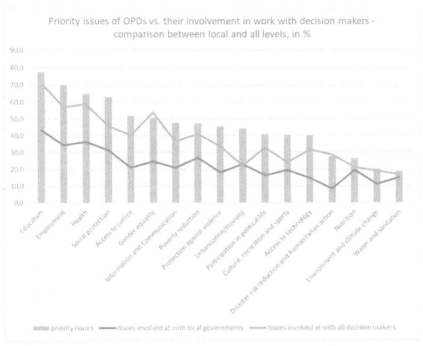

Preconditions for participation – Lastly, but very importantly, a crucial finding from the second IDA Global Survey is that the preconditions for participation with governments have decreased in comparison to 2018. This involves accessibility adjustments and reasonable accommodation provisions such as funding and other types of support given to facilitate OPD participation. Local governments perform slightly better on average than governments overall. However, regardless of the type of precondition (i.e., physical and informational accessibility, positive attitudes towards persons with disabilities, knowledge of what is required for meaningful OPD participation or financial support by governments for OPD participation), required provisions are only made in some ways, thus not meeting the standards set by the CRPD (see figure 6).

40 % of participants report that no financial support at all is given by governments for OPD participation in local decision-making processes; in addition, other provisions for accessibility are still not provided at all, such as informational accessibility (35%) and physical accessibility (31%) (see figure 7).

Figure 4: Levels of accessibility, on average on a scale from 1 (not at all) to 3 (fully)

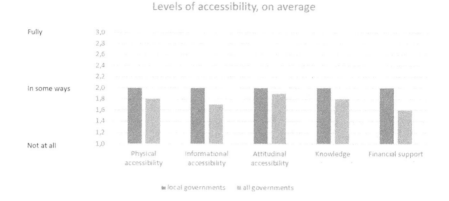

Table 3: Preconditions for participation with local governments, in %

Preconditions for participation with local governments, in %	Not at all	In some ways	Fully	Total
Physical accessibility	31	61	8	100
Informational accessibility	35	58	7	100
Attitudinal accessibility	24	64	12	100
Knowledge of what is required	26	61	13	100
Financial support	40	51	9	100

The following quotation exemplarily illustrates which barriers prevent OPDs from participating in local decision-making processes:

> "Lack of materials that are easy to use, understand and accessible for persons with disabilities. Lack of support and personal assistants, lack of information and advice, lack of proper prior planning as they only include them at the last minute in a very rushed manner." (respondent from Kenya).

3 Summary and recommendations

Local decision-making should be:

> "responsive (doing the right thing—delivering services that are consistent with citizens' preferences or are citizen focused); responsible (doing the right thing the

right way—working better but costing less and benchmarking with the best); and accountable (to citizens, through a rights-based approach)" (Shah 2006: 2).

Taking the voices from OPDs presented here into consideration can be one important step forward on this path. The second IDA Global Survey has revealed that OPDs (1) are increasingly participating (in formal ways, on an equal basis with other groups) in decision-making processes at the level of local governments, on (2) all issues that affect their lives. OPDs report (3) increasing capacities to influence decision-makers and to make a meaningful impact on decisions concerning their priority issues. Nevertheless, (4) OPDs are not satisfied with the level of participation they have with local governments, which might be due to other critical findings, i.e., the (5) reported lack and decrease of enabling preconditions for meaningful participation (such as accessibility, reasonable accommodation or funding), (6) perceived exclusion of many groups from decision-making processes, as well as (7) experienced low levels of involvement in different stages of decision-making processes in often not very influential roles. While slight differences could be observed between local level OPDs and those working with national or regional governments, the findings for the local level did not differ significantly from the global findings for all decision-makers. The differences mentioned are two-fold: On the negative side, OPDs are involved in local governmental work on their priority issues to a lower extent than with national ones. This might be due to the fact that many of the OPDs' priority issues are subject to national decision-making (e.g., employment, education, health), while others (such as housing, culture, recreation or sports as well as nutrition), are more likely to also be treated on the level of local governance. On a more positive note, local governments are perceived as providing more reasonable accommodation and accessibility than their national counterparts. Overall, this might be due to more flexibility in participatory settings on a local level, with more *"approachable"* or sensitised decision-makers. Since the differences are not significant, this finding should not be over-interpreted without additional contextual analysis, which can help to see whether certain countries are performing better than others on the local level.

For further interpretations, explorative analysis can look into potential reasons and relations amongst the findings. It could, e.g., be interesting to explore the extent to which the outcome level (satisfaction, impact/influence) and the conditions for participation (accessibility, reasonable accommodation, funding) are related. It will also be interesting to examine whether significant differences can be found when comparing data disaggregated by constituencies of persons with different disabilities – not least due to the fact that necessary preconditions can differ per constituency.

The findings from the second IDA Global Survey call for the unique perspective, role and expertise of OPDs to be more comprehensively recalled and recognised in local decision-making to ensure equal participation based on social justice. This can and should happen at multiple levels (individual, organisational and governmental/international), as each level complements the others and contributes to meaningful participation in decision-making. Necessary preconditions for meaningful participation need to be ensured in local governance to guarantee that all groups can participate. This comprises the removal of barriers (including legal ones and inaccessibility of digital and online information) and the provision of funding for OPD participation. The latter includes investing in reasonable accommodation provisions and OPDs' technical capacities to participate in local decision-making. OPDs' efforts to improve their capacity to participate also need to be supported (such as their knowledge of local political decision-making processes). All groups or constituencies need to be involved to ensure that the diversity of the movement is heard and given resources necessary to facilitate their participation. Since the needs of different groups in decision-making processes vary, only by taking the whole range of them into account will meaningful participation also become possible for those left furthest behind. OPDs also need to be consulted regularly by local decision-makers, i.e., on a frequent basis and not only occasionally. They need to be given impactful roles to participate effectively and to influence decisions, which means not only being informed about decisions taken or about to be taken, but also going beyond consultation to – in the best case – playing a fully decisive role in local political decisions. Power relations in local governance processes need to be challenged in order to achieve this. OPDs also need to be consulted on all issues that affect their lives (not only on disability-specific ones) and in all stages of local decision-making or project/programme cycles – not only in the implementation of decisions made but also in more impactful stages such as planning, budgeting, monitoring and evaluation, or data collection on a local level. In addition, sector-specific approaches (e.g., with decision-makers and administrative bodies responsible for issues such as education, work, health etc.) need to be combined with cross-cutting inclusion efforts that bring together all activities in an integrated approach. This is necessary to ensure that participation does not take place in silos with individual decision-makers but can fully be mainstreamed throughout local decision-making processes on all issues. OPDs on the local level should be given more opportunities to be meaningfully engaged on all issues which are important for them – even if these are primarily decided at national level. Further structures and activities that can be of help in this regard are consistent promotion, protection and monitoring of the CRPD at the level of local governance and the inclusion of formal mechanisms for the participation of persons with disabilities in local-level decision-making through the involvement of local focal points and other governmental authorities. Specific requirements and recommendations for meaningful OPD participation at the local level in individual countries can be identified in future follow-up analyses, taking into account specific country-contextual conditions and also the perspectives of other actors, e.g., local decision-makers.

In summary, the IDA Global Survey has provided an important insight into OPDs' perceptions of their participation in local, national, regional and international decision-making. It outlines the conditions needed for OPDs to also participate meaningfully in local governance, and the added value of OPD participation in implementing the CRPD at local level. The survey can serve as a tool to operationalise inclusive local programming in the future. Consistent attention to the view of OPDs can thus contribute to greater legitimacy and accountability for all groups of persons with disabilities on the road to inclusive localities for all.

References

Arstein-Kerslake, A./Maker, Y./Flynn, E./Ward, O./Bell, R./Degener, T. (2020): "Introducing a human rights-based disability research methodology". In: Human Rights Law Review. 20 (3). pp. 412-432.
Brühl, T. (2010): Representing the people? NGOs in international negotiations. In: Steffek, J./Hahn, K. (eds.): Evaluating transnational NGOs. legitimacy, accountability, representation. New York/London: Palgrave Macmillan. pp. 181-199.
CIVICUS (2021): 13 countries downgraded in new ratings report as civic rights deteriorate globally. New York/Geneva: CIVICUS.
Cote, A. (2020): Towards meaningful participation of Organisations of Persons with Disabilities in the implementation of the CRPD and SDGs. A pilot study by Bridging the Gap. Madrid: Bridging the gap project. https://www.iddcconsortium.net/wp-content/uploads/2021/07/BtG-II-Cote-2020-Study-on-the-participation-of-the-Organisations-of-Persons-with-Disabilities-in-the-monitoring-and-implementation.pdf [accessed: 08.08.2023]
Cunningham, F. (2002): Theories of democracy. A critical introduction. London/New York: Routledge.
Fraser, N. (2007): Die Transnationalisierung der Öffentlichkeit. Legitimität und Effektivität der öffentlichen Meinung in einer postwestfälischen Welt. In: Niesen, P./Herborth, B. (eds.): Anarchie der kommunikativen Freiheit. Jürgen Habermas und die Theorie der internationalen Politik. Frankfurt a.M.: Suhrkamp Verlag. pp. 224-253.
Gaventa, J./Valderrama C. (1999): Background note prepared for workshop on 'Strengthening participation in local governance'. Institute for Development Studies, June 21-24, 1999. https://www.participatorymethods.org/sites/participatorymethods.org/files/participation%20citzienship%20and%20local%20governance_gaventa.pdf [accessed: 08.08.2023]
IDA (2020.): Increasingly Consulted but not yet Participating. IDA Global Survey on Participation of Organisations of Persons with Disabilities in Development Programmes and Policies.

IDA (2022): Not Just Ticking the Disability Box? Meaningful OPD Participation and the Risk of Tokenism.

Habermas, J. (1998): Die postnationale Konstellation und die Zukunft der Demokratie. Bonn: Friedrich-Ebert-Stiftung.

Kanova, S./Siska, J./Beadle Brown, B. (2021): Active Citizenship as a measure of outcomes and the quality of social services. In: Siska, J./Beadle-Brown, J. et al. (eds.): The Development and Conceptualisation and Implementation of Quality in Disability Support Services. Prague: Charles University.

McVeigh, J./MacLachlan, M./Ferri, D./Mannan, H (2021): Strengthening the Participation of Organisations of Persons with Disabilities in the Decision-Making of National Government and the United Nations: Further Analyses of the International Disability Alliance Global Survey. In: Disabilities 2021, 1(3), pp. 202-217.

NDA – National Disability Authority (2021): A review of Disabled Persons Organisations (DPOs) and their participation in implementing and monitoring the UNCRPD. https://nda.ie/uploads/publications/A-review-of-disabled-persons-organisations-and-their-participation-in-implementing-and-monitoring-uncrpd.pdf.pdf [accessed: 08.08.2023]

Niesen, P. (2007): Anarchie der kommunikativen Freiheit – ein Problemaufriss. In: Niesen, P./Herborth, B. (eds.): Anarchie der kommunikativen Freiheit. Jürgen Habermas und die Theorie der internationalen Politik. Frankfurt a.M.: Suhrkamp Verlag. pp. 7-25.

Pateman, C. (1970): Participation and Democratic Theory. Cambridge: Cambridge University Press.

Siska, J./Beadle-Brown, J. et al. (2021): The Development and Conceptualisation and Implementation of Quality in Disability Support Services. Prague: Charles University.

Schädler, J./Wissenbach, L. (2021): The role of local planning in the implementation of the UNCRPD. In: Siska, J./Beadle-Brown, J. et al. (2021): The Development and Conceptualisation and Implementation of Quality in Disability Support Services. Prague: Charles University, pp. 313-331.

Shah (2006). Local Governance in Development Countries. Washington, DC: The World Bank.

UN (2006): United Nations Convention on the Rights of Persons with Disabilities. New York: UN.

UN (2014): General Comment No. 2. Article 9. Accessibility. CRPD/C/GC/2. New York: UN.

UN (2015): Transforming our world: the 2030 Agenda for Sustainable Development. UN General Assembly A/RES/70/1. New York: UN.

UN (2016): 71/256. New Urban Agenda. UN General Assembly A/RES/71/256.

UN (2018): General comment No. 7 (2018) on the participation of persons with disabilities, including children with disabilities, through their representative organizations, in the implementation and monitoring of the Convention. CRPD/C/GC/7. New York: UN.

UN Sustainable Development Solution Network (2016): Getting Started with the SDGs in Cities. A Guide for Stakeholders. https://irp-cdn.multiscreensite.com/be6d1d56/files/uploaded/9.1.8.-Cities-SDG-Guide.pdf [08.08.2023]

Van Deth, J.W. (2016): Political Participation. In: The International Encyclopedia of Political Communication. New Jersey: John Wiley & Sons.

Wescott, H./MacLachlan, M./Mannan, H. (2021): The Macropsychology of Disability Rights and Structural Change: Using Bourdieusian Analysis to Understand Stakeholder Power Relations. In: MacLachlan, M./McVeigh, J. (eds.): Macropsychology: A Population Science for Sustainable Development Goals. Cham, Switzerland: Springer, pp. 175-189.

Wescott, H./MacLachlan, M. (2021): Implementing 'real' change: a Bourdieusian take on stakeholder reflections from the United Nations Partnership on the Rights of Persons with Disabilities project in Uruguay. In: SN Social Sciences 1 (12), pp. 1-23.

Wissenbach, L. (2019): Conceptual Framework. Planning inclusive cities and human settlements. Entry points for International Development Cooperation. In: Zentrum für Planung und Evaluation Sozialer Dienste (Hrsg.) (2019): ZPE-Schriftenreihe. 55. Siegen: Universitätsverlag Siegen.

Inclusion and political representation of marginalised groups. The example of self-advocacy of people with disabilities

Matthias Kempf, Albrecht Rohrmann

Introduction

In democratic societies, political inclusion is established through equal participation in decision-making. The legitimacy of decisions is primarily but not only guaranteed through free elections. However, many citizens at different political levels do not experience equal chances of participation. There is a high risk of political exclusion. Different forms of articulating interest independently from representation in parliaments have been developed at the local or community level. The interests of certain groups, e.g., persons with disabilities, are to be included in preparation for decision-making through special commissioners or advisory boards. This takes into account the fact that preparatory consultation and the inclusion of different perspectives in the sense of deliberative democracy is a necessary basis for good decisions and good government. This article examines whether such expanded forms of political participation can promote the development of inclusive localities or communities. The article refers to empirical research on the representation of the interests of persons with disabilities in municipalities in the federal state of North Rhine-Westphalia (Germany).

We will first discuss the problems of political representation on the local level (chapter 2). After this, we discuss the chances of empowerment and banding together in interest groups to represent the interests of marginalised groups on the local level (chapter 3). In the fourth chapter, we refer to the link between inclusion and participation from a human rights perspective. In the last chapter, we discuss the findings of empirical research on interest groups of persons with disabilities in municipalities in the federal state of North Rhine-Westphalia (Germany).

1. Political representation and participation on the local level through elections?

There is a consensus in democratically organised societies that political participation should be possible at all levels and in all areas of public life. The ability to influence the shape of one's social environment is essential for full and effective participation of individuals on an equal basis with others. It can therefore be understood as an indicator of inclusivity. The goal is a good balance between the possibilities to lead one's daily life in a self-determined way, to find acceptance with regard to one's individual way of life and to exert influence on common affairs. Locality is of great importance here, as it refers to the space in which everyday life is realised. Even though social relations on the local level are determined by social trends and by social conflicts that originate elsewhere and cannot be resolved locally, they are not only manifested but generated in social interactions at the local level.

The political level that is most directly and inextricably linked to locality is the municipality. There are local authorities of various sizes in rural and urban areas. They are endowed by the higher political levels with the right of self-government in very different ways and are used for administrative purposes. Due to their importance for enabling social participation, their democratic constitution is of crucial significance for the development of inclusive spaces.

However, when looking at the municipal constitution and the political practices of decision-making at this level, it is intensively disputed who is involved in what way and how participation has to be organised. The practices can produce inclusion and exclusion at the same time. This will be briefly explained later.

It is controversial whether municipalities are not first and foremost an administrative level in which instructions from higher levels in the political system are carried out and to what extent their right to democratically controlled self-government should range. In the sense of the European Charter of Local Self-Government, "local self-government denotes the right and the ability of local authorities, within the limits of the law, to regulate and manage a substantial share of public affairs under their own responsibility and in the interests of the local population" (Council of Europe 1985 Art. 3). Empirical studies in 39 European countries show a wide range of forms of local autonomy, but overall an increase in the scope for local decision-making (Ladner/Keuffer/Baldersheim 2016).

A central form of participation in democratic decision-making is the active and passive right to vote. However, there are reasons to believe that elections at the municipal level contribute to inclusion only to a limited extent. The most severe form of political exclusion is exclusion from the right to vote. It can be observed that in democratic societies, any general exclusion from the right to vote is on the decline. In Germany, such an exclusion was abolished in the 19th century for people who were dependent on social benefits, in 1918 for women, and 100 years later for people who had legal guardianship in all areas. In certain cases, prisoners are still excluded from voting rights. However, the right to vote is often linked to citizenship. Also at the municipal level, in the Federal Republic of Germany, as in many other countries, exclusion from active and passive voting rights applies to the increasing number of residents who have the status of non-EU foreigners.

With regard to the right to stand for election, social practices lead to varying degrees of opportunity for social groups to assert themselves in the candidate selection process and to be elected to decision-making bodies. For example, women, young people and especially marginalised groups are significantly underrepresented in local parliaments. However, it is also inconceivable that a parliament would fully reflect the population average. But if the interests of all social groups cannot be included in the decision-making process through the elected representatives, or only to a limited extent, this raises questions about the legitimacy of decision-making processes and demonstrates the lack of inclusivity of the democratic forms of representation.

In many European countries, participation in elections is low and declining. This is not equally distributed among the various social groups. A correlation between voter turnout and socio-economic situation can be identified (Bundesregierung Deutschland 2021: 421ff.). Privileged social groups obviously perceive the opportunities to exert influence through elections more strongly as a possibility for participation than people in economically or otherwise disadvantaged life situations.

The decline in voter turnout in local elections is particularly pronounced in Germany, but also in other European countries (Van der Kolk 2019). Moreover, voting at this level often follows trends at higher political levels. This development also demonstrates a lack of inclusivity in the opportunities for political participation at the municipal level. The use of other ways to articulate interests in the municipal sphere, such as citizens' petitions, referendums, involvement in citizens' initiatives or other forms of extra-parliamentary political participation, also tends to favour groups that have resources, assertiveness or proximity to the dominant political forces. Thus, if the importance of electorally legitimised representation at the municipal level for the inclusion of residents is eroding and thus does not provide a sufficient framework for the participatory development of an inclusive community, other complementary or alternative forms of political participation that promote inclusive processes at the municipal level need to be explored.

2. Extended forms of political participation at the municipal level

A significant basis of political participation is the self-organisation of social groups. People become aware of their interests and can acquire competences for political articulation as well as for the assertion of interests. The best-known movements of socially disadvantaged groups are certainly the women's movement and the labour movement. Since the 1960s and 1970s, a differentiation of social movements can be observed, increasingly making social disadvantages a political issue. Self-help can also be understood as a very successful social movement (Kardorff 2014: 11) – local groups and also supra-regional groups and organisations in which those affected by social or health-related problems join together to support each other. It is estimated that in the Federal Republic of Germany, around three million affected people and their relatives work in 70,000 to 100,000 local groups (Nationale Kontakt- und Informationsstelle zur Anregung und Unterstützung von Selbsthilfegruppen (NAKOS) 2020: 32).

In the context of new social movements, the movement of persons with disabilities has formed internationally, and expresses its political claim in the slogan 'Nothing about us without us'. It has been successful in developing a new understanding of disability, which is now understood as a result of "the interaction between persons with impairments and attitudinal and environmental barriers that hinders their full and effective participation in society on an equal basis with others" (UN CRPD, Preamble, No 5). In the context of this paper, this understanding is on the one hand significant as a rejection of pathologising and discriminating attributions through processes of empowerment. At the same time, the example of disability illustrates that interactions in social spaces are the cause of disadvantage for social groups.

Exclusive self-organisation does not contradict inclusive political participation. Rather, a strong form of self-organisation is the basis for becoming aware of the state of social exclusion and disadvantage and combating it. Self-organisation enables empowerment. Despite all the conceptual vagueness, the concept can be understood as a "group-based, participatory, developmental process through which marginalised or oppressed individuals and groups gain greater control over their lives and environment, acquire valued resources and basic rights, and achieve important life goals and reduced societal marginalisation" (Maton 2008: 5). With this very open definition, group-based activities can be linked to the level of policymaking and community development.

Social movements have shown that provocation, conflict and political struggle are important means of asserting expanded rights. In particular, the newer social movements, which often refer to the consideration of the specific

Inclusion and political representation of marginalised groups 131

interests of small groups, not only require equal opportunities to influence majority decision-making, but also expanded opportunities to articulate themselves and deliberate good decisions. This can be illustrated by the example of taking into account the interests of persons with disabilities. This group is not a homogeneous group with completely identical interests. For example, people who use a wheelchair or a walker are interested in lowering pavements completely. However, such markings in public space are important for orientation for people who use a white cane due to visual impairment. In this case, a balanced consultation is required to find a good solution for all parties involved. In order to take the interests of different people into account, it is necessary to extend the principles of majority decision-making through forms of deliberative democracy (Habermas 2005). Here the quality of public, participatory discourses about possible solutions is in the foreground. Such approaches can be implemented particularly well at the local level. Voting processes that relate to very concrete projects can be conducted intensively between experts, those affected and other stakeholders. However, it is often a disappointing experience when the results and compromises of such discourse and consultation processes are not taken up in the decision-making processes of the elected bodies. Clear agreements on the extent of participation are necessary here.

Estimates of the extent of participation are usually based on the 'Ladder of Citizen Participation' developed by Sherry R. Arnstein (1969). The first two levels of participation, 'Manipulation' and 'Therapy', are understood as non-participation "to substitute for genuine participation" (ibid.: 217). The stages of 'Informing', 'Consultation' and 'Placation' are described as "tokenism", "because the ground rules allow have-nots to advise, but retain for the power-holders the continued right to decide" (ibid.: 217). Only the top three levels 'Partnership', 'Delegated Power' and 'Citizen Control' allow for 'Citizen Power' according to Arnstein. The model is strongly focused on decision-making. From the perspective of democratic theory, it can be objected that for the last two levels of the ladder, there is only the legitimate possibility of majority decisions by direct vote or in elected bodies. The designation of the middle levels as tokenism underestimates the possibilities of exerting influence through informed public relations work and consultations, especially in local contexts. Both in the concept of majority decision-making and in the concept of deliberative democracy, it is necessary to clarify empirically what the relationship is between consultations preparing decisions and democratically legitimised decisions. Only if the relationship is transparent and acceptable to those involved can processes of citizen participation outside the bodies of representative democracy promote inclusion through political participation.

3. Participation and inclusion of persons with disabilities

Participation is a significant topic in the development of human rights. The Universal Declaration of Human Rights initially only formulates the individual right "to take part in the government of his country, directly or through freely chosen representatives" (UDHR Art. 21). The conventions that follow the Declaration are enacted through political decision-making processes, but they are not only legitimised by majority decisions. The significance of fundamental and human rights lies rather in the fact that they limit the space for majority decisions relating to political and territorially defined entities. The consideration of the rights of groups at high risk of human rights violations (vulnerable groups) should be realised through expanded participation opportunities that serve the needs of these groups (Rohrmann/Windisch/Düber 2015: 17ff.).

The UN Convention on the Rights of Persons with Disabilities (UN-CRPD) has therefore established a close connection between inclusion and participation. Even beyond securing the rights of persons with disabilities, it thus contributes to the understanding of the human rights significance of participation. "Full and effective participation and inclusion in society" (UN-CRPD Art. 3) is one of the eight general principles of the convention. In all processes to implement the convention, "State Parties shall closely consult with and actively involve persons with disabilities" (UN-CRPD Art. 4, para. 3). In all areas of life, the requirements for the inclusive design of institutions should serve to guarantee full, effective participation on an equal basis with others. Political participation has its own article (UN-CRPD Art. 29). This consists of two parts. The first refers to the formal process of political decision-making through elections and direct participation. The second refers to measures going beyond this "to actively promote an environment in which persons with disabilities can effectively and fully participate in the conduct of public affairs, without discrimination and on an equal basis with others, and encourage their participation in public affairs" (UN-CRPD Art. 29, part b).

The link between inclusion and participation has also found its way into the Social Development Goals (SDGs). Goal No. 16, to "promote peaceful and inclusive societies for sustainable development, provide access to justice for all and build effective, accountable and inclusive institutions at all levels" includes the target No. 7 to "ensure responsive, inclusive, participatory and representative decision-making at all levels". Like the SDGs, the UN-CRPD also points out that all state levels have to address the goal of participation. In Germany, the interests of persons with disabilities are traditionally represented through service providers. But they have their own perspective and interests. The UN-CRPD (Art. 29, part b) therefore demands that "organisations of per-

Inclusion and political representation of marginalised groups 133

sons with disabilities" should be promoted at the "local level". In the following chapter, we look at the results of two research projects that analysed the current situation in one federal state of Germany, North Rhine-Westphalia.

4. Empirical findings of participation at the local level – possibilities and challenges

To enable some understanding of the given example, we will first present an overview of the different forms of advocacy groups and their distribution on the local level in that German federal state. This sets the stage to address three main critical aspects of political participation and how they can promote or limit the inclusion of persons with disabilities in a community. The different challenges and opportunities that can be identified in that context will conclude the empirical example presented here.

At the local level, two different types of self-advocacy groups can be distinguished and only the second will be discussed further. Over the last few years, the existence of advisory boards run by users in social services for persons with disabilities, like sheltered workshops or residential homes, has increased. They focus mainly on aspects within the service or the organisation and not on those of the city or district the service is located in. The collected experiences in these advisory boards can help users to gain confidence in addressing own interests and needs, as Düber (2015) describes for persons with learning disabilities. But they are embedded in the structures of the services and therefore lack an appropriate degree of independence. The second form of advocacy groups is mainly oriented towards improving the situation for persons with disabilities in a municipality or district. As described in chapter three, such organisational structures fulfil the function of self-organisation. There have been different movements that led to their establishment on a local level, and they have formed different structures.

Two research projects explored the situation of self-representation at municipality level in North Rhine-Westphalia. The first (LAG SELBSTHILFE NRW e.V. 2015) used mainly qualitative research methods and produced an overview of the types of advocacy groups in the municipalities and of how widespread they are in that federal state. These are: 1) Advisory board (different stakeholders that represent different groups of persons with disabilities, politicians, service providers, representatives of the municipality, who meet regularly and mostly work together on the basis of some form of statute); 2) Association of self-help groups (these groups usually work as some kind of umbrella organisation for local self-help groups and are less formally organised) and 3) Ombudsman for persons with disabilities (persons who are mandated by the municipality to provide for the interests of persons with disabilities. Some persons are appointed on an honorary basis, others on a full-time basis).

The second project (LAG SELBSTHILFE NRW e.V. 2021) reviewed the situation five years later with a different research approach and evaluated workshops in municipalities that were designed to promote participation possibilities. The results of both studies provide an example of the situation at hand and the general challenges regarding the representation of persons with disabilities at that state level. As an overview, the following chart shows how widespread organised forms of participation are in the municipalities of North Rhine-Westphalia.

Figure 1: Percentage of Communities with advocacy groups in North-Rhine-Westfalia in 2019 (n=215), own graph, based on ibid.: 122

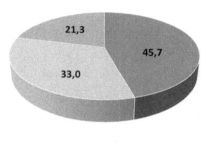

▪ none - ▪ one - ▪ more than one - advocacy group

In one third of the municipalities, one of the described forms can be found, and in around one fifth more than one, but in nearly half of the towns and districts there is no form of advocacy structure. A closer look at the distribution indicates a close link between the number of inhabitants in a municipality and the possibility of finding advocacy groups. In the 22 biggest cities (between one million and 111.000 inhabitants), all have at least one of the described structures and some even one of every type. On the level of the 31 districts (350.000 inhabitants on average), in nearly 90 % at least one structure can be found. But among the 125 smallest towns (between 3.000 and 20.000 inhabitants), only 26 % have any form of participation structure for persons with disabilities (LAG SELBSTHILFE NRW e.V. 2021: 122). In municipalities with only one advocacy structure, these are mostly ombudsmen (ibid.: 121). The representation of persons with disabilities through ombudsmen is the most commonly installed form (124 appointments). The percentage of persons on a full-time basis rose from 50 % to 65 % in the five years between the two research projects (ibid.: 137). Around one third of the appointed persons perceive themselves as persons with disabilities (ibid.: 139). Advisory boards are the next most frequently used form (79 groups) and the most frequent type of newly established structure (14 boards) in the five years between the two research

Inclusion and political representation of marginalised groups

projects. Compared with the other forms, advisory boards have more advanced rights, are better funded and their work is more often based on a legally mandated statute (84.8 % vs. 21.4 % compared to associations of self-help groups) (ibid. 127). In advisory boards and associations of self-help groups, different stakeholders work together. In associations of self-help groups, these are mainly persons with disabilities and their relatives, whereas advisory boards include a broader group of organisations associated with disability, such as service providers and municipality administration. Having the opportunity to discuss topics of barriers and disabilities in a municipality is important. Whether such groups can be seen as "groups of persons with disabilities" (Art. 29 UN-CRPD) is to be decided on the basis of the given rights within such a board. If non-disabled persons are limited to a consulting role, the representative function of these structures is stronger.

The last discussed topic leads to the three critical aspects of political participation, because using political influence to change opportunities for marginalised groups means more than establishing a form of advocacy structure. Working together in a community with the objective to change attitudinal and environmental barriers in a long term arrangement can be seen as the challenge that needs to be addressed. In the first research project, a number of interviews were conducted with persons who had experience working in advocacy groups on the local level. These experts in this field, with and without disabilities, addressed a large number of challenges and chances that can boost or hinder participation. It was possible to summarise these aspects into the following three critical aspects of political participation (LAG SELBSTHILFE NRW e.V. 2015: 9): participative structures, inclusive culture, and political activity. In municipalities where all three aspects merged together, the work was perceived as more effective and successful. Figure 2 shows their relation in the form of a metaphor of a gear transmission to illustrate that all three aspects can propagate motion energy or hinder the movement.

Figure 2: own graph, based on (LAG SELBSTHILFE NRW e.V. 2015: 9)

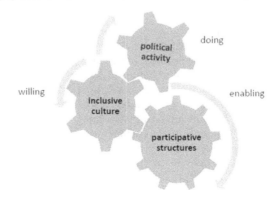

The described forms of advocacy groups or the appointing of ombudsmen by a municipality are part of participative structures and form the frame in which activities unfold. In a statute, the rights and obligations of advocacy groups should be defined, because knowing about such rights can empower persons in the political debate. Since 2004, municipalities have been obliged to regulate by statute how the interests of persons with disabilities are protected (§ 13 BGG NRW) but 15 years later only 18.7 % have done so (LAG SELBST-HILFE NRW e.V. 2021: 131). These results show that in many municipalities the structures have to improve and that the legal obligations for the municipalities need to be more binding. Taking appropriate measures to ensure persons with different disabilities can take part in the advocacy groups is a crucial element of such structures. This also includes the funds and resources, for example for assistance, translation in sign language or providing documents in an accessible form. Only very few advocacy groups cover all expenses and half of the researched forms cover just one form of support (ibid. 148-150). Here, the link between the three aspects of participation is quite easy to identify, because the funding of these measures enables activities on the one hand and reflects the inclusive culture in a municipality on the other. Indications for such an inclusive culture are the willingness to learn from the expertise of persons with disabilities so that barriers are recognised and dealt with. Acknowledging the need for an accessible and useable infrastructure for all inhabitants as a general mindset encourages marginalised groups to express ideas that can make a community more inclusive. To keep motivation high and the process moving it is important that, besides the adequate structures and the willingness to live in an inclusive culture, there really is an experience of change. Advocacy groups that are perceived as successful by the interviewed persons are characterised by political activity. Doing something that aims at reducing the experience of being disabled enhances the motivation to work in structures that sometimes feel bureaucratic. Structures that were able to bring own topics into the political discussion at the local level and that were more active than reactive to input from the outside, are perceived as more successful (LAG SELBST-HILFE NRW e.V. 2015: 284ff.).

After an overview of the structures of advocacy groups and the three critical aspects of political participation, two examples can help to shed light on the possibilities to enhance the political representation of persons with disabilities through activities to implement inclusion. Part of the second research project were 17 workshops that were scientifically evaluated (LAG SELBST-HILFE NRW e.V. 2021: 63). The workshops were intended to help municipalities to develop more binding advocacy structures. The one-day educational workshops were designed to develop concrete measures which the participants committed to implementing in the following six months. Another important goal was to strengthen the network in the community by bringing together persons with disabilities, local politicians from different parties and local administrative staff. When representatives of these three groups worked together, the work was perceived as more successful (LAG SELBSTHILFE NRW e.V. 2015: 284ff.). The three main stages (complain, dream, reality) were based on the group working method "Future Workshop" (Nanz/Fritsche 2012: 81) and helped to establish a dialogue about the specific situation in that community. Part of the workshop was an input on political participation rights and on concepts for establishing (new) participatory structures in the community. A few of the planned measures reoccurred in different municipalities and also reflected general challenges for participation, such as: 1) Establishing more legally binding structures of political participation for persons with disabilities; 2) Making political participation more accessible (documents, interpreters, assistance and public budgets); 3) General accessibility in the community and of public services and 4) Awareness raising in general and for advocacy work in particular (LAG SELBSTHILFE NRW e.V. 2021: 63).

Two surveys of the participants were part of the evaluation of the workshops (on site and six months later) and were useful in identifying to which extent the workshops had been helpful. Besides knowledge building on the topic of the rights of persons with disabilities and the pragmatic "down-to-earth" measures that were easy to continue working on, the change in the assessment of the participatory situation is worth noticing. Especially the local politicians tended to see the possibilities for participation in the community for persons with disabilities more realistically and to recognise the need for more improvement (ibid.: 96). It is important to improve the possibilities to participate in the community. Still, such activities need to be accompanied by a strategy to enhance the living conditions by making the community more inclusive.

Projects on planning inclusive communities (Lampke/Rohrmann/Schädler 2011) can be used as the second example of how political participation of persons with disabilities can be promoted on the local level. Instead of providing a full overview of this topic we will here just offer a glimpse of how it relates to the question of representation. The German constitution (Art. 28 para. 2) grants municipalities the guarantee of self-government, which forms the basis for planning on the local level. This right is to some extent limited by the established social system that is defined by legal guidelines on higher state levels. But on the one hand, around 80 % of the laws from the federal level are implemented on the local level (Bogumil 2018: 773). On the other hand, there are areas of planning in which the municipality has more autonomy (e.g. youth welfare services, public transportation). Besides the formal structures, the municipalities can moderate processes with different stakeholders and conduct planning for 'inclusive communities'. This term is understood as a programmatic approach to establish opportunities in a local community that allow persons (with disabilities) to develop their life in settings which are common for the life course (cf. Schädler et al. 2008: 324ff. The CISCOS Project Consortium (2020) has produced a training package that explains the approach more closely in English. As mentioned in chapter 4, implementation processes should involve persons with disabilities closely (Art. 4, para 3 UN-CRPD). This gives them the opportunity to use their important knowledge as to when, where and how in a given community the interaction with barriers hinders full and effective participation in society. Furthermore, using that expertise in a planning process changes the role in which persons with disability are perceived in a community – from a 'problem-bearer to a problem-solver' (Hoffmann 2015: 263). Such local planning processes provide many opportunities to actively involve persons with disabilities in executive committees, in public discussions and empirical research that should help to understand the specific living conditions (cf. Kempf 2015). Established advocacy groups can easily take on an important role in such processes and widen the scope of their political activity. In communities without these participative structures, these planning activities can serve as the impetus for the formation of advocacy groups. Political representation of persons with disabilities in local planning processes plays a fundamental role for the implementation of the UN-CRPD and more inclusive structures in the general infrastructure. Despite these opportunities, there are still many challenges such as the insufficient involvement of different groups of persons with disabilities in such processes (cf. Laub 2021; Jacobi 2018; Bertelmann/Konieczny 2018) and a high degree of uncertainty regarding the best way to conduct such planning processes (Rohrmann et al. 2014).

5. Conclusion

The interests of different marginalised groups of society are less well represented in the political discussion and in processes of decision-making. This leads to exclusion, declining willingness to participate in politics and problems with the legitimacy of democratic processes. Expanded forms of political participation help to promote the interests of these groups. However, this should not be understood as a substitute for democratic rights. Rather, it is about the expansion of participation rights through advice and proofing options in the run-up to decisions.

The established advocacy groups show the opportunities connected with self-organisation and the empowering effects of standing up for important interests. Such voices are essential for overcoming negative attitudes and for providing specific expertise for the development of inclusive communities. Localities need structures in which marginalised groups can express their needs, interests and ideas for change and local policies for all. The concrete nature of the local level provides an opportunity to change perceptions through pragmatic activities. These actions require planning on a local level to orient existing structures to be more accessible and to provide services that truly fulfil the needs of all. On the other hand, these developments should be further monitored and cannot overcome shortcomings in the needed assistance that is provided by laws on higher state levels.

References

Arnstein, Sherry R. (1969): A Ladder of Citizen Participation. In: Journal of the American Institute of Planners 35, 4, pp. 216–224.
Bertelmann, Lena/Konieczny, Eva (2018): Sozialraumerkundung als partizipative und sektorübergreifende Datenerhebungsmethode? In: Schädler, Johannes/Reichstein, Martin F. (Ed.): Sektoralisierung als Planungsherausforderung im inklusiven Gemeinwesen. Siegen: Universität Siegen, pp. 133–146.
Bogumil, Jörg (2018): Kommunale Selbstverwaltung – Gemeinden/Kreise. In: Voigt, Rüdiger (Ed.): Handbuch Staat. Handbuch. Wiesbaden: Springer VS Verlag, pp. 765–774.
Bundesregierung Deutschland (2021): Lebenslagen in Deutschland. Der sechste Armuts- und Reichtumsbericht der Bundesregierung.
CISCOS Project Consortium (2020): CISCOS Training Package. Siegen.
Council of Europe (1985): European Charter of Local Self-Government. https://rm.coe.int/168007a088 [accessed: 31.07.2022].
Düber, Miriam (2015): Politische Partizipation von Menschen mit Lernschwierigkeiten in kommunalen Behindertenbeiräten. In: Düber, Miriam/Rohrmann, Albrecht/Windisch, Marcus (Ed.): Barrierefreie Partizipation. Entwicklungen, Herausforderungen und Lösungsansätze auf dem Weg zu einer neuen Kultur der Beteiligung. Weinheim, Basel: Beltz Juventa, pp. 190–204.
Habermas, Jürgen (2005): The inclusion of the other. Studies in political theory. Cambridge: Polity Press.
Hoffmann, Friedhelm (2015): Mitwirkung der Selbsthilfe im politischen Raum auf kommunaler Ebene am Beispiel des Kreises Olpe. In: Düber, Miriam/Rohrmann, Albrecht/Windisch, Marcus (Ed.): Barrierefreie Partizipation. Entwicklungen, Herausforderungen und Lösungsansätze auf dem Weg zu einer neuen Kultur der Beteiligung. Weinheim, Basel: Beltz Juventa, pp. 263–270.
Jacobi, Lisa (2018): Die Partizipation von Menschen mit chronischen psychischen Erkrankungen an kommunalpolitischen Prozessen – eine Analyse am Beispiel der Teilhabeplanung des Landkreises Waldeck-Frankenberg. Masterthesis. Siegen: University Siegen
Kardorff, Ernst von (2014): Partizipation im aktuellen gesellschaftlichen Diskurs – Anmerkungen zur Vielfalt eines Konzepts und seiner Rolle in der Sozialarbeit. In: Archiv für Wissenschaft und Praxis der sozialen Arbeit 45, 2, pp. 4–15.
Kempf, Matthias (2015): Kommunale Teilhabeplanung. Ein Beispiel partizipativer und inklusiver Planungsprozesse im politischen Raum. In: Düber, Miriam/Rohrmann, Albrecht/Windisch, Marcus (Ed.): Barrierefreie Partizipation. Entwicklungen, Herausforderungen und Lösungsansätze auf dem Weg zu einer neuen Kultur der Beteiligung. Weinheim, Basel: Beltz Juventa, pp. 218–234.

Ladner, Andreas/Keuffer, Nicolas/Baldersheim, Harald (2016): Measuring Local Autonomy in 39 Countries (1990–2014). In: Regional & Federal Studies 26, 3, pp. 321–357.
LAG SELBSTHILFE NRW e.V. (2015): Politische Partizipation von Menschen mit Behinderungen in den Kommunen stärken! Abschlussbericht zum Projekt. Münster: LAG Selbsthilfe
LAG SELBSTHILFE NRW e.V. (2021): Abschlussbericht zum Projekt "Mehr Partizipation wagen!" der LAG SELBSTHILFE NRW e.V. Münster: LAG Selbsthilfe
Lampke, Dorothea/Rohrmann, Albrecht/Schädler, Johannes (2011): Kommunale Teilhabplanung. Einleitung. In: Lampke, Dorothea/Rohrmann, Albrecht/Schädler, Johannes (Ed.): Örtliche Teilhabeplanung mit und für Menschen mit Behinderungen. Theorie und Praxis. Wiesbaden: VS Verlag für Sozialwissenschaften/Springer Fachmedien Wiesbaden GmbH Wiesbaden, pp. 9–24.
Laub, Matthias (2021): Der inneren Existenz Raum geben. Partizipation von Menschen mit psychischer Behinderung in Prozessen Örtlicher Teilhabeplanung. Dissertation. Weinheim: Beltz Juventa.
Maton, Kenneth I. (2008): Empowering community settings: agents of individual development, community betterment, and positive social change. In: American journal of community psychology 41, 1-2, pp. 4–21.
Nanz, Patrizia/Fritsche, Miriam (2012): Handbuch Bürgerbeteiligung. Verfahren und Akteure, Chancen und Grenzen. Bonn: Bundeszentrale für politische Bildung.
Nationale Kontakt- und Informationsstelle zur Anregung und Unterstützung von Selbsthilfegruppen (NAKOS) (2020): Selbsthilfe im Überblick. Zahlen und Fakten 2019. https://www.nakos.de/data/Fachpublikationen/2020/NAKOS-Studien-06-2 019.pdf [accessed: 30.07.2022].
Rohrmann, Albrecht/Schädler, Johannes/Kempf, Matthias/Konieczny, Eva/Windisch, Marcus/Frensch, Lena/Kaiser, Mario (2014): Inklusive Gemeinwesen Planen. Abschlussbericht eines Forschungsprojektes im Auftrag des Ministeriums für Arbeit, Integration und Soziales in Nordrhein-Westfalen. Siegen: Universität Siegen.
Rohrmann, Albrecht/Windisch, Marcus/Düber, Miriam (2015): Barrierefreie Partizipation – Annäherung an ein Thema. In: Düber, Miriam/Rohrmann, Albrecht/ Windisch, Marcus (Ed.): Barrierefreie Partizipation. Entwicklungen, Herausforderungen und Lösungsansätze auf dem Weg zu einer neuen Kultur der Beteiligung. Weinheim: Beltz Juventa, pp. 15–29.
Schädler, Johannes/Rohrmann, Albrecht/Aselmeier, Laurenz/Grebe, Katharina/Stamm, Christoph/Weinbach, Hanna/Wissel, Timo (2008): Selbständiges Wohnen behinderter Menschen – Individuelle Hilfen aus einer Hand. Abschlussbericht. Siegen: Universität Siegen.
Van der Kolk, Henk (2019): Lokale Wahlbeteiligung in Europa: Befunde, Veränderungen und Erklärungen. In: Vetter, Angelika/Haug, Volker M. (Ed.): Kommunalwahlen, Beteiligung und die Legitimation lokaler Demokratie. Tagungsband. Wiesbaden: Kommunal- und Schul-Verlag, pp. 26–41

Moderation, coordination, mediation – Participatory implementation of the UN Convention on the Rights of Persons with Disabilities under the leadership of the municipal administration[1]

Lena Bertelmann

Introduction

With paragraph 5 of its General Obligations (Article 4), the UN Convention on the Rights of Persons with Disabilities (CRPD) also addresses the lowest of the German administrative levels, the municipalities[2], with regard to the implementation of its provisions. It states: "The provisions of the present Convention shall extend to all parts of federal states without any limitations or exceptions" (ibid.). Involving relevant actors from the local level in the project of shaping a local community in which full and effective participation and inclusion are possible (cf. Art. 3c CRPD) can be understood as a meaningful and goal-oriented, but at the same time demanding condition. The participation of persons with disabilities in the implementation of the inclusion-oriented provisions of the CRPD is also required under Article 4 (3) CRPD.

---

[1] This article presents study results first published in German in 2022 in the 'News Service of the German Association for Public and Private Welfare' (Nachrichtendienst des Deutschen Vereins für Öffentliche und Private Fürsorge) (cf. Bertelmann 2022).

[2] The term 'municipalities' is understood here to mean all kinds of German administrative units on the district level and local level (NUTS 3-level and LAU-level according to the classification of the European Union, 2022: 6). In Germany there are towns and cities belonging to a county (Local Administrative Unit-level) as well as cities independent of a county and counties themselves (Nomenclature des Unites Territoriales Statistiques 3-level). Counties are associations of towns and cities and at the same time independent territorial authorities. The counties are located one administrative level above the towns and cities and assume certain tasks for the municipalities belonging to them. Independent cities perform these tasks on their own.

Despite existing efforts, there is still a general need for development in Germany in the context of political participation of people with disabilities at the municipal level (cf. LAG Selbsthilfe NRW 2015; LAG Selbsthilfe NRW 2021). This particularly applies to participation opportunities of people with disabilities in municipal processes for planning participation (cf. Aichele et al. 2020: 54; Jacobi 2018; Laub 2021). Since the ratification of the CRPD in 2009, action plans have been developed, and in some cases updated, not only at federal and state level. Municipalities are also dealing with the implementation of the CRPD – under different headings. The German municipalities are, unless state or federal laws stipulate otherwise, (self-)responsible for the overall municipal activities. It is therefore obvious that the municipal administration/an agency of the municipal administration should take the lead in inclusion-oriented activities and planning. There are no binding guidelines for municipal planning aimed at inclusion. Various, more or less structured approaches to municipal participation planning can be observed. These are known to be located at different municipal planning levels, such as general development planning, departmental planning and social planning (cf. Rohrmann 2019: n.p.). If the municipal administration understands the inclusive shaping of the community as a cross-sectional task and a participatory process, it has the demanding task of shaping the planning project as a whole in terms of content and form. This task falls in particular to the office or person within the administration who has the main responsibility for the activities and/or planning. This office or person has an important role within the administration and in relation to the stakeholders outside the administration when it comes to organising, moderating, coordinating and mediating between the various interests of the different participants within and outside the administration.

The data on the nationwide dissemination of municipal activities and plans to implement the CRPD is still unclear[3]. There has been no systematic survey of experiences with and assessments of corresponding activities and plans from the perspective of the German municipal administrations in charge of such activities. This article first discusses the importance of the municipal level in terms of participation conditions (for people with disabilities) (1). It then takes a look at the development and planning of an inclusive community[4] under the

---

3   The German Federal Ministry of Labour and Social Affairs is funding the project "UN Convention on the Rights of Persons with Disabilities in the Municipalities" from 2023 to 2025, which is being carried out by the Centre for Planning and Development of Social Services at the University of Siegen in cooperation with the Monitoring Centre for the UN Convention on the Rights of Persons with Disabilities of the German Institute for Human Rights. The project is taking stock of the ways in which municipalities in Germany have become active in developing an inclusive community (www.unbrk-kommunal.de).

4   The English term 'community' translates to different German terms, among others to 'Gemeinde' and 'Kommune' as words for municipalities. 'Community' is also

leadership of the municipality (2). Furthermore, the article presents study results on assessments and experiences from municipal administrations in one of the German federal states, North Rhine-Westphalia (3). In the last section, a summarising conclusion focuses on the office or person within the administration who has the main responsibility for the activities and/or planning, with his or her tasks, requirements and competences necessary to shape the development and planning of an inclusive community as a cross-cutting task of the democratically legitimised municipal administration and as a joint task of the various locally relevant community actors (4).

1. The multiple importance of the municipal level for participation

With regard to participation and the shaping of the community, as well as participation in the shaping of the community, it can be assumed that the municipality is of importance in multiple ways. For example, Beck (2016: 11ff.) traces various aspects of 'municipality' in connection with 'inclusion in the community'. In the social space 'community', the everyday life of individuals takes place; ideally, they can move around, meet each other, be active, use the existing infrastructure, and receive support if needed (on the concept of 'way of life' in connection with participation and risks of exclusion, see Wansing 2016: 244f.). The community as a place of everyday living – 'place' here is not only meant geographically but also has spatial content as a 'localisation of spaces in places' (cf. Löw 2015: 198ff.) – is closely connected to the community as a municipality in the sense of an administrative unit. The latter is endowed by the German Constitution with the right to self-administration (cf. Article 28 (2) GG). This goes hand in hand with the municipalities' responsibility for the provision of services of general interest to citizens (cf. Böhmer 2015: 138). The state municipal codes similarly state that the municipality has the task of providing "within the limits of its capacity, the public facilities necessary for the economic, social and cultural care of its inhabitants" (cf. § 8 para. 1 GO NRW). In addition, municipalities are subject to regional and global influences, which can have different effects on the conditions of everyday life at the municipal and local level (cf. Löw 2015: 198ff).

---

translated to the German word 'Gemeinschaft' which relates less to the administrational aspects of on association of people but more to the social aspects of a group. The matching English adjective would be 'common', for example as in 'common interest'. To make things complicated, the German word 'Gemeinwesen' is frequently translated to 'community' as well, but its content relates more to the concept of 'polity' or 'body politic' in the sense of 'res publica'.

The municipality is of further, essential importance in particular because the design of its local structures in Germany takes place with the democratically legitimised participation of the citizens. For example, the mayor is elected directly by the citizens entitled to vote and the municipal parliament is elected by list. In addition to these representative forms of 'classic' political participation, 'new', dialogue-oriented forms such as 'round tables' or 'future workshops' have been gaining popularity for several years.

The municipality is thus the nearest space where people can potentially realise social and political participation. At the same time, it is the nearest space in which people can potentially encounter obstacles to participation. In accordance with the UN Convention on the Rights of Persons with Disabilities (cf. preamble lit. e CRPD), "disability results from the interaction between persons with impairments and attitudinal and environmental barriers that hinders their full and effective participation". It is therefore crucial that barriers and disability are made issues of municipal planning and strategies of sustainable development (cf. preamble lit. g CRPD).

2. Planning an inclusive local community led by the municipality

The UN Convention on the Rights of Persons with Disabilities refers to the community as well. The local community as a *place of living* is taken up in Article 19 on "living independently and being included in the community". In the German version of the CRPD, in addition to the term 'community', there is talk of "community-*based* support services" (lit. b; author's emphasis) and "community-*based* services and facilities for the general population" (lit. c; author's emphasis). If one looks at the binding English version closely, this is also a reference to the community as an *administrative unit*. The English version of the CRPD refers to community support services and community services and facilities (UN n.d., n.p.). Welti (2013: 91f.) believes that the German translation "gemeindenah" does not adequately reflect the meaning of the English version ("community-based"). He fears that "gemeindenah" is understood in a purely geographical sense and that the reference to local self-government is insufficiently captured. As stated at the outset, the provisions of the CRPD also apply to the administrative unit of the municipality (cf. Art. 4 para. 5 CRPD). According to Welti (2013: 91), "this does not result in a clear obligation to carry out certain planning processes at a certain level" – at least not as long as the federal state has not made corresponding regulations (cf. op. cit.: 92). The municipality, however, is at least addressed with the implementation of the provisions, and thus also with working towards the development of an inclusive community. As explained above, it has a duty to help shape the living conditions of its citizens. In addition, an obligation of the municipality to plan participation through state legislation would hardly be considered a disproportionate encroachment on local self-government due to "the importance of the topic resulting from constitutional law and the CRPD and the need to enable people with disabilities to have equal living conditions [...]" (ibid.).

In the context of planning and shaping an inclusive community – i.e. creating conditions in the local community that enable people (with disabilities) to "shape their lives in a self-determined way in the usual social institutions of the life course" (Rohrmann et al. 2014: 22) – the municipality is on the one hand "a place of mediation between different interests" (Rohrmann 2016: 154), and on the other, one of the planning and shaping actors (cf. ibid.). It is primarily there that "the community and the social space [...] are shaped" (DV 2012: 16). This is "the essential starting point for developing inclusive social spaces" (ibid.). Consequently, the municipality is seen as the leader and role model in the planning of an inclusive community (cf. Rohrmann et al. 2014: 9; 11; 41-44). Here, the municipality is thus seen as having fundamental and far-reaching significance both as a place and as an actor in connection with the participation of persons with disabilities.

Since the ratification of the CRPD, the development of inclusive communities and thus participation planning for and with persons with disabilities have been increasingly discussed for the German context (for a 'new municipal planning optimism' see Steinfurth 2011). However, the question to what extent municipalities strive to improve – and ultimately equalise – the participation of persons with disabilities at the municipal level seems to be answered differently 'on site'. Following the tradition of disability assistance (cf. Rohrmann 2016: 151f.), the responsibility for the concerns of persons with disabilities and the improvement of the participation of persons with disabilities is still often attributed to providers of services for persons with disabilities and supralocally operating providers of social services for persons with disabilities – thus separated and thus excluded. In view of the goal of inclusion – and the associated abolition of special worlds – this neither makes sense nor is it appropriate. (cf. Bertelmann 2019) With the third reform stage of the Federal Participation Act (BTHG), the term social space found its way into the German SGB IX (Social Code Book Nine – Rehabilitation and Participation of Persons with Disabilities) in 2020[5]. There, it is used in the context of "social participation benefits" (§ 76 SGB IX) to designate the place of living outside one's own home (cf. § 76 para. 1 SGB IX). Exactly which meaning of the term social

---

5 The BTHG was a legislative package to improve the opportunities for participation and self-determination of persons with disabilities. It was designed to contribute to the implementation of the CRPD in German social law in a total of four stages (2017-2023). Among other things, the BTHG incorporated the CRPD's understanding of disability into the legal definition of disability.

space is used in the legal text remains open – whether related to administratively defined spaces or rather as an overlap of several living spaces or as a compromise, as it is based on the concept of 'social space orientation' in the profession of Social Work (cf. Noack 2015: 77). Its use in the same breath as 'Lebensführung' (way of life) and 'Lebensverhältnisse' (living conditions) indicates an understanding of social space that assumes the proximity of the individual to the community as a place of everyday living – and thus also concerns the administrative unit. If the aim is to design inclusive social spaces and inclusive living conditions, it is obvious that the municipality should also be involved in the planning of social participation services (cf. Bertelmann 2019).

In connection with the 'planning and development of flexible and inclusion-oriented support services' (as one of the dimensions to be considered in the development of an inclusive community according to Rohrmann et al. 2014), reference should be made, for example, to the obligation of the German states to work towards "comprehensive, needs-based, social space-oriented and inclusive offers by service providers" (§ 94 para. 2 SGB IX). Some of the states, such as North Rhine-Westphalia or Hesse, oblige the providers of integration assistance to conclude cooperation agreements with the counties and independent cities in their state's implementation law for the Social Code Book Nine, which aim at binding planning at the district or local level (cf. § 5 para. 1 AG- SGB IX NRW; § 5 para. 3 HAG/SGB IX). Considering the different local planning traditions and realities within the system of social services in Germany, which is characterised by subsidiarity, it can be assumed that in this planning context alone, the municipal authorities in charge have to deal with very different actors (cf. Rohrmann 2019 n.p.). "The legislator can oblige the autonomous and partly competing actors to cooperate and coordinate only to a limited extent through legal requirements. An integrative planning approach at the local level can in fact only be based on the mandate for municipal provision of services of general interest in the context of the right to self-government and leads to a role of the municipalities as coordinating partners with soft steering options" (ibid.). The widespread dissemination of municipal participation/inclusion planning, i.e. the implementation of the CRPD in the local community – and thus also the participation of persons with disabilities in it – is slowed down in Germany by the fact that it is not defined as a mandatory municipal task and that there are no binding regulations for its design. The expectation that the municipalities (nevertheless and also independently of the offers of integration assistance services) should undertake measures and planning that take into account the well-being of all people living in their area – i.e. also that of persons with disabilities – seems entirely appropriate on the basis of the preceding explanations. (cf. Bertelmann/Konieczny 2022)

This means that the development of an inclusive local community requires a municipal political mandate for action and a planning approach with which municipalities create conditions in participatory and coordinating processes to overcome the exclusion of people with disabilities and other social groups in the local community and to enable people with disabilities to develop their lives in a self-determined way in the usual social institutions of the life course (cf. Rohrmann et al., 2014: 7; Kempf et al. 2014: 56). It initiates a learning-oriented and participatory process in which the locally relevant actors, under the political leadership of the municipalities, set out to realise the objectives of an 'inclusive community' under the specific local conditions (cf. Lampke et al. 2011: 15). Experience shows that on the one hand the special and active role of local government, on the other hand the cooperation of different actors in the community as well as the participation of the group of persons with disabilities can be identified as essential aspects for and in the development of inclusive communities (cf. for example Rohrmann et al. 2014; Aktion Mensch n.d. a; Aktion Mensch n.d. b). 'Participation' is the complex object and goal of planning. At the same time, it is also to be understood as a mode of the planning process. The participation of the various relevant actors, especially the 'experts in their own right', offers the potential to enrich the inclusive design and further development of the community. Effective participation of the relevant actors, especially people with disabilities, can succeed if participation is considered on three levels: participation structure, participation culture and participation activity. Participation must therefore be enabled (structure), desired (culture) and practised (activity) (cf. LAG SELBSTHILFE NRW, 2015: 271). This requires inclusion and participation to be anchored and thought of as cross-cutting issues in the municipal administration and by the office or person within the administration who is primarily responsible for the development of an inclusive community. (cf. Bertelmann/Konieczny 2022)

As mentioned at the beginning, the data on the implementation of the CRPD at the municipal level in Germany is so far rather sparse.

3. Assessments and experiences from municipal administrations in North Rhine-Westphalia

In order to gain insights about the existence and nature of activities and planning for the implementation of the CRPD, as well as on assessments and experiences of municipal administrations with regard to the participation of actors outside the administration, especially persons with disabilities, all administrations of the 427 North Rhine-Westphalian municipalities – counties, independent cities and cities and towns belonging to counties – were invited by the author of this article to participate in an online survey in the first quarter of 2021. The administrative heads of all municipalities were addressed with the request to forward the invitation to the main office or person responsible inside the administration for issues relating to the implementation of the CRPD. In addition, a total of 191 representatives and/or contact persons for the interests of persons with disabilities/for inclusion at the municipal level were addressed with the same request. Despite the municipal burdens due to the Corona pandemic, we were able to include the responses of 155 municipalities in the evaluation (response rate of about 36 %). For almost half of the municipalities, functionaries from the top administration and the management level of the administration responded. A slightly smaller number of questionnaires were answered by commissioners responsible for the interests of people with disabilities in the municipality. The remaining responses came from other administrative levels and stakeholders. With regard to the distribution of the participating municipalities by type of municipality, the independent cities (61 %) and the counties (58 %) were more strongly represented than the cities belonging to counties (33 %) and towns belonging to counties (32 %).

In the following, the results of the feedback are presented first. The last part of the article focuses on the main office or person responsible for the activities aimed at the implementation of the CRPD in the municipal administration.

3.1 Individual Activity – Plan – Update

The majority of participants (119 out of 155) state that there are activities to implement the CRPD in the respective municipality (77%).[6] The following chart shows the occurrence of different types of activities in the various types of municipalities. Activities occur significantly more frequently in counties and independent cities than in cities and towns belonging to counties. This probably has to do with the resources available in larger municipalities. In the municipalities belonging to counties, there are primarily individual activities. In the municipalities belonging to counties, planned activities occur much less frequently than individual activities. Updates of plans are found there in isolated cases. Individual activities are also carried out in over two thirds of the counties and independent cities. Plans exist in almost three quarters of the cases; in almost one third of the counties and a good fifth of the independent cities there are already updates.

---

6   Based on this feedback, it can be assumed in the extrapolation for all municipalities in North Rhine-Westphalia that at least individual activities are carried out in at least just under a third (28%) of the municipalities. A similar result, but based on the survey of other addressees, can be derived from the data used as a basis in the participation report of the federal state of North Rhine-Westphalia (cf. MAGS NRW 2020: 232f.; LAG Selbsthilfe NRW 2021).

Figure 1: Occurrence of activity types in the different types of municipalities (in %)

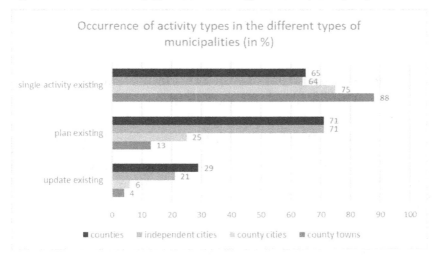

3.2 Lead management by the administration and main responsibility within the administration

The majority of activities and plans to implement the CRPD in the municipality are led by the municipal administration (79%). In cities and towns belonging to counties, it is much more frequent for the municipal administration not to be the leading authority of the activity than in counties and independent cities. There are isolated indications of shared leadership by the municipal administration, for example with interest groups, institutions of disability assistance or commissioners for the interests of persons with disabilities. In 44% of the municipalities where the lead management of activities lies with the municipal administration, the main office or person responsible is located in administrative departments that can be placed under the heading 'social affairs' ('social affairs': 26%, 'inclusion': 12%, 'social planning': 6%). 'Urban planning' is the main responsibility in 6% of the responding municipalities. In a good third (32%) of the municipalities, the main responsibility is held by a commissioned person for the interests of persons with disabilities. In the independent cities in particular, it is the commissioners who act as the main responsible person (in 57% of the independent cities). The management level of the administration assumes the main responsibility in 9% of the municipalities. This is most common in municipalities belonging to counties (in 28 % of the municipalities belonging to counties). There are also indications that the main responsibility within the administration is not centrally determined and controlled but is assigned to several offices of the administration; apparently more in the sense of an implementation responsibility for their own area of responsibility.

3.3 Participation from outside the administration – opportunities, addressing, extent

From the point of view of the municipal administrations in which there are planning activities under their leadership, the participation of actors from outside the administration is associated with the idea of greater expertise in the development of measures. In addition, there is the expectation of greater acceptance of decisions through participation. The municipal administrations also consider the participation of non-administrative actors, especially people with disabilities, to be an opportunity to (already) realise participation (during the planning process). The fact that the participation of non-administrative actors gives the administration the opportunity to coordinate with actors in whose areas of interest the administration itself has no authority, plays a subordinate role for all respondents. However, from the point of view of the respondents from the highest management level of administrations, it is the most important opportunity of participation, along with the increase in expertise. The same applies to the potential linkage of planning to the social spaces of the municipality. From the point of view of the respondents from the administrative levels below the management level, this is essential.

Persons with disabilities are mainly addressed by the administration for participation in planning to implement the CRPD via self-help organisations and representative bodies. They are less frequently addressed as individuals. It is also evident that persons with disabilities are not systematically informed about projects that affect their interests. There are indications that those persons with disabilities involved are the 'few usual suspects'.

According to the responses, the extent of participation of persons with disabilities in planning processes seems to reach the level of 'partnership' in isolated cases, following the 'Ladder of Citizen Participation' (cf. Arnstein 1969), but is probably mainly at the level of 'informing' and, in some cases, 'consultation'[7]. The participation of persons with disabilities in working groups and in steering groups, as well as participation in decision-making, is not established across the board in the municipalities.

---

7 Arnstein differentiates eight rungs on her ladder. Between 'manipulation' as non-participation and 'citizen control' as the highest degree of citizen power, 'informing', 'consultation' and 'partnership' are the third, fourth and sixth rungs of the ladder.

3.4 Environmental and attitudinal barriers to participation

Questions of accessibility are in the foreground of the assessments from the municipal administrations with regard to the participation of persons with disabilities. Accordingly, administration-specific processes are not accessible and resources for creating accessibility are not sufficiently available in the administrations. Individual measures to overcome barriers, such as the use of personal assistants and assistive devices as well as adjustments to organisational framework conditions can be realised sooner than interactional framework conditions. This means, for example, that it is possible to schedule appointments in such a way that participants from the group of people with disabilities can also take part, or to provide rooms that are accessible to and usable by people with different impairments. On the other hand, it is more difficult to provide information in such a way that it is accessible and understandable for people with different impairments or to design communication in such a way that people with different impairments can participate in it.

With regard to cooperation in working groups with participants from within and outside the administration, according to the assessments, not all participants are experienced in dealing with people with various impairments. In 15% of the municipalities, it is assumed that the participants have experience. With regard to the experience of those responsible for planning, the figure is twice as high. The respondents are optimistic about the willingness of the participants to adapt to 'unfamiliar' situations caused by impairments. There are indications that people with disabilities are attributed characteristics by the respondents that deviate from what members of the administration are accustomed to: Non-objectivity, emotionality, subjectivity. These deviations are in some places seen as enriching, in others as a hindrance.

3.5 (Dis-)Advantages of participation from outside the administration

The respondents from the municipal administrations see both advantages and disadvantages in the cooperation between intra-administrative participants and participants from outside the administration. Purely administrative groups are said to have the advantage of easier scheduling, rationality of experts and a more open discourse. The one-sidedness of looking at the issues, which does not lead to the core of the problem, is seen as disadvantageous. In addition, there is the opinion that the hierarchical organisation of the administration makes cooperation as equals difficult. Working groups composed of members from inside and outside the administration required more time. This is seen as a disadvantage by the respondents. The low level of knowledge and understanding of the municipal administration and its processes, as well as of politics and legal frameworks, on the part of those outside the administration, proved to be an aggravating factor. Mixed groups are perceived, with positive connotations, as less hierarchically organised; procedural steps would be reduced in such groups. The respondents see the proximity of the externals to practice as a benefit of mixed groups. This contribution is seen as giving the discussions a broader substance. Different approaches were attributed to the two groups, both of which had their justification. In the cooperation of mixed groups, respondents stated that moderation was needed to create a better balance. Mixed groups are seen as having the potential to sensitise the administration to the external perspective.

3.6 Challenges for municipal administrations regarding participatory activities and planning

The availability of human and/or financial resources is considered a major and the biggest challenge for municipal administrations. The shortage thereof is seen in connection with the fundamentally difficult financial situation of numerous municipalities and the degree to which the legal requirements for implementing the CRPD are binding. In this context, some municipalities invoke their right to self-administration. They argue that, as long as (the planning of) the implementation of the CRPD is not specifically designated as a mandatory task by state or federal law, they are not obliged to free up funds for it. The respondents also consider the sensitivity for the topic within their own organisation to be a challenge, whereby the support of the top management of the municipality is attributed a high degree of importance. In the responses from the municipalities as a whole, support from the municipality's top management is considered to be less of a problem. However, half of the responding contact persons/officials for the interests of persons with disabilities consider support to be a medium to great challenge.[8]

The mediation between the interests of the different stakeholders is another challenge from the respondents' point of view. On the one hand, respondents see a connection within the administration with the large number of adminis-

---

8 Representatives of the highest level of administration and the management level of the administration made up a significant part of the respondents. The self-assessment of the top administration/the management level and the external assessment of the contact persons/officials do not seem to match. The different assessments of the various functionaries may indicate that there is no congruence in the views of or demands for "support".

trative departments to be involved, and on the other hand with the cumbersome nature of the hierarchical municipal structures. With regard to mediating stakeholders outside the administration and between their interests, there are experiences that point to difficulties in cooperation between full-time staff and volunteers. The heterogeneity of the group of people with disabilities, which is based on the composition of the group of persons with different impairments, is also perceived as challenging in connection with the mediation of interests. The accessibility of the process has already been shown to be relevant above. It is also seen by municipal administrations as a challenge with regard to activities and planning for the implementation of the CRPD as a participative process.

4. Mediation through expert opinions and authority

Despite the lack of binding guidelines for municipal planning aimed at participation, municipalities see themselves as responsible within the framework of their overall responsibility for working towards the inclusive design of the community. Ideally, this is done with the participation of relevant stakeholders, especially persons with disabilities. Efforts to implement the CRPD at the local and district level offer the opportunity to improve the conditions for participation and the quality of life of the inhabitants.

The aim of this study conducted in North Rhine-Westphalia was to narrow the knowledge gap regarding the existence and nature of activities and planning for the implementation of the CRPD at the municipal level as well as regarding the experiences and assessments of municipal administrations. It can be seen that dealing with the participation of persons with disabilities as a subject and as a mode is still so new that no habit has yet been able to develop in this regard within municipal administrations which are oriented towards legal requirements and tend to be formal and hierarchical. Activities to implement the CRPD in the municipalities of North Rhine-Westphalia have not yet been established systematically and participatively across the board. Nevertheless, approaches for municipal participation planning are discernible in North Rhine-Westphalia at the level of the municipalities. In particular, the counties and independent cities are already dealing more systematically with questions of participation for persons with disabilities and are treating inclusion orientation as an important topic for municipal development. In the case of the towns and cities belonging to counties, the perceived insufficient resources seem to be of greater importance. In addition, it can be assumed that the relevance attributed to the topic increases with the size of the administered population, and thus the number of people with impairments living in the municipality's area of responsibility (cf. Bertelmann 2019). At the same time, it is conceivable that municipalities belonging to the same county have joined forces with the county and are engaged in activities to implement the CRPD under its leadership.

Looking at the overall results, three aspects can be focussed on, which put the person in the municipal administration who is designated as being primarily responsible at the centre of events and which can serve as a link to dealing with the challenges described: Expertise, authority and mediation. In activities and planning for the shaping of an inclusive community, which are understood as a joint cause of different actors, the participants not only bring in their own interests, but also their expertise. People with disabilities can, for example, contribute their knowledge, experiences and assessments regarding the development of disabilities due to barriers in the social space. Other actors from outside the administration can, for example, point out possibilities for design and cooperation within their areas of action and responsibility. The municipal administration is represented in two roles in such a participatory process. As one of the participants, it is, for example, an expert in matters of municipal (action) planning. In the role of the leading actor, however, further expertise is required from the municipal administration in terms of the person with the main responsibility for the participatory implementation of the CRPD. In order to design a participatory process, this person needs knowledge and understanding of the structures, cultures and concerns of the respective 'others'. This knowledge is useful as a basis for understanding. In order to win over representatives of the actors relevant to the planning project, knowledge about and networking in the social spaces is required, as well as the creation of appropriate publicity within the framework of citizen participation. Internally, the person with the main responsibility needs an insight and overview of which areas are indispensable for the project and to what extent there are already content-related and, if applicable, structural points of connection and linkage to the subject matter. In order to be able to take this insight into administration departments to which he/she is not assigned, it requires the backing of the top level of administration and the willingness and openness of the administrative departments to grant insight. In addition, the responsible person must be (or become) authorised to invite other administrative areas to cooperate. In view of the still unfamiliar cooperation with people with various impairments, the responsible person has to be aware of potential barriers, create accessibility and sensitise all participants to barrier-free interaction. It is also important to take into account the fact that bureaucratic procedures may not be familiar to those from outside the administration and that those inside the administration may first have to adjust to a deviation from these procedures. The mediation of interests is not only about the moderation between the interests directed at the subject matter pursued by those inside and outside the administration. The different interests within the administration must also be explored and mediated.

Moderation, coordination, mediation

It becomes apparent that taking on the main responsibility is a demanding undertaking. The person responsible acts as a mediator within the administration, in the relationship between the administration and external parties, and between all parties involved. Figure 2 summarises the previous explanations in graphic form.

Figure 2: Tasks, requirements and necessary competences of the main responsible person within the administration (illustration by author)

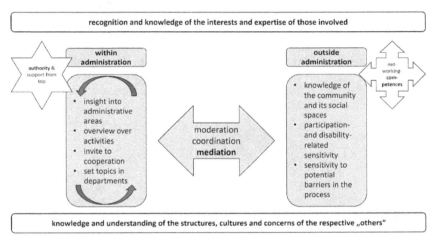

With regard to the person with the main responsibility and his or her equipment, the question therefore arises as to what extent the above-mentioned expertise and powers directed towards mediation are available due to the profession, the previous professional experience and the location within the administrative hierarchy, or to what extent this can be established through the support of the expertise in-house, possibly through the experience of similar or neighbouring municipalities, possibly through cooperation with the county and through recourse to other external offers as well as through the backing of the administrative leadership. Ideally, the concerns of people with disabilities and inclusion as a subject should become so firmly established as cross-cutting issues in all areas of the municipal administration that they are considered as a matter of course within the respective departments. As long as this has not yet been achieved, a central figure, such as the one described here, can contribute in its function to bringing the topic into the departments and thus into the breadth of the administration. Centralising the main responsibility while aiming to decentralise the concern of implementing the CRPD can be seen as a contradiction. It remains to be seen how successful such an approach can be and, if successful, how long it will be necessary as transitional solution on the way to an inclusion oriented municipal administration.

How do activities and plans for the design of inclusive communities succeed under municipal leadership and with the participation of relevant actors, especially people with disabilities? In order to shed light on this question with all its facets, further research is needed at the municipal level. A nationwide inventory of the occurrence of approaches to implementing the CRPD has the potential to trace possible differences in the approaches of the various types of municipalities and municipalities of different sizes even more precisely, to determine possible effects through requirements in the various federal states and to elicit practices of participation of persons with disabilities. It also seems worthwhile to take a closer look at the facet of the role of the municipal administration as the leader of such activities and planning and to pay attention to the question of the location of the leadership within the administration and the main person or office responsible in order to identify obstacles to participation and to create barrier-free opportunities for participation in the joint development of an inclusive local community.

References

Aichele, Valentin/Litschke, Peter/Striek, Judith/Vief, Nils (2020): Zukunftspotential entfalten. Die Aktionspläne der Länder zur Umsetzung der UN-Behindertenrechtskonvention, Berlin: Deutsches Institut für Menschenrechte.
Aktion Mensch (n.d. a): Das ist die Initiative Kommune inklusiv. https://www.aktion-mensch.de/kommune-inklusiv/initiative-kommune-inklusiv [accessed: 28.05.2023].
Aktion Mensch (n.d. b). Inklusion vor Ort – Das Programm für die modellhafte Förderung inklusiver Sozialräume in Nordrhein-Westfalen. https://www.aktion-mensch.de/kommune-inklusiv/neue-foerderung/nordrhein-westfalen [accessed: 28.05.2023].
Arnstein, Sherry R. (1969): A Ladder of Citizen Participation. In: Journal of the American Institute of Planners 35,4, pp. 216–224, DOI: 10.1080/01944366908977225.
Beck, Iris (Ed.) (2016): Inklusion im Gemeinwesen, 1. Aufl., Stuttgart: Kohlhammer.
Bertelmann, Lena/Konieczny, Eva (2022): Aus der inklusionsorientierten Verwaltung ins inklusive Gemeinwesen – Möglichkeiten und Herausforderungen der Vermittlung mit dem Ziel der vollen und wirksamen Teilhabe und Partizipation. In: Bertelmann, Lena et al. (Ed.): Planung und Entwicklung von Sozialen Diensten für Menschen mit Behinderungen. ZPE-Schriftenreihe (Band Nr. 57). Siegen: Universi, pp. 201-223. https://dspace.ub.uni-siegen.de/bitstream/ubsi/2302/3/ZPE%20_57_Planung_Entwicklung.pdf [accessed: 28.05.2023].
Bertelmann, Lena (2022): Aktivitäten und Planungen zur Umsetzung der UN-Behindertenrechtskonvention unter kommunaler Federführung – Hauptverantwortliche in der Kommunalverwaltung als Zentrum des partizipativen Geschehens. In: Nachrichtendienst des Deutschen Vereins (NDV) 2022, 10, pp. 486-493.

Bertelmann, Lena (2019): "Im Moment stellt sich die Frage nicht." – Zur Rolle der Gemeinde und des Ortsbezirks bei der Planung und Gestaltung eines inklusiven Gemeinwesens: In: Zeitschrift für Inklusion 3, n.p. https://www.inklusion-online.net/index.php/inklusion-online/article/view/519 [accessed: 28.05.2023].

Böhmer, Anselm (2015): Verfahren und Handlungsfelder der Sozialplanung. Grundwissen für die Soziale Arbeit. Wiesbaden: Springer VS.

DV – Deutscher Verein für öffentliche und private Fürsorge e.V. (2012): Eckpunkte des Deutschen Vereins für einen inklusiven Sozialraum. In: Nachrichtendienst des Deutschen Vereins für öffentliche und private Fürsorge 92, 1, pp. 15-19.

European Union (2022): Statistical regions in the European Union and partner countries. NUTS and statistical regions 2021. 2022 edition. https://ec.europa.eu/eurostat/documents/3859598/15193590/KS-GQ-22-010-EN-N.pdf [accessed: 25.06.2023].

Jacobi, Lisa Marie (2018): Die Partizipation von Menschen mit chronischen psychischen Erkrankungen an kommunalpolitischen Prozessen – eine Analyse am Beispiel der Teilhabeplanung des Landkreises Waldeck-Frankenberg. Masterarbeit, Siegen, Universität Siegen. https://nbn-resolving.org/urn:nbn:de:hbz:467-12828 [accessed: 28.05.2023].

Kempf, Matthias/Konieczny, Eva/Windisch, Marcus (2014): Die Verwirklichung von Menschenrechten oder: Kann man Inklusion planen? In: Teilhabe. Fachzeitschrift der Lebenshilfe 53, 10, pp. 55-62.

LAG Selbsthilfe NRW e.V. (Ed.) (2021): "Mehr Partizipation wagen!". Abschlussbericht zum Projekt. https://www.lag-selbsthilfe-nrw.de/wp-content/uploads/2021/01/Abschlussbericht_mehr-Partizipation-wagen-1.pdf [accessed: 28.05.2023].

LAG Selbsthilfe NRW e.V. (Ed.). (2015): Politische Partizipation von Menschen mit Behinderungen in den Kommunen stärken! Abschlussbericht zum Projekt. www.lag-selbsthilfe-nrw.de/wp-content/uploads/2018/05/LAG-Abschlussbericht_final_2016-01-12_barrierefrei-1.pdf [accessed: 28.05.2023].

Lampke, Dorothea/Rohrmann, Albrecht/Schädler, Johannes (Ed.) (2011): Örtliche Teilhabeplanung mit und für Menschen mit Behinderungen. Theorie und Praxis. Wiesbaden: VS Verlag.

Laub, Matthias (2021): Der inneren Existenz Raum geben. Partizipation von Menschen mit psychischer Behinderung in Prozessen Örtlicher Teilhabeplanung, Weinheim und Basel: Beltz Juventa.

Löw, Martina (2015): Raumsoziologie. 8. Auflage, Frankfurt am Main: Suhrkamp.

MAGS NRW – Ministerium für Arbeit, Gesundheit und Soziales des Landes Nordrhein-Westfalen (Ed.) (2020): Teilhabebericht Nordrhein-Westfalen. Bericht zur Lebenssituation von Menschen mit Beeinträchtigungen und zum Stand der Umsetzung der UN-Behindertenrechtskonvention. https://www.mags.nrw/sites/default/files/asset/document/teilhabebericht_2020_nrw_barrierfrei.pdf [accessed: 28.05.2023].

Noack, Michael (2015): Kompendium Sozialraumorientierung. Geschichte, theoretische Grundlagen, Methoden und kritische Positionen. Weinheim und Basel: Beltz Juventa.

Rohrmann, Albrecht (2016): Lokale und kommunale Teilhabeplanung. In: Beck, Iris (Ed.): Inklusion im Gemeinwesen, 1. Aufl., Stuttgart: Kohlhammer, pp. 145-183.

Rohrmann, Albrecht (2019): Kommunale Teilhabeplanung. Socialnet Lexikon. Bonn, 5. Juni 2019. https://www.socialnet.de/lexikon/Kommunale-Teilhabeplanung [accessed: 28.05.2023].

Rohrmann, Albrecht/Schädler, Johannes/Kempf, Matthias/Konieczny, Eva/Windisch, Marcus (2014): Inklusive Gemeinwesen Planen. Eine Arbeitshilfe. published by Ministerium für Arbeit, Integration und Soziales des Landes Nordrhein-Westfalen.

Steinfurth, Kerstin (2011): Ein neuer kommunaler Planungsoptimismus und seine Chancen für die Behindertenpolitik. In: Lampke, Dorothea/Rohrmann, Albrecht/Schädler, Johannes (Ed.): Örtliche Teilhabeplanung mit und für Menschen mit Behinderungen. Theorie und Praxis, 1. Auflage, Wiesbaden: VS Verlag, pp. 79-88.

Wansing, Gudrun (2016): Soziale Räume als Orte der Lebensführung. Optionen, Beschränkungen und Befähigungen. In: Beck, Iris (Ed.): Inklusion im Gemeinwesen, 1. Aufl., Stuttgart: Kohlhammer, pp. 239-267.

Welti, Felix (2013): Rechtliche Grundlagen einer örtlichen Teilhabeplanung. In: Becker, Ulrich/Wacker, Elisabeth/Banafsche, Minou (Ed.): Inklusion und Sozialraum. 1. Aufl., Baden-Baden: Nomos, pp. 87-100.

"Giving space to the inner existence" – what to learn from inclusion-oriented action planning for local empowerment strategies

Matthias Laub

Since ratification of the UN Convention on the Rights of Persons with Disabilities (UNCRPD), it can be observed in Germany that many municipalities are setting out to develop action plans to make communities more accessible and inclusive for people with disabilities. The following article focuses on those strategies and elaborates on the actual core of this convention: the participation of persons with disabilities. To do this first the basics of local respectively municipal action planning are explained before the results of a qualitative study are discussed. Finally, the article presents conclusions for local empowerment strategies.

1. Participation – the core element of the UNCRPD

The UN Convention on the Rights of Persons with Disabilities (UNCRPD) consists of two international treaties in the form of the Convention on the Rights of Persons with Disabilities and an Optional Protocol, which contains statements on special procedures for the implementation of this Convention. The overarching purpose of the Convention is first and foremost to make clear that the numerous subject-related human rights, as already set out in the Universal Declaration of Human Rights and the Social and Civil Covenants of 1966, are to be understood universally and hence apply without restriction and indivisibly to persons with disabilities as well (Degener 2015: 59).

The actual normative core of the UNCRPD, however, is the full and effective participation of persons with disabilities, directed towards the societal goal of inclusion. Article 3 in particular and the general principles formulated therein give this claim to full and effective participation such an original human rights normative framework that participation is the actual guiding theme at the center of the treaty[1] (Wansing 2015: 43f; Degener 2015: 58; Deutscher Verein für öffentliche und private Fürsorge 2015: 57).

A comparison of the original English version of the UNCRPD with the German translation shows that in Germany, unfortunately, they avoided using the direct equivalent of *participation* (= Partizipation). Instead, they chose the much more reserved word *Teilhabe* (analogous to *have part*). This should not obscure the fact that an important paradigm shift has taken place, because there is an essential difference between *participation* and *having part*: Instead of granting people the right to be part as an individual with a disability in a non-disabled society, it is now a question of full civic participation in a society that understands disability as a natural part of its own diversity (Deutsches Institut für Menschenrechte Monitoring-Stelle zur UN-Behindertenrechtskonvention 2010: 2f). That is why the concept of participation in the sense of *Teilhabe* used in German social legislation as a prerequisite for the societal perspective of inclusion is not viable as a synonym of the English term *participation*, as it does not include the powerful activity of taking part and the question of the political dimension of exerting influence. On closer inspection, *Teilhabe* turns out to be merely an indeterminate threshold value for a need for benefits under social law: A benefit-granting authority determines a (threatening) impairment of participation and thereupon grants benefits (e.g., integration assistance for people with disabilities[2]), rather to ensure social peace than to enforce a human right (Nieß 2016: 69f).

Participation as the main agenda, however, does not only appear as an abstract ideological construct. It is linked to concrete state obligations to respect, protect and guarantee, or target and promote, as well as recommendations on disability policy of the States Parties. These are intended to ensure and promote the full and non-discriminatory realisation of participation, as far as possible in a subject-related and direct manner, rather than via pure interest groups, e.g., through welfare associations (Degener 2015: 59f). Moreover, this national effort for participation extends not only to private and social coexistence, but to all spheres of civic life and the associated public and political issues (Deutscher Verein für öffentliche und private Fürsorge 2015: 59). A logical consequence of this aspiration is inevitably the need to create corresponding participation structures and orientation towards the possibilities and ideas of people with disabilities (Hinte 2008). In a nutshell, the UNCRPD is based on an under-

---

1 Gudrun Wansing vividly sets out and identifies the articles through which the guiding theme of participation unfolds (Wansing 2015: 43f).
2 Integration assistance is the legal area in Germany that is responsible for all assistance that contributes to the participation of people with disabilities, such as counseling centers, assisted living facilities or day care centers. The basis for this is the German Act to strengthen the Participation and Self-Determination of Persons with Disabilities or in short form Federal Act on Participation. People with mental disabilities are also included in group of the eligible persons.

standing of participation that is composed of three aspects and gives the UNCRPD the necessary verve: Persons with disabilities have a full right to accessible infrastructure, social participation and active civic participation (Kardorff 2010: 267).

2. Participation from a scientific point of view

So, if the concept of *Teilhabe* used in the German translation of the UNCRPD corresponds to participation in the sense explained above, then it requires a fundamental contextualisation of this concept, which becomes an *arena of discourses*, as noted by Schwanenflügel and Walther (2012).

According to Schnurr (2005: 1330f.), the term participation appears first and foremost as a constitutive feature of democratic forms of society and state. This localisation of the origin of the term in political philosophy refers to processes in which decisions are made that affect the lives of individuals and at the same time of the respective community[3]. This is based on an image of the human being as a subject and citizen who has a right to free decision-making and embedding of this decision-making in the community. The subject acts autonomously and maturely while at the same time being aware of his or her social dependence on fellow human beings. Communicative, trust-based negotiation processes in the sense of democratic co-determination are indispensable for this (Schwanenflügel/Walther 2012).

On the other hand, Schnurr (2005: 1330f.) traces the concept of participation back to origins in service theory, i.e., the use of social services. In this context, Schnurr sees participation in the field of social work as a structural maxim of the concept *lifeworld orientation*[4]. "In today's parlance, participation

---

[3] The concept of community has its roots first of all in political philosophy. In terms of democratic theory, it refers to Aristotle and his attempt to define the oikos in relation to the polis, as well as all subsequent concepts, such as those put forth by Hegel, Habermas, Marx or Arendt. A systematic discussion can be found, for example, in May (2017: 17ff). It appears prudent and useful here to undertake a needs-theoretical conflation in the sense of emergent systemism (Obrecht 2005: 110): therefore, community can be understood as a social system in which individuals maintain networks of relationships in order to satisfy human biopsychosocial needs. The satisfaction of those needs depends essentially on a structure of interaction and position as well as rules of power regarding the distribution of resources (Laub 2021: 47ff). Participation and effective accessible power greatly determine how adequately these needs are met.

[4] Thiersch/Grunwald (2014: 934), who essentially shaped the concept of lifeworld-oriented social work, describes it as follows: "Lifeworld-oriented social work sees the addressees in their lives determined by the confrontations with their everyday

in social work/social pedagogy refers to the fact or the goal of *"participation and involvement of users (clients) in the choice and provision of social work/social pedagogy services, programmes and benefits* across all fields of work"[5] (Schnurr 2005: 1330, emphasis in the original).

Even if service theories associated with the concept of participation do not directly address the subject of discussion here, insights can nevertheless be indirectly obtained from the perspective of the users involved as to how participation, user satisfaction and the effectiveness of problem-solving attempts correlate. Empirical evidence shows, for example, how participation positively influences the satisfaction with results and the assessment of interventions[6]. Participation increases people's ability to take part in processes of will formation and decision-making as a co-producer of (here: social) intervention and to optimise subjective as well as collective resources for discovering, articulating, and asserting their interests (Messmer 2018: 5f). One might say that it is participation by itself factually experienced which promotes corresponding participation skills, intrinsic motivational states and democratisation processes was well as sustainable participation structures (Schnurr 2005: 1336; Schwanenflügel/Walther 2012).

However, individualised forms of socialisation and diverse life courses make it less and less possible for people to recognise the connection between participation and its relevance for their own self-determination and their own biographical life course. Participation behaviour is influenced by a person's education and social affiliation, so that the form and content of participation are equally important. Often only institutionalised, formal forms of participation are recognised as opportunities at all (e.g., citizens' assemblies/town hall meetings), but the communication and interaction there are often perceived as dominant. Many people do not perceive such settings as appropriate fora for their concerns. As a result, respective participation structures themselves become another "place of exclusion" (Munsch 2003: 7) or at least perceived as such[7]. Corresponding initiatives quickly develops into an oxymoron, i.e., a construction of inner contradictions: people whose everyday life is massively characterised by restricted scope for participation are supposed to participate in action planning processes (Evangelische Fachhochschule Rheinland-Westfalen-Lippe 2002).

---

living conditions. It sees the addressees in their problems and resources, in their freedoms and limitations; it sees them – against the background of material and political conditions – in their efforts to shape space, time and social relationships."
5 All direct quotes are translated from German into English by the author.
6 For example, participation studies such as those by Abele et al. (2003) in child and youth welfare.
7 Or, as one of the author's interviewees aptly put it when discussing participation in the creation of action plans for the implementation of the UNCRPD: "You're barely in and you're already out!"

These forms of communication and interaction of common participation opportunities are also related to real and latent power relations between decision-makers and participants, which are decisive for the degree of participation. With the *ladder of citizen participation,* Arnstein (1969) made an important contribution to reflecting on participation in political processes that is still valid today, albeit supplemented by many derivatives. Arnstein distinguishes between non-participation, sham participation and actual participation. Actual participation takes place when decisions arise in a process of negotiation based on partnership and when the subject is given actual decision-making competences for certain programmes/planning sections combined with powers of control. Arnstein therefore sees participation as the sharing of decision-making power, whereas mere information or explanations of how the respective decisions came about do not fulfil this criterion. This means it is about influencing the decision itself rather than just informed consent. Another model put forth by Blandow, Gintzel and Hansbauer (1999) assesses the degree of participation in interactive decision-making processes depending on the degree to which the person participating has the possibility of beard heard and the extent of his or her veto rights. It defines a successful participation event in a balanced relationship of these variables for all participants in the interaction.

Another relevant element in this fundamental consideration is the significance of the socio-spatial[8] reference in order to bring participation in line with the person's own, subjective way of life. Participation often seems to fail decisively because of different ideas of space. The residential spaces that are subjectively significant for the individuals often lie at cross purposes or outside of the spaces that are perceived by others as supposedly formable units (Schwanenflügel/Walther 2012). Many people see themselves as residents in a city district, a small town or municipality – or at most a county. This is the maximum dimension in which they have still the feeling that they can have any influence with proposals in such that they can experience the effects in their direct living environment and everyday life. The less this is the case and can be experienced subjectively, the lower the motivation to participate (Schwanenflügel/Walther 2012). Consequently, participation is decisively dependent on subjectively experienced influencing factors and positive experiences of participation. Successful participation itself leading to self-efficacy creates a willingness and ability to participate. Finally, the activities and access

---

8 Social space is the (residential) area in which people and members of social groups dynamically interact with peers and their environment (Bitzan et al 2005: 532). Here, patterns of behavior and use, structures of action and interaction, forms of self-organisation and social networks converge and constitute the social capital of the individuals living there (Kirschniok 2011: 69f, Strauss 2005: 76). This space, then, not only becomes a place of collective socialisation and cultural-normative orientation, but also creates or prevents access to resources and information through its infrastructure and social networks (Häussermann et al. 2010: 5).

to such processes are also dependent on individual characteristics in interaction with disabling environmental conditions (barriers).

3. Participatory social spaces design

It has been clarified above that participation with the goal of an inclusive society cannot be regarded merely as *being there* or *having part*, but as a self-evident possibility of active co-creation and co-determination by influencing social spaces that can actually be shaped (Palleit/Kellermann 2015: 275). However, a social space perspective is not solely based on considerations of participation research. In the case of people with disabilities, the original characteristic of a disability is of crucial relevance. According to the *International Classification of Functioning, Disability and Health* (ICF), disability arises from the interplay between a health impairment, a disabling environment and the effects on individual activity and social participation. According to this biopsychosocial understanding of diseases and disabilities, it is insurmountable attitudinal and environmental obstacles (barriers) that turn an impairment into a disability in the first place (Wohlgensinger 2014: 67f).

Participation can only be realised if the immediate socio-spatial environment in which people with disabilities live is free of infrastructural and/or attitudinal, financial, legal, political or other barriers. Thus, in order to create equal participation opportunities, strategies are required for identifying and removing such access issues (Bethke et al. 2015: 171ff). A community-oriented perspective is therefore indispensable:

> "With the goal of promoting social participation, it is important [for people with disabilities] [...] to locate themselves more strongly in society, to help shape the community with their activities and competences, and to have a preventive and supportive effect locally" (Schäfers 2013: 102).

As defined above, social spaces are statistically and/or politically defined areas in the community in which social integration of the people living there takes place and human needs are satisfied. Social spaces and the risk of segregation of citizens that may be associated with them have a significant influence on individual socialisation, personal development, living conditions and lifestyles and correlate directly with the radius of action. In this context, the lower the mobility, the greater the bond to the social space (Kuhn 2013:107). Therefore, it can be stated that people with disabilities are highly bound to their social space due to mobility restrictions and the receipt of early pensions or social assistance/basic social security. This exposes them to an increased risk of exclusion, as a German study in the city of Munich also points out (Landeshauptstadt München 2014: 172f).

An accessible social space can be understood as an inclusive living environment if all people living in it can use it together and help shaping it, if the material and non-material conditions for this are provided, and if there are counselling and support services as well as open networks that promote participation. The decisive factor here is respect for the diversity of the living environment and participation in planning, design and decision-making processes (Kuhn 2013: 108ff). In summary, it can be argued that the legal aspiration of the UNCRPD to achieve participation in the sense of active participation with the goal of inclusion of persons with disabilities can only be realised if these people are also involved in the design of their social spaces without barriers. This, in turn, requires appropriate participation, coordination, cooperation and communication structures that consider the available resources of persons with disabilities and the processes of self-initiative and self-help (Hinte 2008). Such a structure is offered by municipal action planning as a community-based empowerment strategy, which is outlined below.

4. Doing participation by municipal action planning: a strategy of inclusion-oriented social space design

In order to effectively implement the UNCRPD in the living environments of people with disabilities and to enable accessible social spaces with the direct participation of people with disabilities with the goal of an inclusive society, a grassroots strategy has developed that can be called municipal action planning. Today, it represents the essential action strategy for a participatory implementation of the UNCRPD in Germany (Deutscher Verein 2011: 4ff.).

This strategy is a participatory, learning-oriented collaborative process of different actors working together under the leadership of the municipalities to develop programmes and concepts on how accessibility is to be realised in the common social space. The actors involved in this collaboration include all the relevant stakeholders, such as representatives of the local government and administration, urban and municipal development planning, the supra-local social welfare agency[9], the associations and agencies of the voluntary welfare sector, the housing industry, civil society self-advocacy organisations, as well as affected and non-affected persons. One product of such planning processes is usually action plans that list goals, measures, implementation steps and responsibilities for designing social spaces. Such a process is legally based on the sovereign self-administration and planning law of federal cities, districts

---

9 In Germany, this refers to the authorities that are responsible, among other things, for integration assistance for people with disabilities.

and municipalities within the framework of the German Basic Law (Constitution of the Federal Republic of Germany) and the constitutions of the federal states, the socio-spatial care obligation within the framework of social legislation, the planning requirements of building legislation as well as the obligation for accessible construction through federal states equality or disability equality laws (Deutscher Verein 2012: 2f).

An essential part of such processes is also the often-preceding survey of the current care situation, which compromises a potential and resource analysis of a social space and the development of targets, indicators and monitoring systems. This is done using milieu analyses, surveys of civic engagement through activating surveys, social space inspections/visits, social space reports, etc. with evaluation in workshops, future workshops, etc. (Deutscher Verein 2012: 10).

It is crucial to develop appropriate participation instruments and procedures, forms of cooperation and communication in order to involve all relevant actors in an overall social planning process (Rund et al. 2011: 90). The actual implementation and quality of those planning processes depends crucially on the participation of people with disabilities, and on the fact that ideally the entire population of a social space is addressed and represented (Deutscher Verein 2012: 6). Against the background of the UNCRPD's understanding of participation, it should be pointed out that *"purely advocatory participation by individual representatives – whether disabled or not – is not sufficient, as it is important to reach disabled people in the diversity of their impairments and life situations"* (Welti 2011: 61). Therefore, it is important to reflect the diversity of people with disabilities in these processes, if possible, through direct participation. Such direct participation can take the form of involving key persons from the population or through the formation of advisory councils that represent as many people as possible in the municipal community (Welti 2011: 60f).

However, an exploratory study of such action plans by the author has shown that the participation of one particular target group fails to lead to the desired success: people with mental disabilities (Laub 2021: 116f). For them, spaces of participation seem to become spaces of exclusion, as aptly described by Munsch (2003: 7). This is all the more astonishing because there is a decades-long tradition of community-based, outpatient-complementary care in German social psychiatry compared to the traditional institutions for the disabled. This includes a cross-case orientation, socio-spatial planning and the inclusion of relatives' and self-help associations in the sense of a trialogical communication culture. Of course, assistance for people with chronic mental illness does not provide for social space design services. German integration assistance refers to the individual person in need of assistance and his or her individual needs rather than to accessibility or coexistence in the social space (Rohrmann/Weber 2015: 228). Nevertheless, it was surprising that this target group, which should actually be easily won over for their participation, is not even visible in action plans. Therefore, the author conducted a qualitative-reconstructive study, the results of which are outlined below.

5. When participatory action planning creates new spaces of exclusion! – Illustrated by the example of people with mental disabilities

This section presents key results of a qualitative study about the participation of people with chronic mental illness – people with mental disabilities as defined in Art. 1 of the UNCRPD – in municipal inclusion-oriented action plans. This is followed by a concluding discussion of what can be inferred from these findings for local empowerment strategies such as municipal action planning. The study consisted of qualitative interviews which were conducted iteratively-circularly according to grounded theory methodology (Strauss/Corbin 2010). Interview partners were mentally ill participants, social planners and social psychiatric professionals. The data were analysed based on theoretical coding (open, axial, selective) and were used for a modeling of this special participation event (Laub 2021: 115ff). The following explanations for the aforementioned non-participation of this group of people in municipal action panning processes can be outlined on the basis of the study conducted:

Participation in processes of local action planning was found to be crucially dependent on the success in bringing others closer to one's *inner existence* and with this one's subjective experience of reality and the associated contexts of meaning and concepts of meaning, and in establishing (social) spatial references. The main issue is

> "…to somehow bring something close to, so to speak… the, the, the…the inner existence, the state of mind or what it means to be mentally ill" (Laub 2021: 149)

The difficult questions to answer here are: what do I exactly experience as being impaired and hindered by the socio-spatial environment and attitudes in social interaction as a person with mental disability? In the absence of a commonly experienced, physical environment, the communication and connectivity of such spatial concepts (e.g., *barrier*) are considerably more difficult and because of that dependent on interpretation and prone to distortion due to power dynamics.

> "It's a hell of a job to make it plausible what the specific mental disability constitutes. Also, vis-à-vis the other disabled people, yes. that is…that is…not easy." (Laub 2021: 151)

From the respondents' point of view, mental illness manifests itself externally at best in behaviour and social interaction and becomes a recognised impairment on the basis of observations of these external manifestations, through the narratives of those affected as well as through the formation of phenomenological clusters, which then lead to diagnostic attributions. These attributions and the *inner existence* of this experience are often only partially congruent for those affected. Local participation is therefore faced with the challenge of creating a communication space that is free of stigma and domination and that is accessible to all.

Such a communication space in the context of local participation must therefore not serve to establish the truth regarding the legitimacy of claims, but must promote a symmetrical social exchange in which the non-discriminatory articulation of individual needs is central. Such a communication process is supported (but sometimes also made more difficult) by *gatekeepers* (e.g., social psychiatric professionals, relatives, peers) who, if necessary, create access through translation services and carry out appropriate agenda setting. It is therefore not to be underestimated how important it is to win over social psychiatric networks for assistance and to create a shared reality of the possible implementation of the UNCRPD for people with mental disabilities.

In this context, it is essential to bring the large holistic perspectives of an accessible, inclusive environment into harmony with the diverse, atomistic needs of the addressed citizens and to strike a balance between socio-spatial diversity on the one hand and the grouping of needs into operationalisable topics and measures on the other.

> "We always face the problem…that it is, uh, highly individual…what is an inclusive experience, let's say, if we think of the individual…what is an inclusive life? That's actually what it is about. And that looks like this for one and different for the other. And when I think about all the people who live there., um, I just see…a convention helps nothing. So a general plan, uh, that really has to permeate society." (Laub 2021: 160)

Otherwise, there is a danger that the planning process will be perceived as too abstract and controlled, or that the final municipal action plan will not gather any political momentum to have an effect on the daily living environment of the citizens. Success therefore depends on how diversity is dealt with strategically and how both the connectivity of one's own identity on the one hand and transformative impact on the other are created.

The way society deals with mental health also has an impact on this participation process. How can we talk about human rights, accessibility and inclusion without giving space to the powerlessness, the experiences of psychiatric institutionalisation, the fact of compulsive acts and social blame for not having got one's life back on track again, even if this is beyond the scope of community contexts? The study has shown that the institutionalised lifeworld of people with a mental disability continues to be based on a paradigm of illness that is at odds with the understanding of the ICF and the UNCRPD and also corresponds only slightly to the concept of identity of people with a mental disability. An undiminished nosological understanding of disorders and cause-related treatments only slightly raises the question of how impairment and environmental barriers interact and lead to disability. The understanding of disability that prevails in such planning processes is not only inaccessible to people with mental disabilities, but quite the opposite: The attribution of a disability is perceived as stigmatising and discouraging and causes internalised hopes of treatment, recovery and a life unaffected by illness to fade (Laub 2021: 183ff).

For participation processes to function as intended, it is, therefore, indispensable to create and allow one's own understanding of disability, barriers and inclusion, and to jointly question the prevailing conditions in the subsystems relevant to people with mental disabilities. Human needs and socio-spatial opportunities for self-efficacy serve as a common basis for experience and communication. In Keupp's sense (2020: 42), this can be understood as *identity work* and as the joint development of a suitable, coherent model that recognises individual concepts of meaning and understands inclusion as a social condition in which society grants the individual an identity that allows cohesion and, at the same time, contrariety.

The results of this study show that strategies for action such as local action planning for the implementation of the UNCRPD, for the design of accessible social spaces and finally for a discrimination-free, inclusive society are themselves not free of power processes and access barriers. Therefore, the following and last section discusses what this means for local empowerment strategies and why diverse needs and socio-spatial realisation opportunities, as well as the democratic negotiation of *inner existences* (Laub 2021: 187ff) must be taken into account.

6. The 'E' in empowerment stands for equal opportunities! – What we can learn for local empowerment strategies

The research results show that against the backdrop of the UNCRPD's goal of a participatory world and the problems outlined above, more willingness is needed in the future to design participatory structures in local planning processes that are free of barriers and domination – both in communication or spatial conditions and in the conceptualisation of inclusion, disability and society. It is important to establish a culture of discussion oriented towards the diversity of people with disabilities and to develop standards for good participation structures already at the beginning of planning processes (Palleit/Kellermann

2015: 276ff.; Arnade 2015: 99). This is often prevented by *blind spots* of the actors involved in the planning process, i.e., preconceived notions regarding disability and inclusion, lobby interests or stigmatising attributions of actors with and without disabilities, who are no less prone to this than the rest of society. The design of inclusive social spaces through local action planning is therefore inextricably linked to self-reflexive process management and the acquisition of inclusion and participation competence.

Such an understanding must be placed at the centre of a process of local action planning, if participation is to be pursued and developed as an independent strategic field of action, if the participation provided for by human rights is to be real and not just a sham. In processes of local action planning, it is therefore central to ask

> "how the various groups of people concerned, their self-help organisations and associations are involved, how they come together with the experts and those responsible in the municipality, and how jointly supported proposals for action emerge from this. Special requirements for communication with people with impairments must be taken into account and fulfilled [...]. The quality and implementation of... [inclusion-oriented action] planning depends to a considerable extent on how participation succeeds" (Deutscher Verein 2012: 6).

This necessarily includes a negotiation of the paradigmatic framework (what do we mean by disability, barriers or an accessible community?) and the expectations of inclusion or of the UNCRPD. One could say that it is about nothing less than identifying and breaking down barriers in the planning process itself in order to be able to negotiate those of social coexistence in the first place. It is also recommended to actively use existing socio-spatial networks and to involve social psychiatric professionals who, as gatekeepers, can make participation opportunities visible through their life-world expertise and trust-based access to the target group.

The invisibility of people with a mental illness in municipal action plans has made it clear how much – just as with the concept of inclusion – empowerment through participation, which often forms the basis of local action planning processes, is a so-called "programme concept" (Schädler 2013: 1). This means a concept which, due to its programmatic nature, represents good values and generates a high degree of approval even by those in power, despite – or precisely because of – the given scope for interpretation and its associated indeterminacy. The danger, of course, is that this indeterminacy would transform empowerment, participation and inclusion into *buzzwords* and with this into empty phrases that everyone can connect to. As a result, these concepts are in danger of losing their transformative power through mass-compatible schematisation, toning down of the claim to redistribute power through mainstreaming and detachment of the concepts from their historical-political contexts (Batliwala 2007: 563f). Local action planning, mandated by municipal politics or the service providers it represents and shaped by those who are affected by potentially costly changes, leaves the power of interpretation of a discrimination-free *good life* with the powerful and allows them to assign empowerment and participation. This is often done in conjunction with making the concerns of groups affected by experiences of discrimination conform to systemic rules (e.g., unpleasant topics such as forced psychiatric treatment in a closed institution are better left unaddressed) and generating renewed pressure for normalisation. The goal is then to create a politically usable action plan without initiating any real structural changes (Quindel/Pankofer 2000: 39-41; Enggruber 2014: 5-7). The research described here suggests that local action planning is susceptible to an empowerment concept that is more of a "neoliberal embrace" (Herriger 2010: 84) and is compatible with the model of an activating welfare state focused more on self-responsibility, insight and subject-oriented optimisation rather than on genuine empowerment and the elimination of social inequality (Enggruber 2020: 46-48). Therefore, the question must be proactively asked whether social inequality and new experiences of exclusion are not reproduced in the process and, above all, whether, following Uwe Becker's polemic *The Inclusion Lie*, about the process is some manner of a *participation* and *empowerment lie* (Munsch 2003: 7; Becker 2016).

Instead, participatory empowerment processes such as those of local action planning must be designed in the sense of the professional understanding of social work. This is in order to do justice to the right to accessibility and inclusion. It is about nothing less than dealing effectively with social inequality and "risky opportunities" (Keupp 2020) in between self-determination on the one and vulnerability on the other hand. The aim here should be reducing compulsory choice, increasing opportunities for choice and ultimately contributing to more social justice (Lambers 2018: 296). Participation and Empowerment therefore are not an act of mediation, but the consequence of action aimed at equal opportunities and social justice, which also in such processes constantly reflects the immanent structural power relations and discrimination mechanisms and examines the empowerment space *local action planning* for structures of domination and exclusion mechanisms (Haug et al. 2021: 29). In any case, local action planning does not take place in an idealistic, vacuum space, "but in a dynamic of habitual patterns, social structures, interests and symbols of power" (Laub 2021: 188). It is therefore about participation that sees itself as "identity fitting work" (Keupp 2020: 42) in a diverse-heterogeneous society and that is prepared to discuss different experiences of reality democratically, open-endedly and with a view to realisation opportunities. In other words, it is about giving space to the *inner existence* of people with disabilities in the truest sense of that expression (Laub 2021: 187-199).

References

Abele, Melanie/Bollweg, Petra/Flösser, Gaby/Schmidt, Mathias/Wagner, Melissa (2003): Partizipation in der Kinder- und Jugendhilfe. In: Sachverständigenkommission Elfter Kinder- und Jugendbericht (Ed.): Kinder- und Jugendhilfe im Reformprozess. Materialien volume 2. München, pp. 225-309.

Arnade, Sigrid (2015): "Nichts über uns ohne uns!" – Die Zivilgeselllschaft spricht mit. Staatliche Koordinierungsstelle und Parallelbericht. In: Degner, Thomas/Diehl, Elke (Ed.): Handbuch Behindertenrechtskonvention. Teilhabe als Menschenrecht – Inklusion als gesellschaftliche Aufgabe. Bonn: Bundeszentrale für politische Bildung, pp. 93–101.

Arnstein, Sherry R. (1969). A Ladder of Citizen Participation. In: JAIP 35, 216–224.

Batliwala, Srilatha (2007): Taking the power out of empowerment – an experiential account. In: Development in Practice 17 (4-5), pp. 557–565.

Becker, Uwe (2016): Die Inklusionslüge. Behinderung im flexiblen Kapitalismus. 2. Unveränd. Aufl. Bielefeld: transcript Verlag.

Bethke, Andreas/Kruse, Klemens/Rebstock, Markus; Welti, Markus (2015): Barrierefreiheit. In: Degener, Thomas/Diehl, Elke (Ed.): Handbuch Behindertenrechtskonvention. Teilhabe als Menschenrecht – Inklusion als gesellschaftliche Aufgabe. Bonn: Bundeszentrale für politische Bildung, pp.170–188.

Bitzan, Maria/Hinte, Wolfgang/Klöck/Tilo/May, Michael/Stövesand, Sabine (2005): Diskussionsbeitrag Gemeinwesenarbeit. In: Kessl, Fabian/Reutlinger, Christian/Maurer, Susanne/Frey, Oliver (Ed.): Handbuch Sozialraum. Wiesbaden: VS Verlag für Sozialwissenschaften, pp. 529–557.

Blandow, Jürgen/Gintzel, Ullrich/Hansbauer, Peter (1999): Partizipation als Qualitätsmerkmal in der Heimerziehung. Eine Diskussionsgrundlage. Münster: Votum-Verlag.

Degener, Theresia (2015): Die UN-Behindertenrechtskonvention – ein neues Verständnis von Behinderung. In: Degener, Thomas/Diehl, Elke (Ed.): Handbuch Behindertenrechtskonvention. Teilhabe als Menschenrecht – Inklusion als gesellschaftliche Aufgabe, Bonn: Bundeszentrale für politische Bildung, pp. 55–74.

Deutsches Institut für Menschenrechte Monitoring-Stelle zur UN-Behindertenrechtskonvention (2010): Partizipation – ein Querschnittsanliegen der UN-Behindertenrechtskonvention. Berlin.

Deutscher Verein für öffentliche und private Fürsorge (2011): Eckpunkte des deutschen Vereins für einen inklusiven Sozialraum. Berlin.

Deutscher Verein für öffentliche und private Fürsorge (2012): Empfehlungen zur örtlichen Teilhabeplanung für ein inklusives Gemeinwesen. Berlin.

Deutscher Verein für öffentliche und private Fürsorge (2015): Recht der internationalen Konventionen. Textausgabe zum Sozialrecht 9. Berlin.

Enggruber, Ruth (2014): Kritische Notizen zum Empowerment-Konzept in der Sozialen Arbeit. https://soz-kult.hs-duesseldorf.de/personen/enggruber/Documents/document(3).pdf [last accessed: 04/11/2022].

Enggruber, Ruth (2020): Empowerment, ein Konzept für Soziale Arbeit im transformierten Sozialstaat? In: Jagusch, Birgit/Chehata, Yasmine (Ed.): Empowerment

und Powersharing. Ankerpunkte – Positionierungen – Arenen. Weinheim: Beltz (Diversität in der Sozialen Arbeit), pp. 43–53.
Evangelische Fachhochschule Rheinland-Westfalen-Lippe (2002): Lexikon der Sozialen Arbeit. Bochum.
Haug, Lean/Strähle, Borghild/Kechaja, Maria (2021): Antidiskriminierung im Zusammenspiel von Beratung und Empowerment. In: Bauer, Gero/Kechaja, Maria/ Engelmann, Sebastian/Haug, Lean (Ed.): Diskriminierung und Antidiskriminierung. Beiträge aus Wissenschaft und Praxis. Bielefeld: transcript Verlag (Gesellschaft der Unterschiede, 60), pp. 23–42.
Häussermann, Hartmut/Schwarze, Kristin/Jaedicke, Wolfgang/Bär, Gesine/Bugenhagen, Ina (2010): Lebenslagen in Deutschland. Armuts- und Reichtumsberichterstattung der Bundesregierung: Möglichkeiten der verbesserten sozialen Inklusion in der Wohnumgebung; Schlussbericht.
Herriger, Norbert (2010): Empowerment in der Sozialen Arbeit. Eine Einführung. Kohlhammer: Stuttgart.
Hinte, Wolfgang (2008): Sozialraumorientierung: Ein Fachkonzept für die Soziale Arbeit. Vortrag für den Fachtag Sozialraumorientierung am 28.05.2008. https://www.dowas.at/media/filer_public/4e/fd/4efdc58a-98c0-492a-871d-ff51a29e4439/sozi alraumorientierung_vortrag_hinte_08-05-28.pdf [last accessed: 04/11/2022]
Kardorff, Ernst von (2010) Evaluation beteiligungsorientierter lokaler Enabling Community-Projekte. In Evangelische Stiftung Alsterdorf (Ed.): Enabling Community – Gemeinwesen zur Inklusion befähigen! Elf Empfehlungen für innovatives Handeln in Kommunalpolitik, Verwaltung und Sozialer Arbeit. Berlin/Hamburg, pp. 263-275.
Keupp, Heiner (2020): Individualisierte Identitätsarbeit in spätmodernen Gesellschaften. Riskante Chancen zwischen Selbstsorge und Zonen der Verwundbarkeit. In: Deppe, Ulrike (Ed.): Die Arbeit am Selbst. Theorie und Empirie zu Bildungsaufstiegen und exklusiven Karrieren. vol. 74 (Studien zur Schul- und Bildungsforschung, volume 74). Wiesbaden: Springer VS, pp. 41–65.
Kirschniok, Alina (2011): Analyse sozialräumlicher Behinderung und Ressourcen. In: Flieger, Petra/Schönwiese, Volker (Ed.): Menschenrechte Integration Inklusion. Aktuelle Perspektiven aus der Forschung. Bad Heilbrunn: Klinkhardt, pp. 67–73.
Kuhn, Andreas (2013): Inklusion im Sozialraum aus Sicht des Deutschen Vereins. In: Becker, Ulrich/Wacker, Elisabeth/Banafsche, Minou (Ed.): Inklusion und Sozialraum. Behindertenrecht und Behindertenpolitik in der Kommune. Studien aus dem Max-Planck-Institut für Sozialrecht und Sozialpolitik. Baden-Baden: Nomos, pp. 107–114.
Lambers, Helmut (2018): Theorien der Sozialen Arbeit. Ein Kompendium und Vergleich. 3rd edition. Stuttgart, Opladen, Toronto: UTB; Barbara Budrich.
Landeshauptstadt München (2014): Studie zur Arbeits- und Lebenssituation von Menschen mit Behinderungen in der Landeshauptstadt München. Endbericht Teil 2. Allgemeine Lebenssituation. München.
Laub, Matthias (2021): Der inneren Existenz Raum geben. Partizipation von Menschen mit psychischer Behinderung in Prozessen Örtlicher Teilhabeplanung. Weinheim: Beltz.
May, Michael (2017): Soziale Arbeit als Gemeinwesen. Ein theoretischer Begründungsrahmen. Opladen, Berlin, Toronto: Barbara Budrich.

Messmer, Heinz (2018): Barrieren von Partizipation: Der Beitrag empirischer Forschungs für ein realistisches Partizipationsverständnis in der Sozialen Arbeit. In: Dobslaw, Gudrun (Ed.), Partizipation – Teilhabe – Mitgestaltung: Interdisziplinäre Zugänge. Opladen: Budrich, pp. 109–127.

Munsch, Chantal (2003): Lokales Engagement und soziale Benachteiligung. In: Munsch, Chantal (Ed.): Sozial Benachteiligte engagieren sich doch. Über lokales Engagement und soziale Ausgrenzung und die Schwierigkeiten der Gemeinwesenarbeit. Weinheim-München: Juventus, pp. 7–28.

Nieß, Meike (2016): Partizipation aus der Subjektperspektive. Zur Bedeutung von Interessenvertretung für Menschen mit Lernschwierigkeiten. Wiesbaden: Springer.

Obrecht, Werner (2005): Ontologischer, Sozialwissenschaftlicher und Sozialarbeitswissenschaftlicher Systemismus – ein integratives Paradigma der Sozialen Arbeit. In: Hollstein-Brinkmann, Heino/Staub-Bernasconi, Silvia (Ed): Systemtheorien im Vergleich. Wiesbaden: VS Verlag für Sozialwissenschaften, pp. 93–172.

Palleit, Leander/Kellermann, Gudrun (2015): Inklusion als gesellschaftliche Zugehörigkeit – das Recht auf Partizipation am politischen und kulturellen Leben. In: Degener, Thomas/Diehl, Elke (Ed.): Handbuch Behindertenrechtskonvention. Teilhabe als Menschenrecht – Inklusion als gesellschaftliche Aufgabe. Bonn: Bundeszentrale für politische Bildung, pp. 275–288.

Quindel, Ralf/Pankofer, Sabine (2000): Chancen, Risiken und Nebenwirkungen von Empowerment – Die Frage nach der Macht. In: Miller, Tilly/Pankofer, Sabine (Ed.): Empowerment konkret! Berlin: De Gruyter, pp. 33–44.

Rohrmann, Albrecht/Weber, Erik (2015): Selbstbestimmt leben. In: Degener, Thomas/Diehl, Elke (Ed.): Handbuch Behindertenrechtskonvention. Teilhabe als Menschenrecht – Inklusion als gesellschaftliche Aufgabe. Bonn: Bundeszentrale für politische Bildung, pp. 226–240.

Rund, Marion/Lutz, Ronald/Fiegler, Tilo (2011): Kommunale Teilhabeplanung im Kontext Integrierter Sozialraumplanung. In: Lampke, Dorothea/Rohrmann, Albrecht/Schädler, Johannes (Ed.): Örtliche Teilhabeplanung mit und für Menschen mit Behinderungen. Wiesbaden: VS-Verlag, pp. 89–104.

Schädler, Johannes (2013): Überlegungen und Einschätzungen zum Inklusionsbegriff und zur UN- Behindertenrechtskonvention. In: eNewsletter Wegweiser Bürgergesellschaft 8/2013, 27.09.2013.https://www.buergergesellschaft.de/fileadmin/pdf/gastbeitrag_schaedler_130927.pdf [last accessed: 04/11/2022]

Schäfers, Markus (2013): Barrieren im Sozialraum – ein Kommentar. In: Becker, Ulrich/Wacker, Elisabeth/Banafsche, Minou (Ed.): Inklusion und Sozialraum. Behindertenrecht und Behindertenpolitik in der Kommune. Studien aus dem Max-Planck-Institut für Sozialrecht und Sozialpolitik, 59. Ed. Baden-Baden: Nomos, pp. 101–105.

Schnurr, Stefan (2005): Partizipation. In: Otto, Hans-Uwe/Thiersch, Hans/Böllert, Karin (Ed.): Handbuch Sozialarbeit, Sozialpädagogik. Basel: Ernst Reinhardt Verlag, pp. 1330–1345.

Schwanenflügel, Larissa von/Walther, Andreas (2012): Partizipation und Teilhabe. In: Bockhorst, Hildegard/Reinwand-Weiss, Vanessa-Isabelle/Zacharias, Wolfgang (Ed.): Handbuch kulturelle Bildung. München: Kopäd-Verlag.

Strauss, Anselm L./Corbin, Juliet M. (2010): Grounded Theory. Grundlagen qualitativer Sozialforschung. Weinheim: Beltz.

Strauss, Florian (2005): Soziale Netzwerke und Sozialraumorientierung. Gemeindepsychologische Anmerkungen zur Sozialraumdebatte. In: Projekt Netzwerke im Stadtteil (Ed.): Grenzen des Sozialraums. Kritik eines Konzepts – Perspektiven für Soziale Arbeit. Wiesbaden: VS Verlag für Sozialwissenschaften, pp. 73–85.

Thiersch, Hans/Grunwald, Klaus (2014): Lebensweltorientierung. In: Otto, Hans-Uwe/Thiersch, Hans (Ed.): Handbuch Soziale Arbeit. 5th ext. edition. München, Basel: Reinhardt, pp. 934–943.

Wansing, Gudrun (2015): Was bedeutet Inklusion? Annäherung an einen vielschichtigen Begriff. In: Degener, Thomas/Diehl, Elke (Ed.): Handbuch Behindertenrechtskonvention. Teilhabe als Menschenrecht – Inklusion als gesellschaftliche Aufgabe. Bonn: Bundeszentrale für politische Bildung, pp. 43–54.

Welti, Felix (2011): Rechtliche Grundlagen einer örtlichen Teilhabeplanung. In: Lampke, Dorothea/Rohrmann, Albrecht/Schädler, Johannes (Ed.): Örtliche Teilhabeplanung mit und für Menschen mit Behinderungen. Wiesbaden: VS-Verlag, pp. 55–67.

Wohlgensinger, Corinne (2014): Behinderung und Menschenrechte: ein Verhältnis auf dem Prüfstand. Opladen/Berlin/Toronto: Budrich UniPress.

Innovation in local social service infrastructure – eco-rational logics and collective learning

Johannes Schädler, Lars Wissenbach

Introduction

Local governments[1] are frequently faced with the obligation to implement new rules and regulations in various political sectors of their territory. The transfer of innovative policies into existing structures and routines poses a major challenge both for the implementing agencies and the stakeholders involved. This seems to especially be the case in the social services sector, where modernisation processes at times not only conflict with traditional assumptions on the role of beneficiaries but also question existing service concepts and organisations. A specific type of policymaking is required from local governments, be it when it comes to introducing new national or regional legislation into local practice, implementing political decisions of their local parliament or reacting to requests from local civil society initiatives. This is due to the fact that the implementation of policies into local practices goes beyond authority-based execution of regulatory prescriptions. New rules have to be explained, adapted and transferred into practicable local solutions. Interventions of policymakers to change routines in the provision of social services usually affect the interests and power relations of all organisations involved, including federal, state and local agencies, non-statutory and private service organisations, political and administrative bodies and the beneficiaries. This can lead to resistance and conflict among powerful local stakeholders who cannot always be expected to consider innovations to actually serve their interests.

This article seeks to discuss the implications of complex local social policy environments for innovation in social service provision with reference to planning and implementation theories. The article basically argues for a broad conceptualisation of local social planning which is understood as an approach for

---

1 The text refers to the 'local level' as districts, cities, towns, villages or groupings of villages that form a sub-provincial entity with a democratically elected local council with budgetary powers and a local administration with the power to take administrative or policy decisions for that area, within the legal and institutional framework of the state.

the implementation of innovative policies framed as processes of collective learning. We develop our argumentation with regard to a policy case in the German district of Siegen-Wittgenstein situated in the state of North Rhine-Westphalia. The respective policy aims to tackle problems of sectoralisation in social services infrastructure in order to realise a more integrated system of care and social support. Hereby we refer to empirical research that was conducted between 2017 and 2021 in cooperation with the Siegen-Wittgenstein district authorities (Schädler/Wittchen/Reichstein 2019; Schädler/Reichstein 2019; Schädler et al. 2021).

Based on this concrete policy case, we will first discuss the implementation of social service innovations against Yeheskel Hasenfeld's and Thomas Brock's (1991) 'political economy model of implementation'. They conceptualise implementation as "a process of organizational change" in a complex political environment. In implementation processes, all actors involved have to learn about discrepancies between existing and planned practices in feedback loops and to adapt "to new symbols, values and institutional rules" (ibid.: 466). Based on reflections on the limitations of the 'political economy model', in a second step, this is complemented by a 'reflexive framework for collective learning and social innovation' suggested by De Blust, Devisch and Schreurs (2019).

1. The policy case: from sectoralisation of services to inclusive social infrastructure

Since the United Nations Convention on the Rights of Persons with Disabilities (CRPD) was ratified by the German government in 2009 it has become one of the main drivers for policies to modernise the service system for people with disabilities. In our understanding, the need for modernisation arises when new superior concepts for a certain social domain are available but the given infrastructure does not allow for their realisation. Recently, the provisions of the CRPD have been codified in national and regional German legislation calling for the reform of traditional service systems[2]. However, when it comes to implementing the Convention's provisions, new local policies for developing inclusive social infrastructure are also needed in order to improve the living conditions of people with disabilities and of other groups who are at substantial risk of discrimination. It is the local communities where barriers take concrete shape and where inclusive infrastructure becomes a local governance task.

---

2   I.e. the Bundesteilhabegesetz (Participation Law) and corresponding legislation on federal level.

Innovation in local social service infrastructure 179

When service concepts change from placing people with disabilities and complex care needs in institutions to individual support arrangements in the community, inherent limitations of traditional service concepts become obvious. The more people with disabilities and major dependencies live in inclusive settings in their community, the more they rely on flexible support arrangements.

In the following, findings from empirical research in the German district of Siegen-Wittgenstein will be outlined (see Schädler/Wittchen/Reichstein 2019; Schädler et al. 2021), in order to illustrate the problem which is to be tackled by the implementation project: Existing boundaries between different social service sectors tend to become disabling when it comes to providing inclusive service arrangements. This is what is meant by sectoralisation and is described in its consequences below.

1.1 Sectoralisation of social services and placing problems

People with major support needs who live in inclusive settings in a local community mostly rely on the support of professional services in day-to-day life. When planning an individual support arrangement, the services which appear to be most appropriate for a person's needs must be identified. Due to various reasons such as professionalism, tradition or legislation, social services tend to be organised in rather segregated sectors that have developed over decades. The sectoral fields[3] examined in the district of Siegen-Wittgenstein were the 'disability field' with around 40 services, the 'mental health field' with around 30 services and the 'long-term care for the elderly field' with approx. 120 ser-

---

3   We use the term 'field' with reference to the understanding of 'organisational field' in neo-institutional approaches in organisational analysis (DiMaggio/Powell 1983). An organisational field can be defined as "those organizations that, in the aggregate, constitute a recognized area of institutional life: key suppliers, resource and product consumers, regulatory agencies, and other organizations that produce similar services or products" (ibid.: 64). On this basis, it can be assumed that single disability services are interconnected to other disability service organisations in their region and thus form a field. Such fields share conceptual assumptions, knowledge, have specific forms of interaction, power structures and are aware of a common purpose. With regard to development paths of organisations and their fields it seems plausible that 'history matters', i.e. "initial choices preclude future options, including those that would have been more effective in the long run (...). Altering institutional rules always involves high switching costs, thus a host of political, financial and cognitive considerations mitigate against making such changes" (Powell 1991: 183). Recognising path-dependency can explain why paradigmatic changes of given institutional practices in disability services are so hard to realise in practice (cf. Schaedler 2018).

vices. Data showed that services in each of the fields tend to operate in parallel and in a rather unconnected manner even in identical territories, while mostly co-operating exclusively with services of their particular field. Such sectoralisation of services is encouraged by a shared legal basis and shared implicit assumptions of the actors involved about the purpose of their service organisation and its target group. Sectoralisation structures the composition of organisations in a service field, work routines and staff qualification profiles. It also shapes administrative governance structures, planning routines and information flows as well as the organisation of self-advocacy. Sectoralisation has a strong impact on the day-to-day routines of service provision for people with major dependencies. When people with complex needs are seeking advice or support, they often end up in a suboptimal situation. While they may require the competencies of different service fields, people with complex needs will still find themselves being assigned to a specific field, no matter whether they fully match the needs profile of that supposed target group. Such 'placing problems' can result in assistance not being provided, hasty client identification or inappropriate forms of support. A high degree of specialisation of certain services within fields regarding target groups (i.e., services for persons with specific types of impairments) further complicates the situation for clients as well as for services. The more services seek to operate in inclusive settings providing flexible support, the more they experience the barriers and interfaces between the different service fields.

On the system level, cooperation of services between the sectors as required for inclusion-oriented service concepts appears to be only weakly developed[4]. Data showed that services from different sectors work on similar day-to-day problems in the same territories in parallel, creating situations with unclear responsibilities for complex cases and lack of transparency for clients. On the one hand, this limits opportunities for sound individual support and, on the other, it leads to parallel, uncoordinated investments into intersecting activities. These tendencies undermine more generic approaches towards an inclusive local social infrastructure. The more service systems aim at specific target groups, the more they produce problems of placing, knowledge deficits and suboptimal results.

---

4   See also the concept of "isolated islands" in social policy governance as described by Schubert (2018).

Innovation in local social service infrastructure

1.2 Sectoralisation and problems of linking with informal community resources

Service fields are likely to develop tendencies of self-reference. In particular, more generic services that could complement professional social services, as well as the resources of informal support, have not yet been adequately integrated into service arrangements. In the three fields examined, management and monitoring of social services were largely driven by the logics of different funding streams and focused on marketable services. Linking community development activities with formal service provision holds potential for inclusive service provision which operates in close connection with the socio-spatial realities of the people for whom it is designed. However, this potential so far remains largely untapped.

1.3 Sectoralisation and labour shortages

The need for modernisation of service concepts is contradicted by the rapidly increasing labour shortage which is seriously affecting all areas of the care and social support infrastructure. Conceptual improvements of the past years such as personalised services, inclusive in-home support and participatory community work are becoming difficult to maintain. Due to staffing problems and fiscal threats, even roll-back phenomena can be observed e. g. when persons with care needs are forced to live in institutionalised settings against their will or are left without appropriate support. Strategies of single service organisations to recruit staff are still highly isolated and sometimes even competitive whereas in the given situation coordinated cross sectoral approaches to tackle staff shortages appear to be more promising.

1.4 Sectoralisation and lack of provision of services in rural areas

Available services in Siegen-Wittgenstein were rather concentrated in urban areas, whereas rural areas were rather underprovided. This poses even more of a problem, as with sectoralisation the counselling centres, support and care services tend to provide support with a narrow focus on their own range of services and field. This creates challenges for people seeking advice and calls for a more cross-sectoral approach, especially in rural areas. Further, with the privatisation and marketisation of in-home care services over the past decade, people with care needs in rural and sparsely populated regions run the risk of becoming unprofitable customers for mobile care services.

Based on such empirical findings, a development initiative termed "Siegen-Wittgenstein 2030 – Inclusion in Sustainable Communities" was conceptualised in 2019 and suggested for implementation. The initiative is based on the principles of integrated planning and care. Its concept is briefly outlined in the following.

2. "Siegen-Wittgenstein 2030 – Inclusion in sustainable communities" – Key elements[5]

The concept is guided by the overall objective of developing the district towards an 'inclusive community'[6] that allows inclusion and full participation of all. A commitment was approved by the district parliament that both the district and all its municipalities are to provide a more accessible and needs-based social infrastructure with inclusive community services. To this end, they are to utilise and promote the potential of intercommunal cooperation and civic engagement. Explicitly, community service arrangements should provide people with disabilities, mental health conditions or elderly people with long-term care needs with the option to live independently in their homes as long as they want to do so. This is to be facilitated by systematic coordination of cooperation between services on the individual case level and on the level of service organisations in the district.

Most relevantly, the concept contains recommendations for the decentralisation of planning and service structures at district level. As a key element, it suggests structuring the district territory with its eleven municipalities into five planning regions. In each of the five regions, a new type of integrated contact

---

5 See: Schädler et al. (2021, paper 9)
6 The objective of developing strategies is to organise thinking on a topic in a certain direction (cf. Healey 2006). The vision of an inclusive community is meant to provide a guiding concept and framework for the desired change process. It refers to a policy approach that seeks to develop inclusive structures, cultures and practices at the local level with a political mandate through which local governments enable participative processes and create conditions to overcome the exclusion of people with disabilities and other social groups. Furthermore, the inclusive community denotes a planning approach that creates conditions in the local community that enable every person to lead a self-determined life within the mainstream social institutions of the life course (cf. Rohrmann et al. 2014).

and clearing point for social and care issues (Teilhabe- und Pflegestützpunkte, TEPS) is to be established.

Figure 1: Suggested structure of integrated contact and clearing points for social and care issues (Teilhabe- und Pflegestützpunkte, TEPS) in the district of Siegen-Wittgenstein

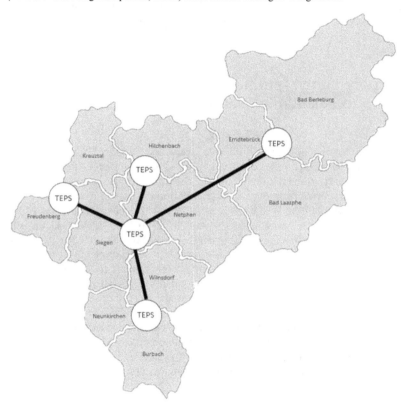

The TEPS concept is based on the idea of a so-called "single window" or "one-stop-shop" approach that guides citizens to appropriate service arrangements based on their needs. The increasing significance of integrating public services through single window approaches since the 2000s can be seen as a reaction to the negative effects of the New Public Management agenda. This had a focus on vertical specialisation and horizontal differentiation, which contributed to a fragmentation of the public sector (cf. Christensen/Filmreite/Laegreid 2006). Among so-called "single window" or "one-stop-shop" approaches, Hagen and Kubicek (2000) distinguish between "first stop", "convenience store" and "true one-stop". A "first stop" is described in terms of an information desk that guides citizens to the appropriate services according to their needs. In a "convenience store", a wide range of services are located in a single location whereas more comprehensive services cannot be provided here (cf. Hagen/Kubicek 2000). With regard to the TEPS concept, a combination of these functions is envisaged. As the model in Figure 1 shows, different services from different sectors are to be offered in such an innovative facility which can evolve gradually over time.

3. Applying the 'political economy model of implementation' for strategy development

The implementation of a more integrated care and support concept outlined above affects existing patterns of service provision in Siegen-Wittgenstein but also cooperation routines within the district administration, aligned district municipalities and service providers. Implementation clearly has to intervene into established local planning structures, service delivery processes and many routinised practices of the stakeholders involved. Even though the reasons and objectives of the reform concept appear generally convincing, implementers face a challenging process that requires organisational changes for a relatively high number of organisational actors involved. This is due to the multi-organisational setting where each of the many organisations affected has its particular goals and decision-making premises that shape everyday activities. In such multi-organisational settings, implementing change through hierarchical decisions does not seem to be an option. Instead, it can be assumed that cooperation, negotiation and compromise in finding common goals and defining change processes will enable joint decisions towards change. Thus, an appropriate strategy is required that might lead to a successful outcome of the implementation process over time.

In the following, the assumptions on implementation as a "political economy model" by Hasenfeld and Brock (1991) will be reflected upon in terms of their relevance to an implementation strategy for the Siegen case. According to Hasenfeld and Brock, an implementation process should be considered as "iterative, time-bounded, and involving organizational learning" (ibid.: 466). We will discuss five key components of the model, namely (1) policymaking, (2) policy instruments, (3) critical actors, (4) driving forces, and (5) service delivery system (ibid.: 466 ff). These key components will be applied to the Siegen case.

3.1 Policymaking

Following Hasenfeld and Brock (1991), the development and implementation of the integrated care reform in the district of Siegen-Wittgenstein can be understood as a process of *'policymaking'* (ibid.: 466). When starting, the implementers will have to frame the problem that is to be tackled. They will have to explain why they prefer the specific solution they want to implement over the current status and other options. Moreover, they will have to specify the political instruments that are intended to be used for implementation. Hasenfeld and Brock (ibid.) indicate that policy making processes often consist of "separate streams of problems, policies, and politics that become coupled into one package when a policy window opens"[7]. Therefore, it will be conducive for the implementation process if no conflicting or incompatible problems or solutions become coupled, and the policy-making environment is stable and allows a coherent use of policy instruments. Given the complexity of local governance systems, this can certainly not be taken for granted but has to be reflected by implementers during the entire process.

For the case of Siegen-Wittgenstein, an implementation strategy is to integrate separate streams of problems, policies and politics in the fields of long-term care, mental health and disability. The overlaps present in the problem settings and solution strategies of the three fields were outlined above. A promising implementation strategy must seek to coordinate field related solutions while considering the specific characteristics of involved stakeholders in order to sustain a stable policy-making environment. It can be assumed that the policy window in the district of Siegen-Wittgenstein is open and favourable for implementation. This is due to various factors such as a decision in favour of a social space-oriented approach to social policy, new legal requirements and, specifically, the current structural realignment of the district's social planning towards an integrated social service approach. Most importantly, this is supported by a relatively strong political will that has already been expressed through a resolution of the local council and through sustained political pres-

---

7   In order to understand a certain field of action, political science suggests differentiating between a field's polity, policies and politics. Polity refers to the set of political actors (stakeholders) in a field, policy is understood as the strategies that those actors develop and pursue, and politics relates to the concrete actions that are undertaken by individuals or organisations. In the context of agenda setting theories, a "policy window" describes a window of opportunity to place a certain topic on the political agenda. According to Kingdon (2011), the opening of such windows is influenced by various factors like e.g. specific events that emphasise the occurrence of specific problems, the specification and compatibility of policy options or alternative solutions at hand as well as organised political forces to support the agenda setting of a specific issue (ibid.).

sure from local political stakeholders. Hence, the policy-making environment seems relatively stable and might allow a coherent use of policy instruments.

3.2 Policy instruments

Effective implementation, according to Hasenfeld and Brock (1991), is generally based on three *'policy instruments'*: authority, programme design and resources (ibid.: 466). The implementers of the Siegen case will need sufficient *authority*, i.e. power to elicit compliance among stakeholders in the political arena in which decisions for change are being made and later realised in practice. In the district governance system, authority is diffused among several agencies within and outside the district government that are not in any direct hierarchy. This increases the risk of interagency conflicts and the need for cooperation and negotiation. As emphasised above, opportunities for decision making through hierarchy are limited in multi-organisational contexts. Therefore, it will be key to establish appropriate forums to communicate and negotiate different interests from the very outset.

Furthermore, the clarity and consistency of the reform programme to be implemented is of central relevance for successful implementation. If the *programme design* of the integrated care reform is questionable, e.g. if it shows major inconsistencies with the organisational goals of individual stakeholders, successful implementation will be at stake. As the reform affects a relatively large group of stakeholders, a diverse sample of needs and interests will have to be considered in the concrete formulation and adaption of a respective implementation concept. *Resources* clearly can be regarded as a very effective policy instrument. They include the availability and allocation of money, personnel, skills, and facilities, but also incentives for stakeholders to participate in the implementation process (ibid.: 466). The more resources are available, the more comprehensively the programme design can be implemented, because stakeholders will tend to adapt their involvement to actively participate in the implementation process. The available resources will also be seen as an indicator of how serious the political will is to realise the planned outcome. The extent to which individual stakeholders are committed to the implementation of common goals will be reflected in their readiness to contribute own resources.

3.3 Critical actors

With regard to *'critical actors'* in implementation processes, Hasenfeld and Brock (1991) differentiate between the implementing agency(ies), typically a government bureaucracy in charge of assembling the programme components, and the stakeholders. Following their argumentation (ibid.: 468) it is conducive for successful implementation processes if a strong and coherent *"dominant coalition"* can be organised on the implementers' side, (i.e. an internal steering group that controls key resources) which is fully in line with the programme design. Otherwise, it will become difficult "to translate programme requirements into coherent technical specifications" (ibid.). For the case of Siegen-Wittgenstein, such an implementing agency is located at an only recently established staff unit for integrated social planning. This staff unit is linked to the head of department of social affairs and seeks to monitor and coordinate all areas of social affairs within the district.

On the other hand, there are the stakeholders that comprise the groups and organisations whose commitment and active participation is needed to operationalise a policy. Hasenfeld and Brock (ibid.) define stakeholders as those who control "commodities" of various kinds needed for the implementation of a programme design. Such commodities can consist of services or expertise but can also have a different form such as political authority, support and legitimation. Again, this creates a political arena in which the implementing agency will have to make compromises with other parties involved in the process. How this will influence the implementation process depends on the number of stakeholders and the degree to which they are organised. For the Siegen case, both the number of relevant stakeholders and their degree of organisation was found to be relatively high (e.g. political parties, government agencies, public service providers, private service providers, users/beneficiaries, self-help groups, neighbourhood initiatives and volunteers, each from at least three different fields). They therefore have a high capacity to influence the implementation process. On the one hand, this can lead to important improvements in the overall outcomes of the implementation process. On the other hand, stakeholders can use their power to ward off approaches that threaten their interests. Such high diversity and power of stakeholders suggests that implementation can only succeed as a moderated and collaborative process.

3.4 Driving forces

Hasenfeld and Brock (ibid.: 469) identify three interrelated *'driving forces'* in the implementation process of social policies: technological, economical and power relations. First, the implementation of a policy such as the integrated care reform in Siegen-Wittgenstein needs the *"technical operationalisation"* of the concept into practical steps. If these steps are rational and coherent, it will be easier to keep to principles of the programme design amid competing perspectives and interests to change or stop the process for ideological, fiscal or political reasons. Both, implementing agencies and stakeholders, consider the effects of costs when engaging in an implementation process (ibid.: 470). These economic considerations refer to the costs that are related to changes in the production of services in a future setting. They also might contain opportunity costs (e.g. possible losses or gains when joining an implementation process) or transaction costs that might arise when new practices are to be established in their organisations. In the case of the integrated care reform in Siegen-Wittgenstein, it can be assumed that the more coherently implementation steps are formulated, the more easily cost considerations can be made.

According to Hasenfeld and Brock, the mobilisation of power – within the implementing agencies and among stakeholders – is the "currency with which cooperation and compliance is attained" (ibid.: 471). Concentrated power on the implementers' side would combine hierarchical authority, resource control and network centrality. If these conditions for *power relations* were to prevail in the case of the integrated care reform in Siegen-Wittgenstein, the chances for successful implementation of the programme design would be high. However, as in the given case, there are multiple stakeholders to be involved, it can be expected that some of them will start coalition building and thus concentrate power. This must not necessarily become a problem for the implementation process as long as these coalitions accept the key elements of programme design and cooperate. In the present case, additional complexity can also arise from the fact that individual stakeholders may compete with each other in a partially privatised market of social services. Generally, Hasenfeld and Brock suggest that the implementers should occupy a central coordinating position in the interorganisational network of actors. This position potentially allows them to "have greater control over the terms of exchanges" and manage potential conflicts that could lower the quality of the expected outcome of the process (ibid.: 471).

3.5 Service delivery system

According to Hasenfeld and Brock (ibid.: 472) *'service delivery systems'* consist of three interrelated components. The "technical core" can be understood as the single service organisations that provide different kinds of support to their target population. These single service organisations form an "interorganisational network" together with other organisations they need for their day-today operations in service provision. Thirdly, this interorganisational network can have "monitoring mechanisms" with which its effectiveness can be measured. Hasenfeld and Brock assume that it is detrimental to the successful implementation of a programme design if the conceptual and economic implications for single services involved are highly uncertain. In the Siegen case, such uncertainty can possibly be limited if a monitoring system were to become part of the implementation process.

4. Beyond the political economy model: local planning and collective learning

In the previous section, we have attempted to apply insights from the political economy model to the development of an appropriate implementation strategy for the integrated care reform in Siegen-Wittgenstein. Certainly, Hasenfeld and Brock (1991) include elements of political power and opportunity in their model. Still, it seems that they base their analysis mainly on rationality assumptions and economic considerations while giving little attention to institutional forces and citizens' interest in collective action. While the approach makes political and technical features of change processes understandable, it remains somewhat vague with regard to the cultural and civic dimension of collective change in social policy development. The political economy model of implementation cannot explain what might motivate local actors to bring in their own resources, to put their own interests at stake and to negotiate collective goals beyond purely eco-rational considerations. With regard to experiences with local community planning (see e.g. Schädler/Wissenbach 2021) we suggest framing the economic understanding of implementation with the concept of 'collective learning' in a given local governance system.

Collective learning can be defined as "a concept that gives insight in how a diverse group of individuals work on processes of shared problematisation and a shared sense of meaning" (De Blust/Devisch/Schreurs 2019: 20). It does not refer to an aggregate of individual learnings (including single organisations) but to a cumulative process of sharing and a co-creative further developing of individual knowledge through a relation of belonging (cf. Garavan/Carbery 2012). Collective learning processes result in the acquisition of new knowledge among the group of collective actors which might help to elaborate the concept and structures to be implemented in more concrete terms and guide future action. Learning thereby becomes the result of the interaction of individual knowledge that is jointly developed further. Garavan and Carbery (ibid.: 646) refer to this as "an evolutionary process of perfecting collective knowledge".

We argue that it is this kind of evolutionary process of collective learning that needs to be built and shaped in implementation processes. Collective learning, as discussed in social innovation studies, is the creation of "the possibility to collectively appropriate, deconstruct and reconstruct information and knowledge, taking into account a diverse set of life-worlds and value alternatives for existing dominant positions" (De Blust/Devisch/Schreurs 2019: 20). With regard to the Siegen case, implementers would not be in the position of merely explaining objectives to other stakeholders but instead facilitating a co-creative development of an innovative agenda in order to review and change existing structures and provide them with new meanings. In such a perspective, the conceptual idea of the TEPS might serve as a starting point for such an agenda development. The "implementing agency" and its "dominant coalition" would not mainly try to achieve implementation of results through hierarchy and decision-making power. Instead, they would rather focus on the initiation and moderation of processes of collective learning. The starting point could be a discussion with stakeholders on the given problem of sectoralisation and what a TEPS approach could actually look like in practice. Thus, the process can be based on "collective sense making" (Healey/Hillier 2008; Healy 2006).

4.1 Multiple loyalties and belongings of actors

Collective learning goes beyond the cooperation of stakeholders. While cooperation usually refers to sharing resources and the division of some labour across stakeholders in order to achieve compatible goals, collective learning rather takes place in processes of collaboration. Collaboration means that stakeholders share risks, resources, responsibilities, and rewards in a process of shared creation and implementation of a programme of activities to achieve a common goal. Collective learning therefore is facilitated when there is a common rather than compatible visions. Such arrangements build on a high degree of trust among stakeholders which cannot be presumed but evolves through common investment of time, effort, and dedication of actors. As in the Siegen case, collaboration can happen because stakeholders from intersecting fields (disability, care, mental health) that share a specific locality decide to implement a place-based reform concept. Actors therefore might act not only in the interest of their particular organisation but due to their sense of belonging to the respective local community and thus develop loyalty to the common interest. This implies a reflection on what winning and losing actually means for single actors in a collaborative endeavour to promote inclusive infrastructure.

Accordingly, the question arises as to how such collaborative stakeholder arrangements can be developed in a concrete region. How can political representatives, government agencies, public service providers, private service pro-

Innovation in local social service infrastructure 191

viders, beneficiaries/users, self-help groups, neighbourhood initiatives and volunteers from different fields enter into a collective learning process that leads to relevant implementation results? How can "implementing agencies" like the Siegen-Wittgenstein staff unit for integrated social planning tackle the coordination of such a highly complex endeavour?

De Blust, Devisch, and Schreurs (2019) propose a reflexive framework that conceptualises social innovation processes as situated trajectories of collective learning. In this framework, learning is modelled along three basic dimensions, namely 'qualification' (capacities), 'socialisation' and 'subjectification'. Moreover, De Blust, Devisch, and Schreurs (ibid.: 21) assume that "five core collective capabilities" can be found in all organisations and systems. These are "(1) to commit and engage, (2) to carry out functions or tasks, (3) to relate and attract resources and support, (4) to adapt and self-renew, and (5) to balance coherence and diversity". They argue that the status of each of these collective capabilities in single organisations indicates "the overall capacity of a group to engage in processes of collective learning" (ibid.) Looking at the diversity of stakeholders in the Siegen-Wittgenstein case, it can be assumed that these capabilities are given, but differ widely among organisations involved.

Such a framework can build a conceptual starting point for implementing agencies like the staff unit for integrated social planning in Siegen-Wittgenstein to (a) create promising conditions for the diversity of stakeholder capabilities to join in (how can we create conditions which encourage relevant stakeholders to make a maximum contribution?), (b) support individual stakeholders in finding and specifying contributive and satisfying roles (what individual requirements and opportunities might stakeholders require to join in?), (c) enhance the collective capabilities of the group (how to help the group with one of their five core capabilities?), and (d) assess the potential of the overall learning process to bring about sustainable change (what does the capability set-up of the group look like?). The development of such capabilities represents a conceptualisation of learning in terms of knowledge and skills acquisition, which is referred to in the first dimension of *'qualification'* mentioned above.

A second dimension of collective learning is defined by De Blust, Devisch and Schreurs (2019) as *'socialisation'*. With this term, they refer to the adaptation of individuals and organisations to existing provisions and dominant ideas. Thus, they contribute to the mere reproduction of an existing order and its related norms and values. Socialisation in the collective learning model reduces learning to reproducing instutionalised routines of working predefined by external decisions (ibid.: 21 f.). In contrast to socialisation, *'subjectification'* is added as a third dimension of collective learning. It entails modes of learning that focus on the development of political agency and thus foster the formation of subjectivity among actors (Biesta 2010). De Blust et al. link to

Biesta's concept of a "pedagogy of interruption"[8] (Biesta ibid.). Here subjectification refers to achieving a certain independence from the existing order and its related norms and values as well as the importance of reflexivity being "the continuous emergence of alternative collective imaginaries and engagement" (De Blust/Devisch/Schreurs 2019: 22). With regard to socially innovative practices, subjectification is crucial to develop a political and transformative potential. For the case of Siegen-Wittgenstein, this requires an implementation strategy that offers room for 'subjectification' which allows for transformative change. When implementers are presenting the design of the reform they should clearly indicate that the concept is wide open for further conceptualisation. If not, implementers may run a high risk of only achieving suboptimal results or even failing.

The reflexive framework of collective learning offers a helpful perspective for conceptualising an implementation strategy for situations with multi-organisational and rather non-hierarchical settings such as in the Siegen case. It provides an understanding of stakeholders as active participants in an open process that can be shaped by collaboration. The process is to be based on a shared vision that makes sense to the actors involved. However, questions arise as to what extent the participation of participants in the process is the only decisive factor for achieving desired results and whether effective strategies can be reduced to the facilitation of stakeholder communication. In spite of efforts to come to a shared vision and to develop innovative measures based on consent, some actors involved may find themselves in a disadvantaged position and may start to obstruct the process. Others might still want to impose their interests on others. Therefore, it would be short-sighted to ignore the significance of power and authority for successful implementation that shapes the Hasenfeld and Brock model. As a consequence, it appears reasonable to integrate the main insights of both approaches to develop an appropriate implementation strategy for the Siegen case.

5. Conclusion

Developing inclusive local communities is an ongoing challenge for both policy makers and civil society actors in municipalities, which is related to the

---

8 Biesta (2010: 91) calls for a "pedagogy committed to the possibility of interruption" and that perhaps itself will interrupt, entailing a process that is not driven by knowledge about what the citizen is or should become according to a socialisation conception of citizenship, but one in which – in line with the basic idea of democracy – the borders of the political order are constantly questioned and re-drawn to allow for new political identities and subjectivities to come into existence.

initiation of change processes in organisations and local infrastructures. It can be assumed that the management of such change processes can be facilitated when based on theory.

This article seeks to contribute to implementation theory in the context of local social politics. It discusses two different theoretical perspectives on the implementation of innovations in the field of social services referring to the Integrated Care Strategy in the German district of Siegen-Wittgenstein as a case. It becomes evident that the perspectives presented differ in their foci and assumptions on how to understand the implementer's role when trying to achieve implementation results. For multi-organisational and rather less hierarchical settings, as described in the Siegen-Wittgenstein case, the political economy model leaves unclear how to bring stakeholders on board. It builds on a rather technical assumption of learning as socialisation where stakeholders are to be convinced to support a strategy or concept developed by the "implementers" that should form "a dominant coalition" of powerful experts. In contexts that, on the one hand, deal with the reduction of social inequalities and the promotion of social inclusion supported by social services and, on the other hand, are defined by stakeholder set-ups with no hierarchical decision-making structures but major power/resource inequalities, a democratic process, that includes all voices and that creates space for social innovation appears ambitious to realise. Such a perspective is based on the idea of controlling or dominating stakeholders' voices in a rational process where assumed innovative ideas of dominant stakeholders are negotiated and where the planner facilitates negotiations among stakeholders.

This has been placed in contrast to a collective learning approach to local social planning that seeks to create space for the empowerment of voices and collective action. Along the reflexive framework of De Blust, Devisch and Schreurs (2019), it was outlined how the example of Siegen-Wittgenstein could be conceptualised as an innovative process of collective learning. The analytic perspective suggested by De Blust et al. can assist implementers in developing a more comprehensive understanding of the process. Assessing collective capabilities of the relevant stakeholders can provide information for implementers on the potential for a joint learning process to achieve the desired change. Assessing the balance between the learning dimensions of socialisation and subjectification can be used for self-reflection and to draw conclusions about the openness and the effective innovative potential of the learning process.

The theoretical framing offers the possibility for implementers, such as the staff unit in the district of Siegen-Wittgenstein, to overcome challenges by providing a conceptual orientation for a meta-perspective on a process. Implementers are to be understood not only as facilitators of the change process but also as participants in a collective learning process. Correspondingly, representatives e.g. of participating service organisations are not only acting as stakeholders for their particular interest but also as collective learners. This is supported by the fact that actors have multiple forms of belonging, which create loyalty both to their organisation and to the locality they share. The combination of theoretical approaches in the context of collective learning therefore opens up a structural-analytical view on the implementation of social innovations beyond traditional notions of planning. The trajectory of collective learning for the Siegen case then can become an iterative process of change in which a group of local stakeholders collectively tries to innovate access to quality services for people with long-term care needs, mental health conditions and dis-abilities in the district.

With this argumentation, we seek to underline a concept of socio-spatial planning as an open learning process for implementing change in complex local settings. Bringing together aspects of collective learning and eco-rational logics of policy implementation can create a reflexive framework for implementers to address a plurality of interests and demands. Within such a perspective, strategic planners are required to take an active, even activist[9] role, balancing but not dominating the power structures in the implementation process (cf. Albrechts 2015). In this sense, they become 'active generators' of collective learning processes.

References

Albrechts, Louis (2015): Ingredients for a More Radical Strategic Spatial Planning. Environment and Planning B: Planning and Design, 42(3), pp. 510–525. https://doi.org/10.1068/b130104p
Biesta, Gert (2010): Good Education in an Age of Measurement: Ethics, Politics, Democracy. London: Paradigm Publishers.
Christensen, Tom/Filmreite, Anne L./Laegreid, Per (2006): Reform of the employment and welfare administrations – the challenges of coordinating diverse public organisations. EGPA Study Group on Governance of Public Sector Organizations, EGPA Conference, Bocconi University, Milan, Sep. 2006.
De Blust, Seppe/Devisch, Oswald/Schreurs, Jan (2019): Towards a Situational Understanding of Collective Learning: A Reflexive Framework. In: Urban Planning 2019, Vol. 4, Issue 1, pp. 19-30. DOI: 10.17645/up.v4i1.1673
DiMaggio, Paul J./Powell, Walter W. (1983): The Iron Cage Revisited: Institutional Isomorphismus and Collective Rationality in Organization Fields. In: Powell, Walter W./DiMaggio, Paul J. (eds.): The new institutionalism in organizational analysis. Chicago: Univ. of Chicago Press (1991), pp. 63-82.

---

9 See e.g. Sager (2016) for the discourse on activist planning.

Garavan, Thomas N./Carbery, Ronan (2012): Collective Learning. In: Seel, Norbert M. (eds.) Encyclopedia of the Sciences of Learning. Boston, MA.: Springer, pp. 646-649. https://doi.org/10.1007/978-1-4419-1428-6_136

Hasenfeld, Yeheskel/Brock, Thomas (1991): Implementation of social policy revisited. In: Administration &Society, Vol. 22, Nr.4.1991, pp. 451-479.

Healey, Patsy (2006): Collaborative Planning. Shaping Places in Fragmented Societies. 2nd Edition. Basingstoke; New York: Palgrave Macmillan.

Healey, Patsy/Hillier, Jean (2008): Introduction. In: Hillier, Jean/Healey, Patsy (eds.): Foundations of the planning enterprise. Critical essays in planning theory (Vol. 1). Aldershot: Ashgate, pp. ix-xxvii.

Hagen, Martin/Kubicek, Herbert (2000): One-stop-government in Europe: an overview. Bremen: University of Bremen.

Kingdon, John W. (2011): Agendas, Alternatives, and Public Policies. Updated 2nd Edition. Boston: Longman.

Powell, Walter W. (1991): "Expanding the Scope of Institutional Analysis,". In: Powell, Walter W./DiMaggio, Paul J. (eds.): The new institutionalism in organizational analysis. Chicago: Univ. of Chicago Press (1991), pp. 183-203.

Rohrmann, Albrecht/Schädler, Johannes/Kempf, Matthias/Konieczny, Eva/Windisch, Markus (2014): Inklusive Gemeinwesen Planen. Eine Arbeitshilfe. Düsseldorf: Ministerium für Arbeit, Integration und Soziales des Landes Nordrhein-Westfalen.

Sager, Tore (2016): Activist planning: a response to the woes of neo-liberalism?. European Planning Studies, 24:7, pp. 1262-1280, DOI: 10.1080/09654313.2016.11 68784

Schädler, Johannes (2018): Vollzugsdefizit? – Örtliche Implementation als unterschätzte Herausforderung für behindertenpolitische Innovationen. In: Teilhabe 4/ 2018, Jg. 57, pp. 150-155.

Schädler, Johannes/Wittchen, Jan-Frederik/Reichstein, Martin F. (2019): Koordinationspotenziale kommunaler Teilhabepolitik in der Pflege, Behindertenhilfe und Sozialpsychiatrie (KoKoP). Düsseldorf: Forschungsinstitut für gesellschaftliche Weiterentwicklung (FGW-Impuls Vorbeugende Sozialpolitik 17).

Schädler, Johannes/Reichstein, Martin F. (2019): Sektoralisierung Sozialer Dienste als kommunales Koordinationsproblem – Empirische Befunde am Beispiel der Behindertenhilfe, Pflege und Sozialpsychiatrie. In: Sozialer Fortschritt, 68 (2019), pp. 819-838.

Schädler; Johannes/Wissenbach, Lars/Reichstein, Martin/Hohmann, Andreas (2021): Integrierte Teilhabe- und Pflegeplanung im Kreis Siegen-Wittgenstein. Siegen: Zentrum für Planung und Evaluation Sozialer Dienste (ZPE), Universität Siegen.

Schädler, Johannes/Wissenbach, Lars (2021): The role of local planning in the implementation of the UNCRPD. In: Siska, Jan/Beadle-Brown, Julie (eds.): The Development, Conceptualisation and Implementation of Quality in Disability Support Services. Prague: Karolinum Press (2021), pp. 313-328.

Schubert, Herbert (2018): Netzwerkorientierung in Kommune und Sozialwirtschaft. Wiesbaden: Springer VS Verlag für Sozialwissenschaften.

Towards a participatory disability policy in Switzerland: Confederation, cantons and municipalities in exchange with civil society

Giulia Brogini, Thomas Schuler

1. Self-determination of people with disabilities

One of the most important concerns of the UN Convention on the Rights of Persons with Disabilities is the implementation of opportunities for self-determination for persons with disabilities. However, self-determination can only be lived if all central areas of life, such as living and working, are designed close to the community and if the associated services are accessible to everyone. Within the framework of the right to self-determination of people with disabilities, it is consequently a matter of enabling each person to have an interplay of freedom of choice or decision, opportunities for participation and barrier-free supportive services that is geared as closely as possible to his or her individual concerns and needs. This is not a *favour* owed in the sense of state welfare to people with support needs. Rather, it is about *living equality* and *meeting* all people *based on equality*.

With the signing of the Convention on the Rights of Persons with Disabilities in 2014 and with the formulation of its first national disability policy in 2018 by the Federal Council, Switzerland has concretised the promotion of equality for persons with disabilities: In the course of the last five years, these foundations were expanded, for example at the federal level through specific multi-year programs as well as through action plans or legislative projects in the cantons, down to measures in the municipalities. The mission of the authorities is to continuously develop disability policy together with people with disabilities and their organisations, so that all decision-relevant information and offers for everyday life are accessible and understandable for everyone. This is particularly complex and challenging in times of rapid technological change or in times of crisis management (e.g., Covid 19 pandemic, migration, energy crisis, inflation).

In Switzerland, more than one fifth of the resident population lives with disabilities (Bundesamt für Statistik 2020: 7). This includes not only elderly people with support needs, but also people who were already confronted with limitations earlier in life. Overall, this population group is very heterogeneous, and the affected people live with various functional limitations and social barriers. According to survey results from the Swiss Federal Statistical Office, people with disabilities are less satisfied with their lives than the rest of the population. The greater the degree of disability, the greater the differences. This refers not only to their overall quality of life, but also to most areas of life, such as leisure time and activities in associations, clubs and political parties. The observed differences between people with and without disabilities have been largely stable since 2014. Other indicators, such as health status, financial situation, satisfaction with personal relationships and housing situation, also show similar findings. In this article, the question 'how can a better quality of life be achieved and how can the self-determination of people with disabilities be promoted?' will therefore be discussed. Therefore, a more barrier-free access to services and facilities for all, such as housing, mobility, shopping, education, work and leisure is required. To achieve this, Switzerland needs more individualised, inclusion-oriented support services, as also called for by the Disability Rights Committee.

2. Confederation, cantons and municipalities: Who implements the UN CRPD?

In Switzerland, all three federal levels of government are responsible for the implementation of the Disability Rights Convention, in particular also of Art. 19 UN CRPD: The federal government, the 26 cantons and the 2,148 municipalities. Compared to other European countries, the cantons have a high degree of autonomy. Each canton is constitutionally obliged to grant its municipalities extensive leeway and to involve them in all phases of political decision-making. Municipal autonomy is the constitutional right of municipalities to manage a substantial part of public affairs on their own responsibility. The scope of this municipal autonomy is defined by the respective cantonal law. It is therefore possible, or even mandatory in some cantons for certain fields of action, for the municipalities to enact their own law on issues relevant to disability equality. For example, the cantonal council of Basel-Landschaft passed the law on the rights of people with disabilities, which came into application in the canton on January 1, 2024. This obliges the municipalities to specify the implementation of the bill for their area of responsibility in a set of regulations. Furthermore, the cantons determine the degree of participation of the municipalities, in particular the forms of consultation in the drafting of cantonal legislation (Schefer et al. 2022: 186). Moreover, the enforcement of federal law is often the responsibility of the cantons as well as the municipalities. Although the

Federal Act on the Elimination of Discrimination against Persons with Disabilities ("BehiG") is a *federal law*, the cantons and the municipalities are still the decisive actors in its implementation in many substantive areas – which in practice has so far also required corresponding coordination among the three levels of government (Egger et al. 2015: 356). With its report on disability policy of 2018, the Federal Council indicated which common legal framework is decisive for the federal government and the cantons and which substantive thrusts should be pursued for the next four years: Two multi-year programs were defined for the period 2018 – 2022, one on *self-determined living* (federal government and cantons together) and one on *equality and work* (primarily federal level). In addition to the two multi-year programs, the thematic focus on *accessibility and digitalisation* was also added. The two programs and the thematic focus set important milestones in terms of content and regulated the interaction of the actors at the various federal levels. In this way, NGOs were also systematically integrated into the decision-making processes, for example by organising joint events and activities between representatives of the authorities and civil society (workshops, conferences, specialist events, project work) and by involving them in working and monitoring groups. The cooperation of all involved bodies of disability policy was thus made more transparent and binding in the last five years. The municipalities have a key role to play within the overall structure of state law, at least where they have core responsibility for disability equality measures. This applies, for example, to the design of public infrastructure (real estate and facilities, e.g. not only administrative and school buildings but also sports facilities or social amenities), the municipality's information and communication channels, and the personnel employed by the municipality.

By international standards, Switzerland is a highly decentralised country. The competences and rights of the municipalities are differentiated in different ways. In general, it can be said that *municipal autonomy* is more broadly defined in the German-speaking part of Switzerland than in the Ticino and the French-speaking part of Switzerland, which is mainly due to the different understanding of the state in the respective language and cultural regions. Thus, about one fifth of the municipalities have their own parliament, especially the cities. The rest of the municipalities organise themselves through municipal assemblies, in which all residents with voting rights can participate. Across Switzerland's national borders, the term "Röstigraben" has become well known. It is used to explain the different mentality – including the different voting results on federal proposals – between German-speaking and French-speaking Switzerland. In general, there is also a larger number of cantonal decrees in French-speaking Switzerland, for example.

For disability policy, this results in a wide range of options for action, action plans and checklists. Bundling this knowledge and making it accessible to all interested parties is not only a task for the state, but also for society as a whole. Important partners in disability policy are the trade associations of service providers for people with disabilities. In this context, the *UN CRPD Action Plan* with its catalogue of recommendations and support for community-based living, for example, should be highlighted. This website is constantly updated with good examples from practice, such as tips for finding housing, finding janitors, finding neighbourhoods, or for having meetings in the neighbourhood, for peer work, for social institutions, for landlords.

With a view to implementing the UN CRPD, the municipalities and cities, as well as the cantons, have already done considerable groundwork in many places. However, especially for smaller municipalities or for economically more burdened cantons, questions of balancing interests increasingly arise, because there is not only a lack of financial resources, but also of expertise and specialised personnel. In the prioritisation of the authorities, the concerns of people with disabilities are thus often put on the back burner. Therefore, the idea of inclusion must be further promoted at the federal level as well as in the cantons, the intercantonal conferences and the municipal authorities, the umbrella organisations of care for persons with disabilities, the associations of service enterprises and finally also in the associations of municipalities and cities. It will be an important task of the new 2023-2026 disability policy to involve *all* stakeholders earlier and more consistently as *active* partners, thus also the decentralised bodies as well as the non-governmental stakeholders. In order to implement independent living and inclusion in the community, the general accessibility of services must be brought into focus: From the most diverse uses of public space, to neighbourhood life, mobility, information and communication, self-determined and obstacle-free living, early intervention and family-supplementary care for children with disabilities, education, work, participation in political life, leisure, and health (Bertels 2022: 18).

3. The participation of people with disabilities in disability policy: examples from administrative practice

How does the interaction between the federal government, the cantons and the municipalities work, and how can disability equality be promoted? The following examples from administrative practice – a survey on the participation of people with disabilities in cantonal authorities and in organisations of people with disabilities as well as the instrument of project funding of the Confederation with five different project descriptions as examples – give an insight into different fields of action.

3.1 Surveys on the participation of people with disabilities

The aim of the surveys on the participation of people with disabilities was to obtain an overview of the inclusion of people with disabilities in the cantons. The term *participation* was understood to mean the *involvement of people with disabilities as experts in their own right*. The general participation in the processes of planning, implementation and evaluation of official measures was examined. It was asked what the challenges were in connection with the participation of people with disabilities and their organisations, and good examples of implementation were identified. In total, two surveys were launched: One with cantonal authorities and the other with civil society organisations. The questionnaire contained approximately the same questions for the two target groups, so that the results could be compared. This also allowed any differences in the assessment of the inclusion to be elicited.

In the first survey, the members of the specialist conference of cantonal commissioners for disability issues, to which all cantons belong, were questioned (EBGB 2021a). These are 26 heads of cantonal specialist offices for facilities for the disabled. The representatives of the authorities reflected critically on the measures taken by the authorities on the whole, which may seem surprising at first glance, since it is to a certain extent a matter of *self-criticism of the state's actions*. The promotion of the participation of people with disabilities was seen as highly complex in itself and also as a lengthy process. The authorities were clearly in favour of dealing with the participation of people with disabilities in greater depth in the future. The question as to whether the most important contact persons for people with disabilities or the most important organisations for people with disabilities were known in the canton was answered positively by the majority of those surveyed. The good cooperation between cantonal authorities and people with disabilities or their organisations was – according to the survey results – in most cases based on the fact that the actors would engage in a regular and constructive exchange of ideas. Concrete projects in the cantons – such as a legislative project, performance agreements, evaluations or cooperation in expert committees – were good opportunities to become familiar with the most important stakeholders in disability policy over a longer period of time and to exchange ideas. The professionalism of the cantonal and municipal specialist offices for people with disabilities that have emerged in recent years was emphasised. The authorities interviewed also wished to increase direct contact with people with disabilities through the organisations for people with disabilities. From their point of view, the authorities interviewed pointed out the gaps and limitations in the cooperation, such as when the resources or structures were lacking on the part of the disability organisations, for example, for longer-lasting project work. Regarding the inclusion of disability organisations in the general political process, for example in consultations, the authorities indicated that they did not give NGOs special treatment (with more time for processing, etc.). However, drafts in connection with disability assistance or disability equality were very much discussed in depth together in advance via industry associations and disability organisations. The survey showed that there is still potential for optimisation on the part of the authorities when it comes to accessibility to information and public relations: The authorities were most likely to pay attention to accessibility at public events, for example for people with limited mobility and for visually impaired people. They paid less attention to the accessibility of websites and the least to ensure that employees in the administration are sensitised and trained in dealing with people with disabilities in customer contact.

A second (parallel) survey, this time among the members of the network of conferences for people with disabilities, was about how the associations of people with disabilities assessed the participation in the general processes of planning, implementation and evaluation of official measures in all areas of life (EBGB 2021b). Of the 19 umbrella organisations contacted, 17 participated in the survey. The following points can be summarised from the responses:

From the point of view of civil society, a clear and reliable division of roles and tasks is necessary for good cooperation between the organisations of people with disabilities and the authorities. The organisations were decidedly critical of what they saw as insufficient opportunities for participation by the authorities in the planning phase, during implementation and in the evaluation of laws, projects and other measures. For successful cooperation in disability policy, more professional structures are needed on both sides – the state *and* civil society – for example with specialist or contact points. This would require sufficient and long-term stable funding of the disability associations as well as individual support for their employees and active members. Most of the disability associations (self-representation organisations as well as organisations of care for persons with disabilities) stated that they wanted to further promote participation also in their own structures. For effective self-representation, however, more people with disabilities with a corresponding interest, with a certain specialist or experiential knowledge and an understanding of socio-political contexts are needed. Furthermore, the activity and commitment of people with disabilities must generally be given greater appreciation (financial compensation, exchange based on equality, media resonance, etc.).

The organisations see the following approaches as necessary for the success of a participatory disability policy: People with disabilities and their organisations should be involved in all disability policy projects from the very beginning. Accessibility should be demanded not only in construction, housing, infrastructure and public transport, but also in all public services and offers. In order to implement this, the participation of people with disabilities could, for example, be a criterion to be fulfilled in service agreements between the authorities and the service providers. In addition, specific counselling and support services are needed to enable particularly vulnerable groups to participate in life in the community.

3.2 Federal financial assistance: Pilot projects to promote independent living

Through the Federal Office for the Equality of Persons with Disabilities ("EBGB"), the Confederation supports projects that sustainably promote the equality of persons with disabilities. Projects from various areas are supported, such as education, work, housing, leisure, culture and sports. Projects are funded that are carried out by an organisation active throughout Switzerland or in a language region, by a canton or a municipality. In the case of pilot projects for professional integration into working life, companies can also be supported. It is the responsibility of the sponsor to provide a certain proportion of its own contributions or other sources of funding. In the following, five projects are presented as examples, which focus in particular on the *participation of* people with disabilities.

3.2.1 Disability Rights Action Days in the Canton of Zurich

The Zurich Cantonal Social Welfare Office – a public authority – and the Disability Conference of the Canton of Zurich – a civil society organisation – organised Action Days for the first time in 2022 in the Canton of Zurich, Switzerland's most populous canton. The Action Days took place from August 27 to September 10, 2022. 113 action partners took part. Among them were municipal authorities, sports clubs, self-advocacy organisations, cultural institutions, institutions for the disabled, universities, banks, administrations, religious communities, foundations, and clubs and associations. During the two weeks, around 100 activities took place.

A success factor for the project was the well-organised, partnership-based project team, which had already been systematically built up in previous years. The core idea of *Participation Canton Zurich* is the inclusion and participation of as many groups of people with disabilities as possible in the implementation of the UN CRPD in the Canton of Zurich. All participating agencies had a professionally led project management at their disposal over the course of the action days, which provided clear framework conditions, such as for the process design, defined the responsibilities and established the quality criteria for participation. All activities had to be related to the UN CRPD, had to include people with disabilities, and had to be organised in a way that people with disabilities had equal access to as people without disabilities. In retrospect, the action days proved to be an important learning field. New forms of communication and cooperation emerged. This project contributed to deepening the society's knowledge about the UN CRPD in the canton of Zurich. Following on from the successful action days, various other cantons and the Conference of Cantonal Social Directors as well as the federal government are now organising a similar action at national level in 2024 – to mark the 20th anniversary of Switzerland's adherence to the UN CRPD.

3.2.2 The inclusion check for municipalities

This offer for municipalities, which is supported by the association "Tatkraft" in cooperation with the canton of Zurich and the financial support of the Federal Office for the Equality of Persons with Disabilities, is about accompanying the municipal authorities in the implementation of the UN CRPD. At the moment, the service is still in the pilot phase, and only a few communities are participating. What is it specifically about? The municipal authority is supported when addressing to people with disabilities who live in the municipality. This is done, for example, via the municipal bulletin, a personal letter or other communication channels. In this way, the active participation of people with disabilities is promoted. Their concerns can be collected first hand. This is followed by an exchange of ideas with the administrative staff and a screening of various publicly accessible municipal spaces and buildings. For example, access to public transport can be examined, or the accessibility of municipal services, such as leisure, sports and cultural activities. After the screening is completed, a report is prepared, and recommendations are formulated for the municipality. One year later, a joint review takes place, the implemented projects are considered and possible improvements for the further implementation process of the UN CRPD are explored.

3.2.3 Disabled in Politics

This project is based on a study that investigated the hindering factors for access to political office as well as the political work of people with disabilities in Switzerland. For this purpose, 41 candidates, active and former politicians with disabilities, were interviewed in all language regions of Switzerland. The results showed that disability can interact differently with political processes. Obstacles were identified in seven areas, namely political dynamics and structures, attitudes towards people with disabilities, financial resources, lack of concrete support and accessibility, discriminatory legal structures, and the context of one's own impairment. The core concern of the project was the empowerment of people with disabilities in order to initiate social change. This goal was to be achieved by mobilising and networking people with disabilities who are either already politically active or who wanted to become active, across party lines. The project should also implement other support measures such as networking of actors, workshops on specific topics such as self-efficacy, addressing hurdles and barriers that exist in current party politics or associations. The project will run until 2025.

3.2.4 Mon Vote, Ma Voix

As mentioned above, the cantons in Switzerland enjoy a great deal of autonomy. Consequently, this also affects the legal situation of persons with disabilities. In Switzerland, people under comprehensive guardianship so far have no political rights at the federal level. The Conference for Child and Adult Protection ("KOKES") calculated that for every 1,000 adults in Switzerland, 14 people are subject to protective measures, the institute of comprehensive guardianship being one of them. In absolute numbers, this means that at the end of 2021, there were 13,546 people in Switzerland under comprehensive assistance. This includes people with disabilities, people with dementia, coma patients, etc. (KOKES 2022). In the canton of Geneva, a constitutional revision was successfully approved at the ballot box in December 2020. The cantonal constitution was revised to the effect that since then, people under comprehensive guardianship (with Swiss citizenship and over 18 years of age) can also exercise their political rights. In some cantons, the exclusion of people under comprehensive guardianship from voting rights can be reversed through appropriate procedures. In the project "Mon Vote, Ma Voix", the path of some affected persons who have claimed their political rights is traced in testimonials in four French-speaking cantons where such procedural possibilities exist. The project – which was completed at the end of 2022 – sheds light on the support that institutions in French-speaking Switzerland offer to affected people so that they can exercise or regain their voting rights, and the challenges they face. These results provide important clues as to how support measures work (or do not work) in individual cases and which bodies play a central role in the (re-)acquisition of political rights.

3.2.5 Training course for administrative staff

The city of Lausanne is the fourth largest city in Switzerland, located in the canton of Vaud. Lausanne has created a training course for the city's administrative staff in collaboration with the canton and regional organisations for people with disabilities. This includes various modules, such as on the technical basics for creating accessible electronic documents, dealing specifically with different disability groups, and raising awareness among public authorities about the concerns of people with disabilities. The project was completed in 2021. A whole bundle of measures is now available for the municipal level, which could easily be used for other cities in Switzerland with minor adaptations (especially the translations into the other national languages).

Overall, the five projects presented here show in their own way approaches to how the participation of people with disabilities and their organisations can be further institutionalised in the cantons and municipalities and thus also more deeply anchored in society. The informal network of Swiss specialised agencies for the equality of people with disabilities (at the federal, cantonal and municipal levels), has taken up several of the projects mentioned above and will organise an exchange of experiences on some of the topics.

4. Outlook: Federal Disability Policy 2023-2026

In spring 2022, Switzerland's dialogue with the UN concerning the implementation of the UN CRPD took place. Based on this, the UN Committee on the Rights of Persons with Disabilities presented its Concluding Observations. These comprise findings and more than 80 recommendations on almost all topics of the UN CRPD 2022. With reference to Article 4 of the UN CRPD, the Committee expressed concern in its concluding observations in paragraph 9 about the lack of opportunities for participation of persons with disabilities in decision-making processes, the lack of financial and other resources to promote participation, and the lack of accessibility of information. The Committee then made three recommendations in paragraph 10 that correspond with its findings in paragraph 9 (CRPD 2022): First of all, mechanisms at the federal, cantonal and municipal levels should be improved to ensure effective support and consultations with diverse organisations of persons with disabilities – including organisations of persons with intellectual disabilities, autistic persons, persons with psychosocial disabilities, women with disabilities, children with disabilities and lesbian, gay, bisexual, transgender and intersex persons with disabilities – in design, reporting and monitoring with respect to legislation and policies aimed at implementing the Convention and achieving the Sustainable Development Goals. Secondly, the availability of adequate financial and other necessary resources must be ensured for the diversity of organisations of persons with disabilities, and such organisations must have access to independent and self-managed funding to improve their capacity to independently promote the effective participation of persons with disabilities and their inclusion in society. Thirdly, organisations of people with disabilities should be provided with accessible information, including information in easy language and sign languages, and it should be ensured to them an adequate time frame for their participation at all stages of legislative, policy and decision-making processes.

The first of the mentioned recommendations recognises that mechanisms already exist at the three levels of government in Switzerland for the participation of organisations for persons with disabilities in the implementation of the UN CRPD. However, these mechanisms should be improved.

According to the Committee, an improvement would consist of ensuring that adequate financial and other necessary resources are available for the organisations of persons with disabilities. For example, according to the second recommendation above, they should have access to *independent and self-managed funding*. The last two mentioned recommendations of the UN Committee on the Rights of Persons with Disabilities can also be seen in connection with the improvement of mechanisms for the participation of organisations of persons with disabilities. Here, on the one hand, it is a matter of the authorities making their information available barrier-free, if necessary, also in easy language and in sign language. This concern is undisputed in principle. In practice, however, prioritisation is mostly unavoidable: Switzerland has three official languages: for example, all documents of the federal authorities are already generally translated into German, French and Italian. There are also several bilingual cantons and even bilingual municipalities and cities. Translating all the information issued by authorities into easy language and sign language is hardly feasible due to resource constraints (and as long as no high-quality, automated tools are available). On the other hand, the committee expresses its opinion on the *adequate time frame* that should be granted regarding the participation of organisations for people with disabilities. It is undisputed and an everyday experience that participation usually prolongs the decision-making process. Thus, what is an appropriate time frame must be decided on a case-by-case basis. In this sense, this recommendation of the committee cannot be concretised further, but must be taken into account in all participation processes from the very beginning and also communicated to the organisations accordingly.

As this article has shown, the implementation of the UN CRPD and the Committee's recommendations in Switzerland is the responsibility of the federal government, the cantons and the municipalities. In order to take into account, the Concluding Observations of the Committee, a classification and prioritisation is now required. The federal disability policy for the years 2023 – 2026, which the Federal Council presented on March 10, 2023, will set content priorities in four fields of action. There will be four federal multi-year programs: On *housing, work, services* and *participation*. Furthermore, the protection against discrimination of people with disabilities is to be increased. Among other things, the need for legislative action in the financing and support of services to enable a self-determined life is to be taken into account. Compared to the first phase of the federal disability policy from 2018 to 2022, the new disability policy 2023 – 2026 specifies a stronger and earlier involvement of all stakeholders, i.e. the federal government, the cantons, the municipalities as well as representatives of civil society. This is also reflected in the joint implementation of program objectives and program activities in the four aforementioned multi-year programs.

References

ARTISET/INSOS/YOUVITA/CURAVIVA/anthroSocial (Ed.) (2019): Aktionsplan UN-BRK. Der Aktionsplan. https://www.aktionsplan-un-brk.ch/de/der-aktionsplan-12.html [accessed: 16.08.2023]
Bertels, Eric (2022): Gleichstellung von Menschen mit Behinderungen. Aktionspläne für Gemeinden und Städte, Riehen
Behindertenkonferenz Kanton Zürich (n.d.): Partizipation Kanton Zürich. https://www.bkz.ch/partizipation-kanton-zuerich-1/[accessed: 13.02.2023]
Bildungs-, Kultur- und Sportkommission des Kantons Basel-Landschaft: Neues Rahmengesetz zur Stärkung der Behindertenrechte, https://www.baselland.ch/politik-und-behoerden/direktionen/bildungs-kultur-und-sportdirektion/medienmitteilungen/neues-rahmengesetz-zur-staerkung-der-behindertenrechte-1 [accessed: 13.02.2023]
Bundesamt für Statistik (2020): Gleichstellung von Menschen mit Behinderungen. Taschenstatistik, https://www.bfs.admin.ch/bfs/de/home.assetdetail.15003394 [accessed: 13.02.2023]
Bundesamt für Statistik (2021): Gemeinden. https://www.bfs.admin.ch/bfs/de/home/statistiken/regionalstatistik/regionale-portraets-kennzahlen/gemeinden.html [accessed: 13.02.2023]
Bundesamt für Statistik (2022): Gleichstellung von Menschen mit Behinderungen. www.bfs.admin.ch/news/de/2022-0216 [accessed: 13.02.2023]
Bundesgesetz über die Beseitigung von Benachteiligungen von Menschen mit Behinderungen vom 13. Dezember 2002 (Behindertengleichstellungsgesetz, BehiG)
Committee on the Rights of Persons with Disabilities CRPD (2017): General comment No. 5 on Article 19 – the right to live independently and be included in the community https://www.ohchr.org/en/documents/general-comments-and-recommendations/general-comment-no5-article-19-right-live [accessed: 13.02.2023]
Committee on the Rights of Persons with Disabilities (2022): Concluding observations on the initial report of Switzerland. https://www.edi.admin.ch/dam/edi/de/dokumente/gleichstellung/bericht/crpd_conculding_observations_2022.pdf.download.pdf/CRPD%20Concluding%20observations%20on%20the%20initial%20report%20of%20Switzerland.pdf [accessed: 13.02.2023]
Der Bundesrat (2018): Behindertenpolitik, Bern. https://www.edi.admin.ch/edi/de/home/fachstellen/ebgb/politique-nationale-du-handicap.html [accessed: 13.02.2023]
EBGB, GS-EDI – Eidgenössisches Büro für die Gleichstellung von Menschen mit Behinderung, Generalsekretariat Eidgenössisches Department des Inneren (2021a):

Auswertung der Umfrage zur Partizipation von Menschen mit Behinderungen. Umfrage der Arbeitsgruppe Behindertenpolitik (AG BePo) bei den Mitgliedern der Fachkonferenz der kantonalen Beauftragten für Behindertenfragen (FBBF), Bern. https://ch-sodk.s3.amazonaws.com/media/files/eecbd99b/3146/4190/a1a2/6727a 2c03645/2021.01.04_Auswertung_Umfrage_zu_Partizipation_bei_FB.pdf [accessed: 13.02.2023]

EBGB, GS-EDI – Eidgenössisches Büro für die Gleichstellung von Menschen mit Behinderung, Generalsekretariat Eidgenössisches Department des Inneren (2021b): Auswertung der Umfrage zur "Selbstbestimmung von Menschen mit Behinderungen". Umfrage der Arbeitsgruppe Behindertenpolitik (AG BePo) bei den Mitgliedern des Netzwerkes der Behindertenkonferenzen, Bern (unpublished)

EBGB – Eidgenössisches Büro für die Gleichstellung von Menschen mit Behinderung (n.d.): Unterstützte Projekte. https://www.edi.admin.ch/edi/de/home/fachstellen/ebgb/finanzhilfen/unterstuetzte_projekte0.html [accessed: 13.02.2023]

Egger, Theres/Stutz, Heidi/Jäggi, Jolanda/Bannwart, Livia/Oesch, Thomas/Naguib, Tarek/Pärli, Kurt (2015): Evaluation des Bundesgesetzes über die Beseitigung von Benachteiligungen von Menschen mit Behinderungen – BehiG. Integraler Schlussbericht im Auftrag des Eidgenössischen Departementes des Innern, Generalsekretariat GS-EDI, Eidgenössisches Büro für die Gleichstellung von Menschen mit Behinderungen EBGB, Bern

Hess-Klein, Caroline/Scheibler, Eliane (2022): Aktualisierter Schattenbericht. Bericht der Zivilgesellschaft anlässlich des ersten Staatenberichtsverfahrens vor dem UN-Ausschuss für die Rechte von Menschen mit Behinderungen, Bern, Editions Weblaw

Kanton Zürich (n.d.): Aktionstage Behindertenrechte: https://zukunft-inklusion.ch/[accessed: 13.02.2023]

KOKES – Konferenz für Kindes- und Erwachsenenschutz (2022): KOKES-Statistik 2021. https://www.kokes.ch/application/files/4216/6307/1978/KOKES-Statistik_ 2021_Erwachsene_Bestand_Massnahmenarten_Details_A3.pdf [accessed: 13.02.2023]

Schefer, Markus/Martin, Céline/Hess-Klein Caroline (2022): Leitfaden für eine behindertenrechtliche Gesetzgebung in den Kantonen. Zum Einbezug der Gemeinden in die Rechtsetzung von Bund und Kantonen, Zürich, Editions Weblaw

Universität Fribourg (n.d.): Projekt Mon Vote, Ma Voix. https://www.unifr.ch/spedu/de/forschung/intellektuelle-beeintraechtigung.html [accessed: 13.02.2023]

VAHS Schweiz/CURAVIVA Schweiz/INSOS Schweiz (2019): Aktionsplan UN-BRK 2019-2023. Umsetzung der UN-Behindertenrechtskonvention bei Verbänden und Dienstleistungsanbietern für Menschen mit Behinderung. https://www.aktionsplan-un-brk.ch/admin/data/files/hero_asset/file/3/191021_a4_ap_lang_de_web_ final.pdf?lm=1571657601 [accessed: 16.08.2023]

Verein Tatkraft und ZHAW, School of Management and Law (n.d.): Projekte. https:// tatkraft.org/projekte/[accessed: 13.02.2023]

Verein Tatkraft (n.d.): Inklusions-Check. https://tatkraft.org/projekt/inklusionscheck/ [accessed: 13.02.2023]

Verordnung über die Beseitigung von Benachteiligungen von Menschen mit Behinderungen vom 19. November 2003 (Behindertengleichstellungsverordnung, BehiV)

Putting citizens into the centre – concepts and lessons learnt for inclusive local governance from German Development Cooperation

Alexander Hobinka

International agendas such as the New Urban Agenda (UN 2016) or the 2030 Agenda for Sustainable Development (UN 2015) with its guiding principles "Leave No One Behind" and "Do no Harm" are recognised by the international community as a binding framework for action to protect and promote disadvantaged population groups. In this context, municipalities around the world offer a central sphere of action in which development processes can be shaped. International development cooperation can contribute significantly both in financial and conceptual terms to improving the living conditions of disadvantaged population groups.

The past few years have put societies to the test: Worldwide refugee and migration movements, the consequences of climate change, crises and wars have caused conflicts as great as the Corona Pandemic and the war in Ukraine. The poverty rate is growing – for the first time since 1990, another 6 to 9 million people are living below the poverty line (Castaneda et al. 2022).

Women, the elderly and people with disabilities without formal social security are particularly affected by unemployment and poverty (UNHCR 2023). In this context, states are challenged to meet the growing expectations of their citizens for a modern and inclusive state, even with scarce public resources and administrative staff. Increasingly educated and organised citizens are demanding greater participation in decision-making and planning processes and better local public services. The delivery capacity of local and regional authorities is also highlighted in the 2030 Agenda as a key challenge for successful inclusive implementation, particularly in the slogan "Localising the SDGs" and the overarching principle of "Leave No One Behind" (LNOB).

The German governmental implementing organisation "Deutsche Gesellschaft für Internationale Zusammenarbeit" (GIZ) conducts many projects at the local level in the Global South.[1] These projects often focus on municipal

---

[1] GIZ is a federal enterprise and acts as a service provider in the field of international development cooperation mainly on behalf of the German Federal Ministry for Economic Cooperation and Development (BMZ). GIZ works in a variety of areas, including good governance, inclusive economic development and employment

and urban development at the level of administrative action. Through a wide variety of project approaches, public services are designed to be inclusive to better reach disadvantaged groups (e.g. older persons, persons with disabilities, refugees) and their specific needs. The inclusive design of municipal core tasks, such as water supply, mobility, political participation, or disaggregated data collection is one principal focus of GIZ's work on the ground. The article gives an insight into promising project approaches from different partner countries. In addition, the article reflects on lessons learnt from previous implementation experiences, and challenges for a cross-sectoral and context-specific approach to inclusive urban and municipal development for German development cooperation are elaborated.

1. Decentralised governance – Bringing the local level into the centre

German Development Cooperation (GDC), particularly the implementing organisation GIZ, has adapted its interventions to the tremendous changes outlined above, particularly in decentralised local governance. In the last 30 years, evidence-based analysis in the field of technical cooperation has shown that decentralised systems of government and administration offer opportunities to address this challenge. The governmental and administrative units at the subnational level – such as the federal states, districts, and municipalities – work closer to the population and can involve them more directly and comprehensively in decision-making and planning processes. Decentralised systems thus offer particularly good framework conditions for administrative action to address the needs, priorities, and rights of the citizens. They can therefore provide important public services – from water supply, and social care to employment promotion – close to where people live and adapted to their region (Ferrazzi 2023; Schlutz 2017). However, whether the regions and municipalities can conduct the public tasks assigned to them to the satisfaction of the citizens depends largely on whether they have the necessary competences, capacities, resources, and room for manoeuvre to do so.

---

promotion, social protection, education and health, energy and the environment, and peace and security.

2. A multi-dimensional approach of (decentralised) governance

Consequently, GIZ supports national and local governments worldwide through advisory services also in the field of inclusive governance. These advisory services are characterised by the fact that GIZ involves all reform actors (such as city councils, civil society organisations, service providers) at all levels of government and administration concerned and strengthens all units of the decentralised system of government and administration. In doing so, the advisory approach is built on in an open-model manner, which integrates different experiences from different good experiences from all over the world (Shakhshir 2023; Schlutz 2017).

For example, in the "Supporting Decentralization and Local Governance Program" (DLG) in Iraq, GIZ develops the capacity of key actors at national and sub-national levels to implement decentralisation in a citizen-oriented manner. This is firstly done through raising awareness about decentralisation and developing capacities of public employees at the central level in the partner structures. Three new curricula were included into the training offers for public employees, and trainers are trained on these new courses. Secondly, organisational units within local public administrations ("local budget sections") were activated and qualified in 14 Governorates (GIZ 2022). Further, micro-projects in selected Districts of 14 Governorates were implemented. In addition, micro-projects were implemented in selected districts in 14 governorates, taking into account local resources, addressing citizens' needs and generating revenues that remain at the sub-national level. Finally, local civil society is empowered through communication tools and participatory mechanisms that enhance citizen engagement in local planning and development. The needs of citizens were surveyed in 14 Governorates with a focus on marginalised groups in corporation with the Central Statistical Organization. In 126 dialogue events, the needs of citizens (in particular: women, youth and people with special needs) were debated together with the responsible district authorities.

Through the provision of technical advisory, for example training on decentralisation and local planning, the project supports the Higher Commission for Coordination among the Provinces (HCCP) in monitoring the progress on decentralisation as well as Governorates in improving their planning capacities.

This example corresponds to a main pillar of promoting decentralised governance through the appropriate allocation and reallocation of decision-making powers, tasks and resources between the levels based on the subsidiarity principle and the decentralised performance of tasks to the satisfaction of the citizens, at the local level (OECD 2018).

3. Promoting political participation

To achieve sustainable structure-building effects that benefit the broadest possible sectors of society, GDC bases its efforts to promote political participation on a multidimensional approach. Political participation and the development of constructive state-society relations are promoted in three dimensions that are interrelated and mutually reinforcing:

1. Building and permanent anchoring of legal and institutional framework conditions. Institutionalised democratic procedures and rule-of-law structures are important prerequisites for the development of active political participation and a stable democracy. Only if an institutional framework and formal legal safeguards exist, civil society can participate in political decision-making. To make this possible, GDC supports the establishment of a democratic environment and rule-of-law structures. It promotes the legal enshrinement of participation rights, the establishment of suitable participation procedures or interaction spaces in which state and social actors can enter exchange with each other (e.g., dialogue forums, round tables, processes), as well as the implementation of complaint and control mechanisms (e.g., ombuds*wo*men). The creation, institutionalisation, and legal protection of opportunities for political participation and involvement also strengthen the rule of law. In this way, political participation is made possible regardless of current power constellations.

2. Strengthening civil society and disadvantaged groups. Political participation presupposes that citizens are aware of their opportunities and rights and can demand them from government agencies. GDC supports them in acquiring the necessary knowledge and skills so that they can articulate their interests and effectively bring them into political negotiation and decision-making processes (empowerment). In this context, the empowerment of disadvantaged groups is of particular importance. Their ability to articulate, negotiate and assert themselves is strengthened, for example, by learning to organise themselves, to bundle their interests and to form networks to increase their assertiveness. The promotion of effective interest groups and representative associations is an important contribution to strengthening civil society. In addition to advising civil society organisations, GDC supports civil society groups in defending their interests through specific projects and measures.

For example, the "Strengthening Civil Society Organisations Program" (CSP) works towards ensuring Palestinian society is more inclusive, and institutions are more approachable and effective. The programme partners with 21 civil society organisations, networks, community-based organisations, women's and youth organisations and Organisations of People with Disabilities (OPDs) in the West Bank, including East Jerusalem, and the Gaza Strip to increase the political participation of the population in line with the Leave No

Putting citizens into the centre 215

One Behind principle of the 2030 Agenda. In line with its commitment to capacity development, the programme encourages initiatives in the areas of advocacy, organisational development, intra-civil society coordination, digitalisation, state-civil society dialogue, and inclusion of persons with disabilities. Main activities of CSP focus on improving the resilience of civil society through better organisational structures and processes; providing accessible digital methods and instruments to represent the interests of communities; fostering participation and integration of marginalised groups in subnational planning processes and strengthening the inclusion of persons with disabilities and other marginalised groups in the programmes of the German Development Cooperation in Palestine (Dämmrich 2022).

3. Promoting free and independent media. Another focus of GDC is the promotion of free and independent media. They play a key role in the democratic development of a society and are a prerequisite for the participation of an enlightened civil society in the political process. Civil society is supported in its function of bundling social interests and representing them vis-à-vis state authorities, as well as demanding and monitoring respect for, and protection and guarantee of, individual and collective rights (triad of duties).

Strengthened in this way, civil society can better fulfil its critical-constructive watchdog and interest representation function. At the same time, the democratic awareness of the population is raised, the integration of disadvantaged groups is promoted, and the transparency of political decision-making processes is increased.

4. Improving the performance of the state. A constructive relationship between state and society is only possible if the state is responsive to the active participation of civil society in political decision-making processes. To increase the responsiveness of the state, GDC promotes democratic awareness among actors in government, parliament and public administration and strengthens democratic institutions. Political decision-makers and state actors learn to design decision-making processes in such a way that the active participation of civil society is possible at both national and decentralised levels: in the initiation of issues, the processes of decision-making, and the implementation of decisions. Representatives of state structures and employees in public administration are supported in dealing competently with citizen participation and in integrating it into procedures and structures. At the same time, they are enabled to make administrative procedures transparent and to be accountable for government and administrative actions. The promotion of political participation strengthens the legitimacy of state structures and the democratic accountability of political actors. It helps them further to institutionalise public participation in procedures and structures. Finally, it increases the transparency of governmental and administrative action, improves the checks and balances on the exercise of

state power and makes it possible to effectively combat corruption, arbitrary state power and abuse of power.

4. Local perspectives for strong social cohesion

As a second pillar in the context of inclusive local governance, GIZ has, over the last two years, developed a complementary conceptual framework for a better understanding of social cohesion. This framework describes social cohesion as the quality of community togetherness within a society and aims at:

- Crisis-resistant social relationships characterised by resilient social networks, trust in fellow human beings and acceptance of diversity.
- Connectedness/community welfare orientation and solidarity, which are expressed in people's positive identification with their community, willingness to help the weak and civic engagement.
- Constructive state-society relations characterised by trust in institutions and acceptance of social rules and regulations, enabling active political participation and civic engagement of all population groups.

GIZ, as the principal, works on many important influencing factors (also see above, the three inter-related principles) that promote and sustain social cohesion. These include access to basic social services, citizen-oriented and legitimate administrations, equal opportunities, and economic, social and political participation. Against the backdrop of current challenges and future trends, GIZ has identified the following five fields of action to make targeted contributions within the good governance portfolio, such as strong social systems; sustainable and inclusive cities; youth as agents for change; crisis management and conflict resolution and finally functioning and legitimate state administrations.

5. Municipalities as principal enablers for social cohesion

By 2050, two-thirds of the world's population will live in cities and the number of people living in informal settlements and slums will rise to as many as 3 billion (UN-HABITAT 2022). Rapid urbanisation exacerbates already inadequate and overburdened infrastructure in many places and often deficient basic service delivery, especially in Africa and Asia. Climate change and natural disasters affect urban infrastructures and populations to an even greater extent than in the Global North. This applies even more to the mostly disadvantaged population groups in slums. In addition, there is a rural exodus, migration and the settlement of refugees, migrants and internally displaced persons in cities. It is already clear that a lack of or unequal access to these aspects can lead to a (further) loss of confidence of the population in the state and administration as well as their loss of legitimacy, social tensions, violence and conflicts. This was intensified by the Corona pandemic. To overcome these challenges, an offensive is needed to enable urban decision-makers and administrations to shape sustainable and inclusive urban development in a forward-looking and participatory way. Based on this realisation, GIZ has put one emphasis on supporting municipalities to strengthen their potential to overcome poverty, counteract social inequality and strengthen social cohesion. The following five areas of intervention play a significant role in addressing these challenges:

Integrated and sustainable planning. In view of the diversity of challenges and opportunities, city administrations need to introduce and apply methods of strategic, integrated, and long-term planning that make complexity across sectors processable. This includes improving the data base (e.g., disaggregated data on the socioeconomic situation of residents, spatial distribution, quality and quantity of basic services, etc.) and analytics to enable evidence-based decisions. Administrations can use this to derive options for measures, introduce them into the public dialogue and evaluate them.

Digitalisation and data management in urban development: In view of the multitude of technological possibilities, cities and municipalities are often faced with the challenge of shaping digitalisation to ensure disaggregated and updated data management in a strategic way and oriented towards a better and more inclusive service provision for their citizens. With the help of suitable analysis and evaluation methods for the context-appropriate selection of tools, the design of collaborative spaces (e.g., planning pilots, household surveys) and appropriate decision-making processes in administrations, these challenges can be met.

Participation. Strengthening inclusive, citizen-oriented, and participatory urban planning and development based on dialogue between urban authorities and the population and effective co-design and participation of all population groups, for example through citizens' offices and participatory urban planning processes.

Encounter. Designing peaceful and safe public spaces, especially in hotspot areas, to serve as vehicles for exchange and encounter. This includes (cultural) offers at the city (sub)urban level to strengthen identity with the urban space, overcome stereotypes and strengthen individual and joint identity, but also specific offers of mediation and conflict prevention.

Income. The development of economic potential in cities serves to increase economic participation, reduces poverty, contributes to social cohesion, and helps to develop cities as liveable ecosystems. Concrete starting points are the vocational qualification of young people (with specific programmes for women), urban economic development as part of regional economic development and the promotion of the local innovation system with a focus on environmentally friendly and digitally based approaches.

In the following third part of the article, the author presents three selected promising practices from the implementation level of three partner regions of the GIZ portfolio (Western Balkan, Sub-Sahara Africa, MENA) to show how the development agency translates these conceptional foundations into inclusive governance programming.

6. Promising practices from the field

6.1 Social mapping – pro-poor targeting in municipalities in the Western Balkan region

The first promising practice, which focuses on the inclusion of marginalised groups at municipal level, is elaborated by the GIZ Social Rights Program (SoRi II). Implemented in five Western Balkan countries, Albania, Bosnia and Herzegovina, Kosovo, North Macedonia, and Serbia, on regional, national, and local levels, SoRi II cooperates with and engages a variety of partners and stakeholders. The aim of the SoRi II project is to improve the living conditions of disadvantaged groups (such as ethnic minorities, girls and women, persons with disabilities, elderly people) in the five project countries, by focusing on the economic, social, and cultural human rights provided by relevant state and non-state actors in line with the overarching "Leave no one behind" principle (LNOB) of the 2030 Agenda. The project's target groups are particularly disadvantaged groups in the five partner countries.

Social mapping is an approach that allows stakeholders to collect data (both quantitative and qualitative) about so-called left-behind groups and the distribution of socio-economic resources in their local communities. The approach takes social services directly to the people in need in their communities. Previously, agencies for social service provision had no validated data about living conditions, numbers, and specific needs of the various target groups. Through social cards, social workers can register all relevant (poverty-oriented) data of individuals and their families. Further, this outreach work leads to more informed citizens in the settlements and a better understanding of whom they can talk to and what claims they can assert and finally what requirements they must meet to receive assistance.

This helps decision makers to understand the needs of the population (which are often invisible due to lack of data), the availability of social services

Putting citizens into the centre 219

and the gaps between needs and offered services. Further, it facilitates the collection and use of data to identify who is being excluded (e.g., from equal access to basic social and health services) or discriminated against, how and on what grounds, as well as who is experiencing multiple and intersecting forms of discrimination and inequalities. Understanding the root causes that exclude these groups is at the heart of social mapping. Therefore, each social mapping report elaborates not only on who is excluded from certain basic services but also on why and, most importantly, what should be done to overcome the situation. Finally, recommendations are provided for further consideration by the municipal authorities so that these can be reflected in evidence-based policy making. Within the framework of the SoRi II project, support is provided for re-alignment of local social protection strategies with the 2030 Agenda, prioritisation of SDGs at local level (based on the mapping) and introduction of policy measures to address the most urgent needs of vulnerable population groups in their communities.

6.2 Main benefits and achieved results

If there is no documentation on the situation, needs and challenges faced by the local population, there will not be a solution to their problems. Using disaggregated data and conducting social mappings represents a step towards tackling the challenges faced by communities. The following benefits are the most essential ones. First, the municipal and civil society stakeholders will be capacitated to conduct social mappings. Second, the planning and decision-making on all municipal levels will be more evidence-based and inclusive and the work on ensuring social, economic and cultural rights will be more effective and efficient. Further, vulnerable groups will be visible and will be included into social policies. Finally, the LNOB principle is applied in practice: those left behind will be reached and supported.

As part of the SoRi II project, 22 municipalities from the Western Balkans region are supported in collecting LNOB data, of which half took a step further and re-aligned their social protection strategies in line with the 2030 Agenda and selected priority SDGs.

At central level, Ombuds Offices in the region are in the process of drafting LNOB specific reports based on the locally collected data. Moreover, the Government in North Macedonia is initiating a multi-sectoral strategy on people with disabilities that takes into consideration the locally collected data. Similar steps are being taken in other countries in the region by the relevant line ministries which are in the process of acquainting themselves with the benefits and use of data for central level policy making. Within the project, a Training Guide Toolkit for Social Mapping was developed. The toolkit can serve as a framework for the identification and description of LNOB across countries and projects. Social mapping was conducted in 22 municipalities in the Western Balkans region. The LNOB data served as a basis for LNOB targeted policy measures within existing municipal social protection strategies, rule books, etc. The mappings have identified eight LNOB groups (Roma and in particular Roma women, victims of domestic violence, persons with disabilities, single parents, young people without access to social protection, rural women farmers, victims and potential victims of human trafficking, elderly people).

Finally, the analysed data revealed gaps between unmet needs of the LNOB groups and availability of social services (e.g., lack of certified personal assistants on local level for persons with disabilities and elderly people; lack of implementation of national policies by local institutions in the field of protection for victims of domestic violence; single parents are not yet recognised by the social protection system, etc.). Around 40 professionals from municipalities and CSOs are receiving further training on conducting LNOB social mapping.

7. Disability Management Information System (DMIS) in Rwanda

While Rwanda has ratified the Convention on the Rights of Persons with Disabilities (CRPD) and is committed towards building an inclusive society, persons with disabilities still face major inequalities. The exclusion of persons with disabilities from participating equally in society makes them invisible. (Kidd/Kabare 2019) The CRPD calls on States Parties to collect appropriate information, including statistical and research data, to enable them to formulate and implement policies and to identify and address the barriers faced by persons with disabilities (UN 2006, § 31). Although disability data is collected occasionally, there is a gap of nation-wide reliable disaggregated data. For follow-up and review of the 2030 Agenda for Sustainable Development and the Sustainable Development Goals (SDGs), it is recognised that high-quality, accessible, timely and reliable disaggregated data will be needed to help with the measurement of progress towards disability inclusion (UN 2015: SDG 17).

Considering the complexity of the institutional landscape and the need for disability-specific knowledge, GIZ in Rwanda collaborates closely with one of the main change agents, the "National Council of Persons with Disabilities" (NCPD).

This council represents the views of persons with disabilities at national and local levels and is a forum for advocacy and social mobilisation on issues affecting persons with disabilities to build their capacity and ensure participation in the national development. NCPD assists the Government of Rwanda (GoR) in implementing programs and policies that benefit persons with disabilities and strengthen the disability network in Rwanda.

The absence of disability-disaggregated data makes it difficult to effectively advocate for the inclusion of persons with disabilities, to actively target measures towards persons with disabilities and to measure change, especially at the local level. Currently, identification and categorisation of persons with disabilities in Rwanda is incomplete and conducted through a medical model instead of the bio-psycho-social model recommended by the WHO whereby Washington Group (WG) questions are included.

The development and implementation of the DMIS is designed as an inclusive and participatory process. Therefore, the involved stakeholders consult all relevant actors in the disability movement. Representatives of Organisations of Persons with Disability (OPD), NGOs, Development Partners (DP) and Government of Rwanda (GoR) institutions at central and local level were asked to participate in Technical Working Groups (TWG) and Steering Committees (SC) to ensure a participatory approach.

An important step during the implementation of the DMIS project is the identification of as many persons with disability as possible. Consequently, in every village, persons with disabilities will be interviewed through a questionnaire developed in collaboration with relevant stakeholders. Identification of persons with disabilities will be administered through a questionnaire where only relevant questions pop up. Answers given are linked with (SDG) indicators about demographics, socio-economic status, functional limitations, assistive devices, health care utilisation, barriers, wellbeing including specific needs and priorities of persons with disabilities and will be the base for on-demand dashboards and maps for M&E purposes.

Besides general types of questions, the questionnaire will make use of the Washington Group (WG) sets of questions. WG questions are the international standard for disability identification which are recommended for identification of persons with disabilities, surveys, research, and the national census. WG questions can capture significant impairments that result in a disability. WG questions focus on functions (such as walking, hearing, seeing) and are easy to administer for local staff. Categorisation and classification as required in the Ministerial Order will be automatically calculated within the DMIS environment including printing of a Disability ID-card.

The work of case managers, who assist persons with disabilities in the assessment, planning, referral, and monitoring of different services also at the district level, plays another important role. Case management is available for those persons with disabilities who have specific needs and additional support requirements assessed during the identification process. In general, these will be persons who have a severe type of disability. A case manager will support, assist, and refer but will not take over the responsibilities of the individual person with disability. Together with a person with disability and/or their family, a case manager will make an Individual Support Plan (ISP) including proposed actions.

Further, the Disability Service Directory provides instant information about all organisations including OPDs working with and for persons with disabilities throughout Rwandan districts. It is designed in a way to help persons with disabilities and their families to look for specific disability-related services and have access to all kinds of information related to disability. The directory utilises a disability inclusive chatbot, which supports persons with disability in an integrated web-based environment to have access to the information. In the directory, annual plans, reports and by-laws of the licensed service providers could also be uploaded for reference.

Within a politically institutionalised and technically feasible DMIS, concerned representative bodies and individuals of Rwandan society will be able to express their diversity of needs, challenges, barriers, and priorities in disability-relevant areas of life. It will support NCPD and stakeholders in the disability sector at local and national level to make coordinated and well planned, targeted and evidence-based support plans and advocate for change towards equal participation of persons with disabilities in their communities. Finally, the interlinkage between disaggregated data collection and the assessment of specific needs helps local governments in Rwanda to design better informed and needs-oriented service provision for people with disabilities in their communities.

8. Promoting social engagement among young people in Jordan and Lebanon

Like many states in the region, Jordan and Lebanon face the challenge of implementing comprehensive political, social, and economic reforms, to meet the needs of its people, particularly the young. Over 65% of the population is currently under 30 (World Bank 2023). These young people are playing a "waiting game" and are unable to make the transition from adolescence to adulthood, primarily due to the high rate of youth unemployment and lack of opportunities for economic participation. Not only are young people not involved in shaping policies and reform processes, but those policies and processes also do not reflect their needs. Young women above all are largely excluded from participation, while young men often experience frustration and lack of prospects (OECD 2022).

The key objective of the GIZ project "Social participation and community engagement by young people" (SPACE) is to promote social cohesion and integrate vulnerable groups, especially refugees. By using different participation and dialogue measures, the project aims to foster a constructive relationship between the state and diverse groups in society and by creating spaces for civil society engagement. This project aims to empower particularly young women and men to make a positive contribution to shaping their society. The target group of the project consists of young women and men between 15 and 23 in selected municipalities in Jordan and Lebanon. It provides support and empowers young people to participate in social/political dialogue and activities. The target group comprises young people from host communities and from a refugee background who could be able to share their experiences and ideas. Project activities also explicitly target young people who require special support because of having been traumatised or displaced by the violent conflict that has raged in the region for many years now. An integrative approach that incorporates vulnerable groups (especially women, refugees and/or Internally Displaced Persons) is adopted, in line with the "do-no-harm" approach (UNHCR 2023). In this way, the project aims to contribute to strengthening social cohesion in the partner countries.

The project implements participatory measures that strengthen the influence young people can exert on the peaceful development of their society. Greater capacities for social inclusion and participation can get young people more involved in their communities' social and political development, so that they can have an impact on peaceful and inclusive development. The inclusion and networking of different actors (organised and non-organised/marginalised young people, educational institutions, youth centres, civil society) can facilitate the development. As the project provides support particularly at the local level, where NGOs, youth centres and sport and cultural associations are key cooperation partners, it therefore intends to mainstream measures at this level by closely involving local institutions of target municipalities in the planning, implementation, and evaluation phases of the measures.

Interaction between project outputs not only pinpoints existing successful approaches to participatory, peace-building youth work, it also empowers young people to influence their immediate environment directly and proactively through activities supported financially by a youth fund and create space within society for addressing their needs. This enables the (re)building of young people's trust in their own ability to act. Finally, the sharing of successfully piloted approaches at the regional level also fosters the transnational exchange of information which could facilitate the scaling up of approaches at a later stage.

Since the beginning of SPACE, the project has worked with approximately 2500 young people from both countries combined, with women constituting over 65% and refugees around 24% of the number. The geographical span of the activities includes 11 governorates in Jordan and over 14 municipalities in Lebanon. Through different agreements with 12 partners (3 Lebanese, 8 Jordanian and 1 with both countries), along with collaborating with the Ministry of Youth in Jordan and municipalities in Lebanon, 13 conceptual spaces have been either established or utilised and 94 measures executed, using a participatory approach involving young people, including them in both the decision-making processes and the implementation of tasks and activities. By conducting pre- and post-assessments, over 750 participants reported improved knowledge of social participation practices and a better sense of belonging within their communities, along with enhanced abilities in creating more inclusion in their surrounding environment and coming up with solutions through developed technical and soft skills. Some of these young people were also part of the project's Youth Advisory Committee in Jordan, where they were involved in a participatory manner in decisions related to project activities in four DC projects. In Lebanon, the Youth Advisory Committee is currently in the final steps of creation and will soon follow the same steps as its Jordanian counterpart, with other DC projects. To emphasise the importance of knowledge-sharing and dialogue exchange, national and regional forums are held annually, including youth and partner representatives. So far, over 300 participants have joined across 3 regional (1 virtual and 2 physical) and 4 national ones, discussing youth-related needs and expectations, and developing their skills in various topics.

A fundamental results hypothesis for the project is that young people whose trust in their own abilities is strengthened are accordingly able to participate in a more targeted manner in their social environment and in the social and political development in their communities. As such they will also be able to contribute actively to peaceful and inclusive development. The inclusion and networking of different actors (organised and marginalised young people, local administrations, educational institutions, youth centres and civil society), including at the regional level, will enable the development and implementation of integrated approaches to peaceful and inclusive development.

1. Participation by young people in decision-making processes in DC projects. The project aims at significantly improving the participation of young people in the implementation of selected DC projects in Jordan and Lebanon. Through participatory measures, such as the introduction of a youth council, this participation will give young people a chance, in a modest way, to contribute actively to decision making. The results hypothesis is that the insights gained in this way, being a positive example of young people's involvement in decision-making processes, could provide a model for other acts of participation. This is because there is a need for more physical and virtual public spaces to encourage personal growth and development of young people and enable them to exert influence in the social and political sphere.

2. Improving scope for young people to use physical and virtual public spaces in accordance with their needs. This activity aims to mainstream measures by

closely involving the Ministry of Youth and local institutions in the planning, implementation, and evaluation of measures, in what the project set up a youth fund that will enable young people to design and implement 80 small and micro projects, selected according to an agreed list of criteria, in their immediate environment. Here, the results hypothesis is that young men and women will be able to develop and implement measures that lead to the shaping of peaceful spaces that are defined as safe, non-violent physical or virtual locations where young people can spend time and/or further their personal development.

3. Initiating mutual learning, dialogue and networking events on youth promotion with the involvement of youth organisations from the partner countries. This activity carried out 15 different pilot approaches for participatory youth work by youth organisations supported by the project in both partner countries. The hypothesis here is that the exchange of information (either in virtual or face-to-face forums) between civil society actors from both countries will facilitate an evaluation of the development impacts of the piloted project approaches as well as the long-term provision of digital data for third parties. This will result in scaling up and sharing of approaches that will pave the way for young people to have a greater influence on shaping peaceful spaces.

9. Conclusion

The three GIZ program approaches in three different partner countries (North Macedonia, Rwanda and Jordan) described above, illustrate impressively how the living conditions of disadvantaged population groups are taken into focus in the context of German Development Cooperation. According to these three promising practices, there are key success factors which contribute to a more inclusive community. First, through systematic and disaggregated data collection at local (North Macedonia) and national (Rwanda) level, local governments design social services in a more needs- and demand-oriented manner. Second, a close collaboration with and involvement of representatives of marginalised population groups ensure a better understanding of social grievances and inequalities at the municipal level and improve the communication capacities and ways of dialogue between citizens and the state. And finally, the creation of physical and virtual spaces for political participation at national and local governmental level (Jordan) offers opportunities to young people to express their own interests and needs vis-à-vis state bodies. It helps to further strengthen the trust and self-confidence of young citizens in their ability to influence decision-making processes and in taking on their role as self-advocates to effectively defend and express their own rights in the political arena at local and central level.

References

Castaneda Aguilar, Andres R./Eilertsen, Aleksander/Fujs, Tony/Lakner, Christoph/Gerszon Mahler Daniel/Nguyen, Minh Cong/Schoch, Marta/Baah, Samuel Kofi Tette/Viveros, Martha/Wu, Haoyu (2022): Global poverty update from the World Bank. https://blogs.worldbank.org/opendata/april-2022-global-poverty-update-world-bank [16.08.2023]

Dämmrich, Thomas (2022): Strengthening Civil Society Programme (CSP), February, 2022. giz2022-en-civil-society-programme.pdf [16.08.2023]

Ferrazzi, Gabriele (2023). Decentralization, Local Governance, and Localizing the Sustainable Development Goals in Indonesia. In: Carasco, Bruno/Rahemtulla, Hanif A./Rohdewohld, Rainer (eds.): Decentralization, Local Governance and Localizing the Sustainable Development Goals in Asia and the Pacific. New York: Routledge, pp. 253-274

GIZ Office Bagdad (2022): Supporting Decentralisation and Local Governance in Iraq (DLG). Baghdad: GIZ. https://www.giz.de/en/downloads/giz2022-en-decentralisation-local-governance.pdf [16.08.2023]

Kidd, Stephen/Kabare, Krystle (2019): Social protection and disability in Rwanda. Orpington: Development Pathways. http://Social-Protection-and-Disability-in-Rwanda-Report-.pdf [16.08.2023]

OECD (2018). Maintaining the Momentum of Decentralisation in Ukraine. OECD Multi-level Governance Studies. Paris: OECD Publishing.

OECD (2022): OECD Policy Responses to Coronavirus (COVID-19): Delivering for Youth: How Governments can put Young People at the Centre of the Recovery. Paris: OECD. http://oecd.org/coronavirus/policy-responses/delivering-for-youth-how-governments-can-put-young-people-at-the-centre-of-the-recovery-92c9d060/ [16.08.2023]

OHCHR (2023): About the right to social security and human rights. https://www.ohchr.org/en/social-security/about-right-social-security-and-human-rights [16.08.2023]

Schlutz, David (2017): Decentralisation and Good Governance in Rwanda. Kigali: GIZ. https://www.giz.de/static/en/images/contentimages_320x305px/Factsheet_Decentralisation_and_Good_Governance_in_Rwanda_09032017.pdf [16.08.2023]

Shakhshir, Jehad (2023): Promoting more efficient local governance for inclusive development. https://www.giz.de/en/worldwide/128531.html [16.08.2023]

UN (2015): Transforming our world: the 2030 Agenda for Sustainable Development. UN General Assembly A/RES/70/1. New York: UN.

UN (2016): 71/256. New Urban Agenda. UN General Assembly A/RES/71/256.

UN-HABITAT (2022): World Cities Report 2022: Envisaging the Future of Cities. Nairobi: UN-Habitat. https://unhabitat.org/wcr/ [16.08.2023]

UNHCR (2023): Humanitairian principles. https://emergency.unhcr.org/protection/protection-principles/humanitarian-principles [16.08.2023]

World Bank (2023). Population Data (Jordan). https//:data.worldbank.org/country/JO [16.08.2023]

Enhancing participation at the local level toward inclusive communities. Presumption of the subsidiarity principle for local decision-making from the perspective of Ghanaian decentralisation and local government policy

Paul Kwaku Larbi Anderson

Introduction

The underlying principle of an inclusive community is the maximum involvement of the people in the local decision-making process, especially in the planning and implementation of policies and programs that directly affect them. Accordingly, global policy frameworks such as the United Nations (UN) 2030 Agenda for Sustainable Development and the New Urban Agenda *Quito Declaration on Sustainable Cities and Human Settlements for All* highlight the role of decentralisation and local governance for sustainable and inclusive societies (United Nations 2015, 2016).

Decentralisation reforms have been pursued by various countries across the globe to promote local decision-making and bring governance closer to the people by accelerating and enhancing local development while upholding the rights of the community. On that basis, the decentralisation and local government concept is broadly defined and implemented variously due to differences in the size and structure of governments. Accordingly, international institutions, like the Council of Europe, the European Commission, the United Nations, and the World Bank, mostly employ a general definition of the decentralisation concept. For instance, according to the Organisation for Economic Cooperation and Development (OECD 2019), decentralisation refers to policies that give subnational governments, elected by universal suffrage, a variety of authorities, responsibilities, and resources previously held by the central government to act on behalf of the people. This implies transferring administrative authority such as planning, decision-making, and revenue mobilisation from the central government to local governments, federal units, and semi-autonomous public establishments.

Decentralisation and local governance provide the opportunity for governments across the globe to provide a platform to advance the common good of the people. Such governmental duties are carried out effectively through the transfer of authority, and responsibility for carrying out functions at the local level based on the principle of subsidiarity. Notwithstanding, whenever the local institution or the lower hierarchical level is unable to carry out the assigned function effectively, a higher echelon of government must intervene (Pavy 2023). The subsidiarity principle as applied to decentralisation and local governance seeks to ensure some degree of independence for a lower level in relation to a higher authority, specifically, for a local unit in relation to the central government (Cahill 2016, 2017a).

In this paper, decentralisation and local government are discussed in greater length with emphasis on the various forms, dimensions, policy formulation, and prospects from the Ghanaian perspective. It further scrutinises the presumption of the subsidiarity principle for local decision-making from the perspective of Ghanaian decentralisation and local government policy. Accordingly, it is organised into three sections and employs secondary source material analysis. The first section gives an overview of the concept of decentralisation and local government. It provides a variety of definitions of decentralisation from related relevant literature and an overview of its nature, forms, objectives, and practice from the Ghanaian perspective. In the second section, the background of the subsidiarity principle and its implementation strategies are reviewed. In addition, it examines subsidiarity as a principle for governance and social organisation in the local decision-making process. The third section provides a concise view of Ghana's strategy for encouraging citizen participation in local government on the assumption of the subsidiarity principle.

1. The concept of decentralisation and local governance

Recent years have seen an increase in global interest in decentralisation as a means of removing the burden of centralisation while fostering the growth of an effective democratic culture by enhancing participation in the decision-making process at the local level. Decentralisation is seen as a way of mobilising support for national development policies by making them better known at the local level. The reason being that greater involvement in development planning and administration by allowing people from various backgrounds to participate in decision-making more actively strengthens national unity and thus helps to promote effective democratic culture. It is argued that fairness in the distribution of government resources for investment is more likely to be attained when decision-making is established with input from members of a wide range of political, religious, ethnic, and social groups (Cohen 2002; Martinez-Vazquez/Vaillancourt 2011; OECD 2019).

From the global perspective, the decentralisation concept is broad with numerous sub-components. Therefore, definitions and categorisations are required. According to the United Nations Development Program (UNDP) (Altmann et al. 2000), decentralisation refers to the restructuring or reorganisation of authority so that institutions of governance at the central, regional, and local levels share responsibility in accordance with the principle of subsidiarity, improving the overall quality and effectiveness of the system of governance while boosting the authority and capabilities of sub-national levels. Similarly, the Organisation for Economic Cooperation and Development (OECD 2019) describes decentralisation as a measure that transfers a range of powers, responsibilities, and resources from the central government to subnational governments, defined as legal entities elected by universal suffrage and having some degree of autonomy. In the view of (Ayee 2008), decentralisation is the practice of transferring significant authority, responsibility, and fiscal and human resources to local government units for the development of their areas of jurisdiction. Mewes (2011a) adds that decentralisation is the practice of administration by which considerable autonomy is given to sub-political governmental bodies and institutions at the local level to make decisions and implement policies and programs to promote socio-economic development. Explaining further, Mookherjee (2006) asserts that decentralisation is not only about the transfer of power, authority, and responsibility from the centre to the periphery but a process of redefining the structures and procedures of governance to bring democracy and development closer to the people, especially at the local level.

Largely, four types of decentralisation are identified in the literature (Antwi-Boasiako 2014; Martinez-Vazquez/Vaillancourt 2011; Schneider 2003) as political, administrative, fiscal, and market-related norms. These types of decentralisation overlap in definition and approach to implementation and come in different forms based on the nature of government. Political decentralisation involves creating sub-national units of administration with the power to make decisions and implement policies within the framework of democratisation to ease the workload of the central government. The sub-units of the statutory structure such as states, provinces, municipalities, or districts are given the legal authority to elect their representatives and to set up a budget. The objective of political decentralisation is to enhance participatory democracy by bringing governance closer to the people. Ideally, political decentralisation requires that sub-national officials are not appointed by or be subject to undue influence from the central government but must be elected through universal adult suffrage. Notwithstanding, political decentralisation is influenced by distinct features such as geography, ethnicity, and language. It is assumed that political decentralisation offers greater opportunities for participation and is relevant to diverse interests at the local level as the selection of representatives allows the people to choose officials with close contact to the community (Ahwoi 2010; Cohen 2002; Schneider 2003).

Administrative decentralisation involves the allocation of authority, responsibility, and resources from the central government to sub-units of administration for public services provision. Administrative decentralisation can take the form of deconcentrating, delegation, or devolution. In de-concentration, the central government grants administrative and supervisory authority to ministries, departments, and agencies to take decisions and implement policies on behalf of the government. The practice which is also known as *decongestion* is aimed at reducing the workload of the central government. Delegation is considered a functional activity where power given to the sub-units of administration to act is not guaranteed and therefore can be withdrawn at any point in time. In the case of devolution, power is legally granted to the sub-governmental bodies and institutions at the regional and local levels. Devolution ensures a strict sense of decentralisation as the transfer of authority is derived from legal rules accompanied by full responsibilities. Until the last decades of the twentieth century, decentralisation was mainly in the form of de-concentration and almost without exception (Ahwoi 2010; Mewes 2011b; Schneider 2003).

Fiscal decentralisation entails the distribution of resources and granting of authority by a central body to sub-units for financial management to enhance the decision-making and implementation process. This involves the authority to raise and collect revenue, make an expenditure, and reallocate resources to sub-national levels of administration. Fiscal decentralisation comprehensive and traceable since it has everything to do with budgetary practices. For local government units to perform their functions effectively, adequate measures such as the authority to source funding from the central government and generate their revenue are put in place through fiscal decentralisation. Depending on the nature of the government set up, fiscal decentralisation takes different forms such as self-financing, co-financing, intergovernmental transfers, and local revenue mobilisation. In most cases, for instance in Ghana, the local government units are assigned the legal authority to impose taxes and levies to raise revenue for development.

Market-related decentralisation takes the form of privatisation and deregulation that seeks to transfer functions and responsibilities from the central government to the private sector and is carried out by businesses, cooperatives, non-governmental organisations, and community groups. It is usually coordinated by central government market growth policies such as value chain development, inclusiveness, and industrial strategy. Decentralisation of national markets aims to enhance participation and inclusiveness by offering job opportunities, products, and financial access to the people. In addition, it offers opportunities for people to take part in economic activities.

2. Policy formulation and implementation of decentralisation and local government in Ghana

The decentralisation and local government policy is an essential element of democratic governance because they create a conducive atmosphere for bringing decision-making and service delivery closer to the people. The political ideology that initiated the decentralisation and local government reform in Ghana was the Provisional National Defence Council (PNDC), a military government led by Jerry John Rawlings in 1988. The objective at the time was to usher the country into democratic governance by increasing civic participation at the local level (Boamah 2018; Gocking 2005; Jumah 2011). According to Ahwoi (2010) and Ayee (2008), the idea behind the decentralisation policy in Ghana was to increase participation at the local level and also to reduce the workload on the central government by devolving power and responsibilities to local units in the area of policy initiation and implementation. Accordingly, a comprehensive local government and decentralisation policy was instituted by the government of Ghana in 1988 with the passage of the Provisional National Defence Council (PNDC) Law 207 establishing Metropolitan, Municipal, and District Assemblies (MMDAs) with remarkable legislative, executive, budgeting, and planning powers.

The decentralisation policy in Ghana was given credence by the 1992 fourth republican constitution when the country was re-legitimised in a multi-party election. Essentially, the country acknowledged political, administrative, and fiscal decentralisation as the fundamental basis of enhancing civic participation in the decision-making process and consolidating democratic values. For effective implementation, the policy framework was replaced by an act of parliament (Act 462) in 1993 which was amended (Act 936) in 2016. The fundamental basis for the act (Act 462) was the provision made in the 1992 Constitution of the Republic of Ghana in Article 240 (1) which recommends that as far as possible local governments in Ghana should be decentralised. According to (Ahwoi 2000), the core objective was "*affording all possible opportunities to the people to participate in decision-making at every level in national life and government*". Under the decentralisation policy in Ghana, the sub-national administration consists of the Regional Coordinating Council (RCC), the four-tier Metropolitan, the three-tier Municipal or District Assembly, the Urban, Town, Area, Zonal (UTAZ) council, and the unit committee. Conventionally, the unit committee forms the basic unit whilst the Regional Coordinating Council (RCC) represents the highest level of decentralised local government structure. The MMDAs are established as the hub of decentralised government administration with deliberative, legislative, and executive functions. They are assigned the responsibility (Act 936) of bringing about the integration of political, administrative, and development support needed to achieve a more equitable allocation of power, wealth, and geographically dispersed development in Ghana. Essentially the MMDAs are constituted as the planning authority for the district. The Local Government Act (Act 936) of 2016 stipulates the functions of the District Assemblies which are principally aimed at improving the quality of life of the people through better political representation.

The decentralisation and local government policy in Ghana as noted in its policy formulation and implementation seeks to ensure that every person has the right to take part in the decisions that have an impact on their community. In decentralisation, the principle of subsidiarity which seeks to guarantee some degree of independence for a lower authority in relation to the higher level or for a local unit in a hierarchical order is often invoked (Cohen 2002; Pavy 2023).

3. Background to the subsidiarity principle

The idea behind the subsidiarity principle is rooted in Catholic social thought. It posits that a person's concerns should first be resolved at the family, community, or parish level, and only when those levels are unable to handle the matter should it be resolved at the central level. The notion behind it was to restrict higher authority from interfering unduly in private or community life, which was seen as a constraint to the (Catholic) church. This implies that the local level is granted some degree of authority and resources to act and operate within the parameters set by the central authority. The general objective of the subsidiarity principle is to ensure some level of independence for a lower authority with respect to a higher entity. Ultimately, it provides the basis for the allocation of powers and responsibilities from the base to the peripheries. The principle is applied purposely to enhance the organisation of social groups in reaction against disproportionate individualism (Cahill 2016).

The subsidiarity principle can be traced back to Althusius (1563-1638), who developed an early theory of it based on Orthodox Calvinism, on the notion that communities and associations have a crucial role in helping ("*subsidia*") individuals to meet their needs for leading holy lives (Follesdal 2013). It was later developed as a social philosophy and Catholic social theory with the publication of the encyclical Rerum Novarum on May 15, 1891, by Pope Leo XIII. Although the publication did not use the term subsidiarity specifically, it did place a strong emphasis on the relationships between the state and society, people's economic well-being, and the duties and obligations that eventually came to be linked with the idea behind it. Later, in 1931, Pope Pius

XI formally endorsed the subsidiarity principle in the papal Quadragesima Anno. Subsequently, from the 1960s onwards, Catholic social theorists such as Oswald von Nell-Breuning and Gustav Gundlach embraced subsidiarity as a principle in governance and social organisation (Cahill 2016).

As it relates to the European Union (EU), the adoption of a single European Act (Article 130 R, 4) on jurisdiction popularised the application of the subsidiarity principle in modern times. The act permits certain matters to be addressed adequately by individual member states. However, it mandates the European Union to intervene in areas where the competencies of member states are in question. (Kersbergen/Verbeek 2004).

In the framework of governance, the subsidiarity principle has anchored the assumption that the autonomy of local units should be recognised and supported, and that the central authority must provide sustenance when the lower (local unit) is unable to address pressing challenges. This means that even though a local unit is given some level of autonomy, the central authority has a role to play to ensure that the right things are done, and the local authorities are given the resources needed to complement what could be mobilised locally to enhance development (Drew/Grant 2017).

4. Subsidiarity as a principle in governance and social organisation that holds the people together and as a presumption for local decision-making

An important feature of the subsidiarity principle is situating the individual at the core of the social organisation. In that context, the principle goes beyond organisational structure but is applied to connect the welfare of the individual and society as well as define state-society relationships. Ultimately, it provides the basis for the allocation of powers and responsibilities from the centre to the peripheries. As a normative principle of justice, it links to three basic ideas. The first is philosophical acceptance, which serves as a prism through which modern societies are analysed and as a tenet for institutional development. The second is technical acceptability, which serves as the foundation for examining power imbalances between levels of government and potential power redistribution. The context for philosophical and technological difficulties is provided by the third, which is legal acceptance (Cahill 2016; Mulé/Walzenbach 2019).

When the subsidiarity principle is used in local decision-making, it typically results in a differentiated functional distribution of tasks and responsibilities. For instance, in line with the decentralisation and local governance policy in Ghana, the national government sets principles and minimum standards for the regional and local levels in social and public services delivery. This implies that the subsidiarity principle always relates to the level of the users, the residents, and the local communities, not just the level at which tasks are distributed among the several levels of government. In many instances, only with the participation of the people can a specific problem be solved efficiently and sustainably. Respectively, the principle requires a higher authority to ensure a certain level of independence for a lower authority and to promote local accountability. However, if a lower authority lacks the resources and ability to act efficiently, the principle requires that a higher authority step in and regulate when necessary (Follesdal 2013; Komonchak 1988). Presumably, it encourages interventions as a way of helping people to help themselves. Moreover, the subsidiarity principle necessitates the localisation of social problem-solving, including the duty to make sure that people are ready to fully engage in group decision-making over issues that impact them and their communities. It serves as a guide for defining power, and redistribution of authority to make it more operational (Cahill 2016, 2017b; Mulé/Walzenbach 2019).

The subsidiarity principle is applicable in decentralisation when it comes to local decision-making and helps with the allocative function and responsibilities. In this instance, the lower levels are assigned the responsibility of taxing, local spending, and other regulatory activities unless a compelling case can be established for allocating them to a higher level. For instance, in the Ghanaian decentralisation and local government policy, the district assemblies are charged with the responsibility for the overall development of the districts. It further mandates the zonal council at the bottom of the decentralised structure to mobilise community members to participate in the decision-making process, raise revenue, and implement policies on behalf of the people. Based on this mandate, the local people are given some level of authority and resources to act and operate within specific boundaries defined by the central government. The implication is that, even though the focus on decentralisation at the onset was to decongest central government, a recent shift has been to empower local authorities to mobilise resources and get the people to be actively involved in identifying their needs and be part of the solution (Ahwoi 2000; Anderson 2022a; Popic/Patel 2011).

5. Ghana's strategy for encouraging citizen participation in local government

Ghana has one of Africa's most extensive histories of democratic government and a decentralised local governance system. In accordance with Article 1 of

Chapter 1 of the 1992 Constitution of the Republic of Ghana, *"sovereignty resides in the people of Ghana in whose name and for whose welfare the powers of government are to be exercised in the manner and within the limits laid down in the Constitution"*. This and other articles guarantee citizens the right to unrestricted speech and the ability to participate in the decision-making process whether at the national or local level. For instance, the Local Government Act (462) of Ghana states that local participation initiates the entire planning process from the local to the national level. It stipulates that in the decentralised system, Regional Coordinating Councils (RCCs) oversee regional issues, while Metropolitan, Municipal, and District Assemblies (MMDAs) oversee local matters. This decentralised framework aims to foster effective participation in local decision-making (Anderson 2022a, 2022b; Ayee 2008; Boamah 2018).

Consequently, participation in the decision-making process in Ghana takes different forms, such as information sharing, program input, voting, representation, association, and cooperation. These forms of participation allow the community members to be part of specific discussions and contribute to the local and national decision-making process. For instance, national elections are held in Ghana every four years to choose the president and members of parliament. Correspondingly, local-level elections are also held in all the MMDAs to elect local representatives every four years. The process provides an opportunity for community members not only to choose a leader but to decide who represents them at a higher level. The assumption is that in a democracy, the level of provision of public goods and services that inure to the benefit of members of a given community has some correlation with the level of citizens' participation in the decision-making process (Anderson 2022a; MLGRD 2015).

6. Conclusion

The decentralisation and local government policy play distinctive roles not just to transfer authority, resources, and responsibilities but to broaden civic participation in local decision-making. Therefore, effective implementation of the policy has the potential to strengthen the local government's capacity to reach out to the generality of the people in public service delivery for the common good.

In Ghana, the local government act (Act 936) establishes sub-district structures and accords them functions based on the subsidiarity principle. These structures such as the Urban, Town, Area, Zonal (UTAZ) council, provide a way for members of the community to communicate their needs and aspirations to the municipal assembly. The decentralisation policy stipulates that the devolution of some functions and authority to the local structures has legal implications that make the transfer of certain functions irreversible. As a result, the local authority is required to be equipped with the expertise to carry out the function that is devolved. In the case where the competencies of the local authority are in question, they are required to be equipped with the necessary resources to carry out their functions effectively. Fiscal decentralisation is a major area in which the subsidiarity principle is applied to a significant extent in the Ghanaian local governance system. For instance, the local government act (Act 936) requires the central government to allocate not less than 5 percent of all government revenue each fiscal year to the District Assemblies Common Fund (DACF) secretariat. This fund is then divided among MMDAs in accordance with a formula approved by the Ghanaian Parliament. In addition to that, the local government act gives MMDAs the authority to set rates and to collect taxes as well as non-tax income including rates, license fees, and fines. The main purpose for establishing this fund and the mandate to collect taxes is to offer funding to help the local government's development efforts based on the subsidiarity principle.

Notwithstanding, the subsidiarity principle is predicated on the question of responsibility, albeit with different perspectives. As in the case of Ghana as a unitary state, the upward accountability of the MMDAs to the central government threatens the district assemblies' autonomy. The decentralisation policy just gives off the idea that the MMDAs are in charge, but in reality, the central government exerts greater control over them and so restrains their authority. In this regard, it can be said that subsidiarity as a principle in decentralised governance and social organisation is applied in a different context concerning the domain, objectives, role, and allocation of functions by the corresponding authority. Be that as it may, there is a common ground that builds on the foundation that decision-making should involve the generality of the people as much as possible to allows the people to demonstrate some degree of community control.

References

Ahwoi, K. (2000): Enhancing The Decentralisation Programme: District Assemblies And Sub-Structures As Partners In Governance. Accra: Institute of Economic Affairs (IEA Ghana). https://policycommons.net/artifacts/1444828/enhancing-the-decentralisation-programme/2076574/[08.08.2023]

Ahwoi, K. (2010): Rethinking decentralization and local government in Ghana: Proposals for amendment. Accra: Institute of Economic Affairs (IEA Ghana). file:///C:/Users/Wissenbach/Downloads/CRS%20-%206-%20Rethinking%20decentralization%20and%20local%20government%20in%20Ghana%20proposals%20for%20amendment.pdf [08.08.2023]

Altmann, J./Cariño, L./Flaman, R./Kulessa, M./Schulz, I. (2000): The UNDP role in decentralization and local governance: A joint UNDP–Government of Germany

Evaluation. New York: UNDP. https://erc.undp.org/evaluation/documents/download/5029 [08.08.2023]

Anderson, P. K. L. (2022a): Local Government and Community Participation; Prospect of the Unit Committee Model in Ghana's Decentralization Program. International Journal of Research and Innovation in Social Science, Volume VI, Issue IV, pp. 2454-6186.

Anderson, P. K. L. (2022b): The Trajectory of Traditional Authority in Contemporary Governance; The Ghanaian Experience. International Journal of Research and Innovation in Social Science, 6(5), pp. 94-100. https://doi.org/10.47772/IJRISS.2022.6505

Antwi-Boasiako, K. (2014): The theories of decentralization and local government: Implementation, implications, and realities: A global perspective (1st ed.). Nacogdoches: Stephen F. Austin State University Press.

Ayee, J. R. A. (2008): The balance sheet of decentralization in Ghana. In: Saito, F. (ed.) Foundations for Local Governance. Heidelberg: Physica-Verlag, pp. 233-258. https://doi.org/10.1007/978-3-7908-2006-5_11

Boamah, E. F. (2018): Constitutional economics of Ghana's decentralization. World Development, Vol. 110, Issue C, pp. 256-267.

Cahill, M. (2016): Sovereignty, Liberalism and the Intelligibility of Attraction to Subsidiarity. The American Journal of Jurisprudence, 61(1), pp. 109-132. https://doi.org/10.1093/AJJ/AUW003

Cahill, M. (2017a): Theorizing subsidiarity: Towards an ontology-sensitive approach. International Journal of Constitutional Law, 15(1), pp. 201-224.

Cahill, M. (2017b). Theorizing subsidiarity: Towards an ontology-sensitive approach. International Journal of Constitutional Law, 15(1), pp. 201–224.

Cohen, J. (2002): Administrative decentralization: Strategies for developing countries (2. print.). West Hartford: Kumarian Press.

Drew, J./Grant, B. (2017): Subsidiarity: More than a Principle of Decentralization—a View from Local Government. Publius: The Journal of Federalism, 47(4), pp. 522-545. https://doi.org/10.1093/publius/pjx039

Follesdal, A. (2013): The principle of subsidiarity as a constitutional principle in international law. Global Constitutionalism, 2(1), pp. 37–62. https://doi.org/10.1017/S2045381712000123

Gocking, R. (2005): The history of Ghana. Westport: Greenwood Press.

Jumah, A. B. (2011): Towards Democratic Ownership in Ghana: Strong Progress in Civil Society Engagement. Alliance2015. https://docplayer.net/30622722-Towards-democratic-ownership-in-ghana-strong-progress-in-civil-society-engagement-author-bashiru-jumah-send-ghana-editor-javier-pereira.html [08.08.2023]

Kersbergen, K. van/Verbeek, B. (2004): Subsidiarity as a Principle of Governance in the European Union. Comparative European Politics 2004 2:2, 2(2), pp. 142-162. https://doi.org/10.1057/PALGRAVE.CEP.6110033

Komonchak, J. (1988): Subsidiarity in the Church: The State of the Question. The Nature and Future of Episcopal Conferences. The Jurist, XLVIII, Washington, 1988, pp. 298–349.

Martinez-Vazquez, J./Vaillancourt, F. (2011): Decentralization in developing countries: Global perspectives on the obstacles to fiscal devolution. Cheltenham: Edward Elgar Publishing Limited.

Mewes, K. (2011a): Decentralization Concept. In: Mewes, K. (ed.): Decentralization on the Example of the Yemeni Water Sector. Wiesbaden: VS Verlag für Sozialwissenschaften, pp. 29–52 https://doi.org/10.1007/978-3-531-93051-0_3

Mewes, K. (2011b): Decentralization: Concepts and Definitions. In: Mewes, K. (ed.): Decentralization on the Example of the Yemeni Water Sector. Wiesbaden: VS Verlag für Sozialwissenschaften, pp. 53–75. https://doi.org/10.1007/978-3-531-93051-0_4

MLGRD (2015): Ghana national decentralization action plan 2015-2019: Accelerating decentralization and local governance for national development. Accra: MLGRD. https://new-ndpc-static1.s3.amazonaws.com/pubication/Decentralisation+Action+Plan_2012.pdf [08.08.2023]

Mookherjee, D. (2006). Market institutions, governance, and development: collected essays. Noida: Oxford University Press/Oxford India Paperbacks.

Mulé, R./Walzenbach, G. (2019): Introduction: Two spaces of subsidiarity? Commonwealth and Comparative Politics, 57(2), pp. 141-152. https://doi.org/10.1080/14662043.2019.1573991

OECD (2019): Making Decentralisation Work. A Handbook for Policy-Makers. OECD Multi-level Governance Studies. Paris: OECD Publishing. https://doi.org/10.1787/g2g9faa7-en.

Pavy, E. (2023): The principle of subsidiarity. https://www.europarl.europa.eu/factsheets/en/sheet/7/the-principle-of-subsidiarity [08.08.2023]

Popic, D./Patel, M. (2011): Decentralization: Equity and sectoral policy implications for UNICEF in East Asia and the Pacific. Bangkok: Social Policy and Economic Analysis Unit, UNICEF EAPRO, Bangkok; 2011.

Schneider, A. (2003): Decentralization: Conceptualization and measurement. Studies in Comparative International Development, 38(3), pp. 32-56. https://doi.org/10.1007/BF02686198

United Nations (2015): Transforming our world: the 2030 Agenda for Sustainable Development. UN Genral Assembly A/RES/70/1. http://www.un.org/ga/search/view_doc.asp?symbol=A/RES/70/1&Lang=E [08.08.2023]

United Nations (2016): 71/256. New Urban Agenda. UN General Assembly A/RES/71/256. http://habitat3.org/wp-content/uploads/New-Urban-Agenda-GA-Adopted-68th-Plenary-N1646655-E.pdf [08.08.2023]

Authors' Details

Alisch, Monika, sociologist, Professor of social planning, social space and community work at Fulda University of Applied Sciences, department social work. Director of the Centre of Research for Society and Sustainability (CeSSt). Main research areas: social space, migration, aging, participatory research.
Contact: monika.alisch@sw.hs-fulda.de

Anderson, Paul K. L., PhD, is a research associate at the Centre for Planning and Development of Social Services (ZPE), University of Siegen. His main research interest lies in the field of decentralization and local governance with particular emphasis on civic participation and social inclusion.
Contact: paul.anderson@uni-siegen.de

Bertelmann, Lena, M.A. Education and Social Work, ZPE (Centre for Planning and Development of Social Services),University of Siegen. Main areas of work: implementation of the CRPD at municipal level, participation of persons with disabilities in municipal planning processes and leadership of planning by the municipal administration.
Contact: lena.bertelmann@uni-siegen.de

Brogini, Giulia, Dr. phil. hist, University of Berne. Main areas of work: Implementation of the UN CRPD in Switzerland at the federal, cantonal and municipal level; participation research; evaluations, innovation projects and campaigns in the field of social participation and diversity.
Contact: giulia.brogini@gs-edi.admin.ch

Bulder, Elles, Prof. Dr., PhD in Economics, Research Centre "Noorder Ruimte", University of Applied Sciences Groningen. Main areas of work: Liveability of the built environment with an emphasis on the interactions between men and their environment, in which co-creation with 4-helix partners and participatory action research are important methods.
Contact: e.a.m.bulder@pl.hanze.nl

Daniel, Rebecca, M.A. Empowerment Studies/Development Education, freelance researcher and consultant. Main research interests and/or areas of work: Political participation of persons with disabilities, inclusion of persons with disabilities in international cooperation, full and effective participation in the workplace.
Contact: rebecca.daniel@posteo.de

Hobinka, Alexander, M.A. in Public Management (Leipzig) and in Political Science (IEP Paris). Main areas of work: inclusive governance in the global south, poverty-oriented economic and social development, social cohesion in fragile contexts and participation and empowerment of marginalised groups.
Contact: alexander.hobinka@giz.de

Kempf, Matthias, M.A. Education and Social Work, ZPE (Centre for Planning and Development of Social Services), University of Siegen. Main areas of work: implementation of the CRPD at municipal level, participation of persons with disabilities; diffusion of (social-) innovations; legal guardianship.
Contact: matthias.kempf@uni-siegen.de

Laub, Matthias, Dr. phil., M.A. Social Work, Professor of Social Work Science and Research, University of applied Sciences Landshut. Main research interests: implementation of the CRPD at municipal level, inclusion and participation of persons with mental disabilities, interprofessional cooperation networks for the support of children of mentally ill and/or addicted parents.
Contact: matthias.laub@haw-landshut.de

May, Michael, Prof. Dr. phil. habil., Inter-University Doctoral Research Centre for Social Work in the German State of Hessen. Main areas of work: Politics and Pedagogy of the Social, Professionalism of Social Work, Community Work, Subalternity, Intersectionality.
Contact: michael.may@hs-rm.de

Meier, Sabine, Prof. Dr., RheinMain University of Applied Sciences, Wiesbaden. Main areas of work: Theories of social space, housing and community work, Social space oriented Social Work, Qualitative research methods of social space analysis, participation of migrants in small and large cities.
Contact: sabine.meier@hs-rm.de

Nio, Ivan, PhD in Urban Sociology/Urban Studies, University of Amsterdam. He is an independent researcher and consultant. He has also been working as senior researcher at AUAS (Amsterdam University of Applied Sciences) for many years. Main areas of work: the tension and mutual interaction between the planned city and the lived city; everyday life and the built environment.
Contact: nio@planet.nl

Authors' Details

Reichstein, Martin F., Dr. phil., ZPE (Centre for Planning and Development of Social Services), Faculty II (Education – Architecture – Fine Arts), University of Siegen. Main areas of work: Complex support needs of persons with disabilities and approaches to integrated planning and development of social services – e.g. in the fields of services for persons with disabilities, psychiatric care, and long-term care.
Contact: martin.reichstein@uni-siegen.de

Reijndorp, Arnold, Independent researcher, Em. Professor of Socio-economic and Spatial Developments of New Urban Areas (Han Lammers Chair) at the University of Amsterdam. Main areas of work: qualitative (and ethnographic) research on the cutting edge of socio-cultural and spatial developments of cities, with a focus on the growing diversity of cities and city-district, and the development of new public domains.
Contact: reijn@antenna.nl

Rohrmann, Albrecht, Professor of Social Pedagogy with focus on social rehabilitation and inclusion; Spokesman of the Centre for Planning and Development of Social Services (ZPE), University of Siegen. Main areas of research: social services for people with disabilities, inclusive child and youth care, implementation of the CRPD at municipal level.
Contact: rohrmann@zpe.uni-siegen.de

Schädler, Johannes, Professor for Social Pedagogy with a focus on social planning and inclusion. Centre for Planning and Development of Social Services (ZPE), University of Siegen. Main areas of research: inclusive social infrastructure and local planning, comparative European and international research on development of social services, Chair of EURECO-research platform.
Contact: schaedler@zpe.uni-siegen.de

Schmidt, Marcel, Prof. Dr. phil., Hochschule Darmstadt, University of Applied Sciences. Main fields of work: Ethics, theories and philosophy of social work and ecosocial transformation of communities.
Contact: marcel.schmidt@h-da.de

Schuler, Thomas, Lic. iur., University of Berne. Main areas of work: Implementation of the UN Convention on the Rights of Persons with Disabilities in Switzerland at the cantonal level; support for cantonal activities in the area of housing, work and participation of persons with disabilities.
Contact: thomas.schuler@sodk.ch

Wissenbach, Lars, M.A., Centre for Planning and Development of Social Services (ZPE), University of Siegen. Main areas of work: disability and social protection in Global South contexts and the field of international cooperation, with a particular interest in actors, structures and planning processes at local levels.
Contact: lars.wissenbach@uni-siegen.de

Index

accessibility 8, 12, 15, 19, 40, 51, 55, 57ff., 61, 113, 119ff., 137, 151, 153f., 165f., 168, 171, 199f., 202, 204, 206
actors 14, 16, 18f., 89, 110, 123, 141, 143, 145ff., 150, 154, 156, 165f., 170, 178, 180, 184f., 188–192, 194, 199, 201, 205, 213ff., 218, 221, 223f.
Agenda for Sustainable Development 2030 7, 10, 19, 110, 211, 220, 227
anti-racism 8
barriers 9, 13, 40, 44, 58, 99, 101f., 112f., 120, 122, 130, 135f., 138, 144, 151, 154, 164f., 169f., 178, 180, 198, 205, 220ff.
barriers of accessibility 154
barriers to participation 112
Belgium 16
BTHG (Federal Participation Act in Germany) 29, 31f., 145
care 18, 26, 28, 39, 59, 65–68, 70–77, 143, 160, 166, 178f., 181–186, 188ff., 194, 200, 202, 212
care institutions 16
care services 181f.
caring communities 71, 73, 77
case manager 221
categories of difference 9, 13f.
citizen participation 110, 112, 131, 154, 215, 228
city 13, 15, 30, 40ff., 45, 51–57, 59, 61f., 81, 83f., 89, 133, 163f., 205, 213, 217

civil society 13, 18, 41, 43, 46, 55, 57, 89, 111f., 116, 165, 177, 192, 199, 201ff., 208, 213ff., 219, 223ff.
civil society actors 111, 192, 225
collective learning 18, 178, 190–194
communication space 168
community 11, 14–18, 25, 28, 31f., 37–46, 57ff., 66, 68–71, 73, 76f., 82–85, 109, 111, 127, 130, 133, 135ff., 141–144, 146, 153, 156, 161, 164ff., 168, 170, 179, 181, 189f., 197, 200, 203, 211, 214, 216, 222, 227, 230, 232, 234ff.
community development 37f., 41ff., 46, 130, 181
community work 14, 85, 181
community-based care initiatives 16, 66, 70f., 76f.
concept of inclusion 7f., 12, 25, 27, 38, 52, 61, 170
coordination 10, 14, 165, 182, 191, 199, 215
counterculture 89
counterpublics 87–91
decentralisation 16, 19, 66f., 182, 213, 227–236
dependence 161
design of inclusive communities 14, 156
difference 9, 27, 53, 160
digital 16, 75, 95–101, 122, 215, 225
digital transformation 96, 98, 101
dimensions of inclusive cities 12

disability 9, 14, 17f., 26–30, 52, 58, 66, 96, 98f., 110, 118, 122, 130, 135, 138, 144f., 149, 160, 164, 166–170, 179, 185, 190, 197–202, 204, 206f., 220ff.
disability field 96, 179
disability policy 160, 197, 199–202, 207
disability rights movement 26–30
discrimination 8, 132, 169, 171, 178, 207, 219
diversity 12, 16, 45, 52, 57, 60, 62, 81f., 86f., 91, 110, 112, 122, 160, 165f., 168f., 187, 191, 206, 216f., 222
Dutch cities 51f.
elderly people 58f., 65, 67, 182, 197, 218, 220
empowerment 18, 127, 130, 165, 170f., 193, 205, 214
federal financial programmes/investments 41, 112, 119, 152, 204, 206, 211, 230
finance of services 11
gentrification 11f., 60, 85, 86
Germany 15, 25f., 29, 42, 46, 95f., 98f., 116, 127, 129f., 132, 141f., 144, 146f., 159f., 165f.
Ghana 19, 230ff., 234ff.
Ghent 16, 81, 84, 86, 89
GIZ (Deutsche Gesellschaft für Internationale Zusammenarbeit) 211ff., 216ff., 220, 222, 225
governance 10ff., 15, 17, 110, 122, 180, 186, 211, 213, 216, 218, 227ff., 231, 233, 236
Groningen 67, 75
health care 16, 57, 65, 74f., 221

human rights 8, 37, 101, 110f., 114, 127, 132, 159, 168, 170, 218
ICF (International Classification of Functioning, Disability and Health) 9, 28ff., 164, 169
inclusion 7ff., 11–15, 18f., 25–32, 37ff., 41, 44–47, 51–59, 61f., 70, 88, 90, 99, 109, 112, 122, 127ff., 131ff., 136, 141ff., 145–148, 153, 155, 159f., 165–171, 180, 182, 198, 200f., 203, 206, 215, 218, 220f., 224
inclusion/exclusion 7, 27
inclusion-oriented action planning 159
inclusive cities 10–13, 51ff., 55, 57f., 61, 216
inclusive communities 14f., 19, 37, 39, 46, 129, 137f., 142, 145ff., 154, 182, 225, 227
inclusive development 10, 223f.
inclusive localities 101, 123, 127
inclusive policies 7
inclusive spaces 9, 128
infrastructure 11, 13, 16, 39, 42, 57, 82, 86, 89, 112, 136, 138, 143, 161, 163, 178, 180ff., 190, 199, 202, 216
integration 7, 27, 38, 68, 76, 146, 160, 164ff., 203, 215, 232
intersectionality 8, 117
Jordan 19, 222–225
ladder of citizen participation 163
lead management 149
leadership 143, 147, 149f., 154ff., 165
Lebanon 19, 222ff.
local actors 17, 189
local and regional authorities 211

Index

local decision-making 10, 19, 109, 111, 114f., 117, 119ff., 128, 227f., 233ff.
local empowerment 159, 167, 169
local governance 10, 14, 17, 109–112, 116, 121ff., 178, 185, 189, 212, 216, 227, 233f., 236
local planning 10, 12, 14, 17, 109, 138, 146, 169, 184, 213
local social policies 18, 177
locality 11, 15, 128, 190, 194
mediation 18, 32, 145, 152, 154f., 171, 217
meeting places 16, 59, 83, 88, 90f.
migration 9, 11f., 59, 197, 211, 217
mixed neighbourhoods 16, 54, 58f.
mobility 7, 12f., 16, 164, 198, 200, 202, 212
moderation 32, 152, 154, 190
Munich 164
municipal administration 142f., 147ff., 152, 154ff.
municipal planning 142, 144f., 153
municipality 18, 39, 45, 51, 53–57, 59, 61, 72ff., 109, 128, 133f., 136f., 143–146, 148ff., 152, 163, 170, 199, 203f.
neighbourhoods 13, 16, 32, 40, 51–62, 68, 81–89, 91, 187, 191, 200
neo-institutionalist theory 96
neoliberal land policies 12
Netherlands 15, 51f., 65–68, 70f., 73f., 76f., 82
new social movements 130

New Urban Agenda 7, 10, 19, 110, 211, 227
normality/normalisation 27, 29, 171
North Rhine-Westphalia 17, 127, 133f., 143, 146, 148, 153, 178
pandemic 16, 95–101, 148, 197, 217
participation 7, 10f., 13–19, 28–31, 33, 38, 40, 44, 54ff., 61f., 65, 68, 76, 81, 83, 85, 87f., 90f., 98, 101, 109–117, 119ff., 123, 127–132, 134–138, 141–148, 150f., 153, 156, 159–171, 182, 187, 192, 197f., 200–204, 206f., 211, 214f., 217, 221–224, 228–231, 234f.
path dependence theory 97
person with disabilities 167, 222
persons with migration background 9, 59
places 12f., 18, 31, 39f., 53, 57f., 60ff., 82, 85–88, 90f., 151
policy 10–13, 16, 18, 32, 42, 46, 51–55, 57ff., 61f., 65, 68f., 82, 110f., 177f., 180, 182, 184–189, 192, 194, 197, 199f., 202, 207, 219, 227f., 231–236
policy implementation 194
political 7f., 11–17, 19, 25, 28–31, 37, 42, 53, 65, 84f., 109ff., 113, 117, 122, 127–133, 135–138, 142, 144, 146, 160–164, 168, 170, 177ff., 182, 184–193, 198, 200ff., 204f., 212, 214ff., 222–225, 229, 231
political agenda 185
political participation 8, 12, 17, 19, 110f., 113, 127–131, 133, 135–138, 142, 144, 212, 214ff., 225

political representation 127, 136, 232
real world laboratories 43–46
representation 17, 31f., 55, 127, 129, 133f., 137, 202, 215, 235
representative bodies 150, 222
rural areas 16, 66f., 71, 75f., 181
Rwanda 19, 220ff., 225
SDGs (Sustainable Development Goals) 10, 109, 132, 206, 211, 219ff.
self-advocacy 10, 19, 133, 165, 180, 203
self-criticism 201
self-determination 7, 145, 162, 171, 197f.
self-evident meeting places 81, 90
self-help organisations 16, 150, 170
service providers 110, 132f., 135, 146, 170, 184, 187, 190, 200, 203, 213, 222
shared places 13f.
small-scale places 56, 58, 66, 70–77, 89f.
social cohesion 60, 66, 68, 70, 73f., 87, 111, 216f., 222
social disciplining 26f.
social inclusion 11f., 14, 81, 91, 193, 223
social interaction 90, 99, 167f.
social life/everyday life 8, 13, 30, 38, 46, 51, 62, 69, 83, 95, 128, 143, 162f., 197
social networks 69, 76, 88, 99ff., 163, 216
social participation 31, 38, 128, 145, 161, 164, 224
social policies 83, 187, 219

social relations 7, 14f., 25, 27, 39, 58, 69, 76, 128, 162, 216
social services 8, 18, 39f., 96f., 101, 133, 145f., 161, 177ff., 181, 188, 193, 216, 218, 220, 225
social space development 15, 30–33, 39, 44f.
social space organisation 15, 30, 32f., 39
social spaces 15, 18, 31, 41, 95, 100, 130, 145f., 150, 154, 164f., 169f.
social work 7, 14f., 17, 31f., 37, 39, 45f., 58, 95, 101, 161, 171
socio-spatial infrastructure 54, 61, 85
spaces 9, 11, 16, 19, 26, 31f., 39, 42, 58–61, 90, 143, 146, 163f., 166, 204, 214, 217, 223ff.
Sub-Sahara Africa 218
subsidiarity principle 213, 228, 232–236
Switzerland 18, 197ff., 203ff., 207
UN-CRPD (UN Convention on the Rights of Persons with Disabilities) 25, 27, 132, 135, 138
undivided cities 53
urban areas 42, 67, 128, 181
urban development 10, 37f., 40–44, 46, 53, 81, 212, 217
urban planning 12, 41, 62, 217
vital places 16, 75f., 83, 88, 90
vitality 16, 81ff., 86, 88, 91
voluntary engagement/volunteers 66, 68–73, 75ff., 82, 90f., 114, 153, 187, 191

vulnerable population/social groups 10ff., 44, 129f., 147, 163, 182, 219, 229, 232
welfare 14, 16, 25f., 29, 41, 65–68, 71–77, 84, 110, 137, 160, 162, 165, 171, 197, 216, 233, 235
welfare state 14, 25f., 29, 41, 65f., 171
welfare system 65, 67, 76f.
Western Balkan 19, 218ff.

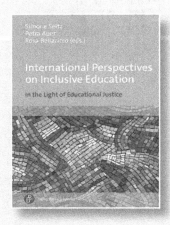

Simone Seitz
Petra Auer
Rosa Bellacicco (eds.)

International Perspectives on Inclusive Education

In the Light of Educational Justice

2023. 268 pp. • Paperback • 59,90 € (D) • 61,60 € (A)
ISBN 978-3-8474-2698-1 • also available as e-book in open access

International developments and impulses call for the equitable and inclusive design of education systems. This book takes this up and focuses on the often blurred relationship between inclusive education and educational equity. By compiling current research results and theoretical contributions from several European countries on the topic, the authors create an overarching framework for discussion.

www.shop.budrich.de

Printed in the USA
CPSIA information can be obtained
at www.ICGtesting.com
JSHW061252050424
60581JS00005B/45